THE
NAVAL
MUTINIES
of
1798

THE NAVAL MUTINIES of 1798

THE IRISH PLOT TO SEIZE THE CHANNEL FLEET

PHILIP MACDOUGALL

PEN & SWORD MARITIME

First published in Great Britain in 2024 by
PEN AND SWORD MARITIME
an imprint of
Pen and Sword Books Ltd
Yorkshire – Philadelphia

Copyright © Philip MacDougall, 2024

ISBN 978 1 39904 459 2

The right of Philip MacDougall to be identified
as the author of this work has been asserted by him in accordance
with the Copyright, Designs and Patents Act 1988.

A CIP record for this book is available from the British Library
All rights reserved. No part of this book may be reproduced or
transmitted in any form or by any means, electronic or
mechanical including photocopying, recording or
by any information storage and retrieval system, without
permission from the Publisher in writing.

Typeset in Times New Roman 11/13.5 by
SJmagic DESIGN SERVICES, India.
Printed and bound in the UK by CPI Group (UK) Ltd.

Pen & Sword Books Ltd incorporates the imprints of Pen & Sword
Archaeology, Atlas, Aviation, Battleground, Discovery,
Family History, History, Maritime, Military, Naval, Politics, Railways,
Select, Social History, Transport, True Crime, Claymore Press,
Frontline Books, Leo Cooper, Praetorian Press, Remember When,
Seaforth Publishing and Wharncliffe.

For a complete list of Pen & Sword titles please contact
PEN & SWORD BOOKS LIMITED
George House, Units 12 & 13, Beevor Street, Off Pontefract Road,
Barnsley, South Yorkshire, S71 1HN, England
E-mail: enquiries@pen-and-sword.co.uk
Website: www.pen-and-sword.co.uk

or
PEN AND SWORD BOOKS
1950 Lawrence Rd, Havertown, PA 19083, USA
E-mail: uspen-and-sword@casematepublishers.com
Website: www.penandswordbooks.com

Contents

Illustrations vii

Terminology ix

Preface xi

Prologue xvi

PART 1	**Pathway to Mutiny** 1
Chapter 1	The Ships 3
Chapter 2	The People of the Ships 17

PART 2	**Liberty and Revolution** 33
Chapter 3	Harsh Laws and Discrimination 35
Chapter 4	The Society of United Irishmen 42
Chapter 5	'Mankind are naturally friends to each other' 49

PART 3	**Ushant: The Key to Irish Independence** 57
Chapter 6	The Blockade of Brest 59
Chapter 7	Bantry Bay 63

PART 4	**The Diabolical Spirit of Mutiny** 69
Chapter 8	*Amelia, Haughty* and *Adamant* 70
Chapter 9	All Not Well Within the Fleet 82

PART 5	**For the Sake of the United Irishmen**	87
Chapter 10	*Captain*	88
Chapter 11	Organisation and Leadership	94
Chapter 12	*Caesar, Defiance, Glory* and *Neptune*	100
PART 6	**All the Officers Must be Put to Death**	107
Chapter 13	Cadiz! Our Country	108
Chapter 14	*Il a mort pour la liberté*	125
Chapter 15	Bloody Mutiny	137
PART 7	**The Admiralty Takes its Revenge**	147
Chapter 16	Hanging, Transportation and the Lash	149
Chapter 17	Trial by Courts Martial	160
Conclusion	What Might Have Been – A Personal View	178
Bibliography		184
Discussion of Sources		190
General Index		198
Index by Name: Rebels, Revolutionaries and Mutineers		204

Illustrations

Illustration 1: Richard Parker, the 'President' of the Nore ships in mutiny, hanged from the yardarm of *Neptune* during the summer of 1797.

Illustration 2: Among those Tone met while in Paris was Ferdinand Dubois de Fosseux, minister of war, who gave his support to the French expedition. De Fosseux was also a prominent citizen of Arras, possessing this stately residence.

Illustration 3: Portsmouth Harbour, the main base of the Channel fleet and where it took refuge during winter. Here was witnessed in 1798 several executions of those found guilty of conspiring to take ships to the enemy, including those identified as leaders of the planned mutinies on *Defiance* and *Haughty*.

Illustration 4: A depiction of those preparing in 1798 to take up arms to free Ireland from English rule. Given that it is drawn by popular early nineteenth century English cartoonist George Cruickshank for a book opposed to the cause of Ireland, it is none too favourable to those who joined the uprising.

Illustration 5: A view across Goulet de Brest with Cornouaille Battery in the foreground. The Cornouaille Battery was one of many strongpoints guarding the entrance to Brest Harbour and could have given protection to British naval warships taken by a crew favourable to the French republic.

Illustration 6: The Rade de Brest showing the vastness of its protected waters, the position of the naval base and its many outlying fortifications.

Illustration 7: A modern-day view of Brest, the French naval base from which most expeditions set out for an invasion of Ireland.

Illustration 8: Ireland showing Bantry Bay and other important locations connected to the events of 1798.

Illustration 9: Admiral Adam Duncan who commanded the North Sea fleet and who witnessed several of his ships in mutiny during the French Revolutionary War.

Illustration 10: Admiralty House, London. Here the Board of Admiralty, the controlling body of the British Navy, met and determined on such matters as strategy to be taken in line with government directives. The board also sanctioned decisions taken by courts martial, including determining the fate of those charged with mutiny and the planning of taking ships into enemy ports.

Terminology

Bugger: an expression of distaste towards another, a swear word frequently annotated into the minutes of a court martial with other words used, probably not annotated as less acceptable to officer-class sensibilities.

Cadre: activists, here used to refer to the inner core of those fermenting rebellion on board British warships during the year 1798.

Club: the term adopted by the rebel seamen for their meetings, a term also adopted by radical and French revolutionary political societies.

Directory: the five-member ruling committee of the French First Republic – *le Directoire*.

Dolly mop: lower deck slang for a part-time street woman.

Forecastle: the forward part of a ship.

Hegemony: the dominance of one social group over another.

Larboard: the term used in the eighteenth century for the port (or left) side of a ship.

Long drop: a hanging at the yardarm.

Lower deck: a collective term for the petty officers and crew.

Nobs: term used by the people of the lower deck to refer to the officers.

People of the lower deck: term used to refer to the crew of a ship.

THE NAVAL MUTINIES OF 1798

Port: The left side of a ship, but a term not introduced until the nineteenth century to replace the use of larboard, which could too easily be confused with starboard (the right or opposite side of a ship).

Quality: the term used by the people of the lower deck to refer to the officers.

Quarterdeck: the upper deck of the stern reserved for the officers.

Radical: during the time of the French Revolution, a term referring to those who were totally opposed to the existing inequalities of society and which included the abolition of the monarchy and destroying the power of the aristocracy through the introduction of universal suffrage.

Revictualling: the taking on by a ship of food, water and other essentials.

Revolutionary: used here as an alternative to radical for the purpose of fully clarifying the nature of societal change being demanded by the activists of the shipboard cadres.

Roundhouse: the uppermost room or cabin at the stern of a ship and normally occupied by the master of a ship.

Starboard: the right side of a ship.

Stern: the rear or aft-most part of a ship.

Wardroom: area of a ship for officers when relaxing.

Yardarm: the outermost points of the yard or spar from which sails are set, but used also for the hanging of a man sentenced to death following a court martial.

Preface

For Ireland, the year 1798 saw a major rebellion breaking out against rule from London, a time in which Britain was in its fifth year of a hard-fought war against revolutionary France. Set in motion by the Society of United Irishmen, an underground organisation with links to Paris, the rebellion was eventually crushed by an overwhelming force of arms. Yet it could well have proved successful should a sizeable military landing have been made by the French at the time of the rebellion first breaking out. It was believed by leading members of the United Irishmen that the Directory, *le Directoire*, in Paris, the ruling body of France, was prepared to sanction the sending of an invasion force, if not at the beginning of the uprising then certainly once the rebellion had broken out. Indeed, such a force was eventually sent, landing at Kilcummin in County Mayo. However, its arrival was both too late and far too limited in the numbers sent. Just a few weeks later, despite two early but minor victories in battle, this French expeditionary force was defeated, the remnants of that army repatriated to France in exchange for British prisoners-of-war.

All of this is relatively well-known, if not in Britain then certainly in Ireland. At Enniscorthy in County Wexford is the National 1798 Rebellion Centre, a permanent memorial to the events of that year. Here the names of many who died in the rebellion are recorded on a casualty database to be found online (www.facebook.com/1798casualtylist/). What is less well-known is the United Irish plot to capture a number of British warships and the planned use of those vessels in support of the rebellion that broke out in 1798. Mentioned only in passing by a few British naval historians, and generally unmentioned in books devoted to the retelling of events in Ireland during that year, it is the rebellion at sea that is the subject of this book. The means by which those ships were to be taken, not by direct external attack but by mutinous intrigue directed from on board, is fully explored. Most frequently, the activists who formed revolutionary cadres were closely linked to the Society of United Irishmen. Sometimes, though, it was English revolutionaries, members or sympathisers of radical organisations that had formed links with the United Irishmen, who were also followers or leaders of these ship-borne cadres.

THE NAVAL MUTINIES OF 1798

In 1798, there was not a single ship in the British Navy that did not possess a substantial number of Irish seamen serving on the lower deck. They were a peculiarly discontented element, for in Ireland a desperate conflict was underway. The Society of United Irishmen, in league with revolutionary France, had inspired a rebellion against the ruling English Protestant hegemony, and to which the majority of the Irish on the lower decks would appear to have been sympathetic. By the early summer of 1798, the United Irishmen were anticipating a landing in Ireland of a sizeable military force from France, with support for the society not simply restricted to those of the Catholic faith. Discontent borne out of poverty and hunger was endemic in Ireland among large elements of both Catholics and Protestants. While rebels drawn to the cause were to fight a number of pitched battles on land, the United Irish leadership also recognised that the sea was vital to their cause. A major obstacle to the landing in Ireland of a supporting military force was the British Navy. Not only did it possess a sizeable fleet that throughout the year was blockading the French port of Brest and other French ports from where a military expedition was likely to sail, but the sea lanes closer to Ireland were constantly patrolled by British warships. If Irish crews on board those ships could be utilised in some way, then a full-scale French invasion force might be unimpeded as it sailed towards a suitable point of disembarkation. Thus, a plan emerged. A plan that was often carefully co-ordinated between seamen of both Irish descent and others sympathetic to the ideals of the French Revolution, seamen serving on different ships, with the object of seizing those ships and handing them over to the French. If successful, not only would the British Navy be seriously weakened but the French Navy would be greatly strengthened. This would also result in impetus by propaganda. Others with a desire to transform society would be encouraged to act in a similar fashion. As for the officers of the Royal Navy, they would be in perpetual fear as to which ship would be next to rebel and the likelihood of one day they being the ones hanging from the yardarm, jeered by a mutinous crew they had once commanded.

There can be little doubt that the governing elite in Britain was extremely fearful of the potential that such a plot might have, with the Board of Admiralty taking robust action against any who were connected in some way with these shipboard conspiracies. Those known to be part of the inner core of leadership, if found guilty in a trial by court martial, were hanged. This fate was also applied to others drawn into the plot, although not all were hanged. Some were flogged around the fleet while others were punished with a lengthy prison sentence or transportation to the penal colony in New South Wales. As for the actual number of rebels brought to trial on the charge of mutiny, no more than a hundred, this

PREFACE

was simply the tip of the iceberg. Many more would have given their support, but against them the Admiralty failed to secure any real evidence.

Despite most of the lower deck being aware of the planned mutinies, of which a number would also have been unsympathetic to the aims of the rebel cadres, the plots went unreported for many months. As a result, all those who knew of the existence of such a plot and failing to report it to an officer, would be considered by the Admiralty to be as guilty as any man active in the plot, and so liable to be sentenced to death if selected for court-martialling. That so many took such a risk through not reporting their knowledge of these plots is a topic picked up within this book. The most obvious explanation, and one for which there is overwhelming evidence, is that any man known to have reported even the slightest hint of what was going on knew that he would face brutal retribution at the hands of those conspiring to take the ship. Daniel Lacey and James Mason, seamen mustered to *Queen Charlotte*, in surreptitiously finding under cover of darkness the master-at-arms, informed him of a conspiracy by some of the Irish seamen on board. Lacey, in later passing this information to one of the ship's lieutenants, and described as being in a very agitated state, made it clear that if the conspirators knew of him speaking to an officer he was 'sure he would be murdered'. Such a reprisal would, of course, be surreptitious but final in its consequence, a possible heaving over the side of the ship during the dead of night or thrown from the height of a topgallant mast. Effectively, much of the crew were trapped between a rock and hard place, damned if they reported the planning of a mutiny and damned if they didn't. For Lacey, this was exactly the situation in which he felt he had been placed, witnessing one of the leading conspirators on the ship approaching an Irish member of the crew to sign a document that was described as subversive in that it referred to 'liberty' and 'rights'. Dennis Callaghan, with whom both Lacey and Mason shared a berth, had refused to sign the document and in doing so had been called 'a traitor to God and his country'. However, in having learnt of the existence of this document, both Lacey and Mason could be court-martialled if not immediately reported. On this occasion, it seems that their fear of Admiralty retribution over that of any retribution by the conspirators, and possibly also through having a better relationship with the master-at-arms, led them to reporting what they knew.

Should these planned shipboard rebellions have proved successful, then history could well have been turned on its head. The ships upon which known cadres were formed were primarily those of the Channel and Mediterranean fleets, and which were, in reality, Britain's first line of defence against invasion. While the fleet in the Channel was engaged in blockading the French Atlantic sea ports, the Mediterranean fleet was blockading the French naval port of Toulon and the Spanish naval port of Cadiz. Here were being assembled ships that might well be used in supporting the Irish rebellion or of mounting an invasion of England. The objective of these two British fleets was to prevent the sailing of ships from those ports, but if they did escape, to chase and destroy them. That task would be made near impossible should mutinies orchestrated by rebel cadres break out on board one or several British ships. Even more serious would be the consequence arising from ships of those fleets being taken into a French or Spanish harbour and then used to assist in the invasion of Ireland. This would be a double catastrophe, reducing the strength of the blockading force while increasing the magnitude of the enemy through the addition of a valuable ship of war.

In working on this book, I have made much use of records held in London at the National Archives (Kew), contemporary newspaper reports and other available primary source material. All these sources are unsympathetic to the Irish cause, a fact reflected in both what went recorded and in the way events were chronicled. Given that those directly involved with the planned mutinies have themselves left no records, this is problematic if an unbiased account is to be achieved. However, one exception, and one upon which heavy reliance was placed, is that of the detailed hand-written minutes of the courts martial held upon those identified as rebel leaders and some of their supporters. In these scrupulously preserved papers can be found the actual words of the people of the lower deck, not just those accused of shipboard rebellion but of the witnesses called both by the prosecuting officer and the man being tried. Admittedly, those standing trial did not provide unadulterated accounts of their actions, for to do so would have been an act of self-condemnation. But witnesses giving their testimonies do provide some of the missing detail that allows for a better understanding of not just what was happening on board these ships but the motivation that led to those actions. Clues are also given as to the organisational structure of the cadres that were established within various ships and the means by which rebel crews of different ships communicated both with one another as well as with the executive committee of the Society of United Irishmen in Dublin. In addition, evidence is given of French involvement in these plots, and the existence on shore of French agents who were there to support the conspirators and encourage them in their endeavours.

One small note I need to add here. In using the minutes made by the judge advocate during the trial by court martial of several of the mutineers, especially those brought to trial on *Caesar*, *Captain*, *Defiance*, *Diomede*, *Glory* and *Neptune*, I have attempted to gain a closer understanding of what was happening on board those ships, the prevailing ambience and the sense of expectancy. To

PREFACE

do this I have sometimes turned reported speech into direct speech and allowed a conversation to flow for the purpose of continuity. At no point has anything been introduced that changes the facts. Where conversation has been given it is for the purpose of creating a factional re-enactment of the kind adopted in documentary dramas. It is designed to allow the story to flow and heighten the interest of the reader. The alternative would be a somewhat dry rendition of the events that underpinned the brave and desperate men who attempted to take British warships into enemy ports. The audience for this book, if written as an academic tome, would have been limited. I wished to open up my research to a much wider audience rather than the book being restricted to a small potential readership. For those who wish to see the evidence upon which I drew, the reported rather than the rewritten direct speech, I refer those readers to my academia site (www.academia.edu) in which I give examples of the reported speech responses by some of the key members of the shipboard revolutionary cadres. It is this website that also contains the full list of names with further details of each and every man executed by the navy for supporting or endeavouring to take naval warships into enemy ports in the cause of ending the rule of Westminster over Ireland.

In writing this book, and supported by detail to be found on my website, I offer the first detailed account of both an aspect of the Irish liberation movement of 1798 and actions of revolutionaries on mainland Britain that has in the past been rarely acknowledged. In doing so, the names of those executed are included within the pages of this book, and to which one day might be added to the Rebellion Casualty Database and fully acknowledged by the National 1798 Rebellion Centre.

Philip MacDougall
January 2024

Prologue
Vive la République!

The French Revolutionary calendar, introduced in 1792, was a decimalised calendar that renamed each month to reflect either the prevailing weather or natural events, such as *Vendémiaire*, the month of the grape harvest, and which in the Gregorian calendar, as used in Great Britain, began towards the end of September. The previous month to *Vendémiaire* was named *Fructidor*, the month of fruit, and it was on the seventh of *Fructidor* in Year VI (24 August 1798) of the calendar of the revolution that could well have marked the opening stage of a grand scheme masterminded by a revolutionary organisation, the Society of United Irishmen.

In a co-ordinated series of ship-board conspiracies, Irish patriots serving on ships of the British Royal Navy, alongside Scots, Welsh and English radicals, planned to mutiny and take the ships upon which they served into Brest or one of the other French Atlantic sea ports. Purposely contrived to both weaken the Royal Navy and strengthen the French Revolutionary Navy, it was one way of helping ensure that an invasion force destined for Ireland would arrive in safety and once there would successfully defeat the minimal British defence forces then in Ireland.

The hopes of the United Irishmen and their revolutionary allies did not stop there. With Ireland occupied, the back door into England would be wide open. Again using its reinforced navy to protect and transport it across the Irish Sea, the French Army, once strengthened by extra infantry and artillery from France and supported by thousands of Irish who were expected to join them, would begin the conquest of England. Here too in Britain it was hoped that those who wanted a new society, one based on the principles of *liberté, fraternité* and *égalité*, would back the invading force in vast numbers to help overthrow the ruling establishment and in doing so create a new republic.

If the seventh of *Fructidor* was the day the conspiracy began to unfold, it would have been the residents of the Atlantic port city of Brest who were its first

PROLOGUE

witnesses. Here, the *citoyens* and *citoyennes*, as men and women had now to be respectively addressed, were faced with an unbelievable sight. Around midday and approaching the roadstead that lay immediately beyond the harbour of this important naval town was a massive British warship. Keen observers would have seen that this vessel was still flying the colours of *Grande-Bretagne* at her stern, but above that flag and proudly fluttering was a large green ensign emblazoned with a harp. On the main topmast, and for all to see, was one further flag – the French *Tricolore*. To those meandering along the sea wall and aware of naval tradition, this clearly proclaimed the vessel to be a British warship that had been captured in some way. Captured not by the French Navy, but by some unknown country, a country whose flag was green and emblazoned with a harp.

At this time, early in the morning, few would have known what all this signified. It was very much an enigma. Had there been a great naval victory at sea? *Non!* Most unlikely. A miracle maybe, for the ship showed no signs of battle damage. As for the flag, this merely added to the puzzle. Who was this new ally of France with a flag that nobody recognised? How had this unknown authority taken on the all-powerful British Navy and captured one of their major warships? A warship that would soon be moored where only French warships normally rested.

Shortly the full story began to spread. The flag was that of the anticipated and hopefully soon to be declared Irish Republic. And it was Irish seamen who had taken the ship. Furthermore, it was now the intention of those seamen that the French Republic take possession of the ship. Her name was *Defiance*, a name that would soon be on everyone's lips. She was a 74-gun third rate, one of the most powerful ships afloat, and one that could boast outstanding qualities as a warship, outsailing most other ships of her class and able to keep pace with much nimbler frigates.

Until this time, *Defiance* had been one of a fleet of warships blockading the Breton coastline, making it all but impossible for ships to enter and leave the port of Brest. As more and more *citoyens* and *citoyennes* learnt of *Defiance*'s arrival, their numbers swelled with the cheering ashore becoming louder and louder. First a steady chorus of '*Vive la Republic!*' In time, and once it had been learnt that she had been taken by Irish republicans, another chant emerged from the crowd '*Vive la Irlande!*' Presently a few hastily gathered musicians came together, breaking into the familiar and catchy *Ah! Ça Ira*, the anthem of the revolution. Helping boost this enthusiasm was a rumour that also began to circulate. Seemingly *Defiance* might soon be joined by other British warships. Perhaps half the blockading force, a possible ten ships, were about to mutiny. One ship would follow another into the Brest roadstead. All who were assembled began to sing even louder, joyously chorusing in unison *Ah! Ça Ira, ça ira, ça ira!*

THE NAVAL MUTINIES OF 1798

William Lindsey, leader of the *Defiance* mutineers, had successfully recruited about forty of the crew upon whom he could totally rely, with a further sixty indicating their support for the taking of the ship. Of the trusted forty, they at different times met on the starboard side of the galley. Here, and proclaiming their meetings to be that of a 'smoking club', the taking of the ship was planned. To show their commitment to the cause, each had sworn upon a book of prayer a solemn oath that they would 'be true to the Free and United Irishmen'. Most, but not all, were Catholics, men whose families in Ireland had long suffered the effects of legalised discrimination, impoverishment and judicial injustice. Some would have also directly witnessed the violence of marauding Protestant gangs, against which the authorities chose to do little. Others were Irish Presbyterians, men who were also discriminated against in Ireland and who desired a more democratic form of government unrestrained from the English controlling hegemony. Finally, there were men like Thomas Goldsmith and John Drinkwater, English revolutionaries who were also prepared to take an oath in support of taking the ship.

Many of those recruited by Lindsey were willing to join him because of a long-entrenched desire to better the position of Catholics in Ireland, with some believing this could only be achieved by a mass slaughter of Protestants. This, however, was not the way of the Society of United Irishmen, of which Lindsey was a member and some of whose leaders were Protestants. They wished to see Catholics and Protestants working alongside each other to create in Ireland a fully democratic society free of England but also free of religious sectarianism. But in his enthusiasm to gain supporters for the cause, Lindsey showed little interest as to why a man would willingly agree to join in the taking of the ship. As far as he was concerned, as long as he swore the oath then he was happy. As well as committing themselves to be 'true to the Free and United Irishmen', those taking the oath also swore to 'afterwards kill or destroy the Protestants'. It was a suitably vague postscript interpreted by some to be an attack only on the Protestant system of government but by others as encouraging acts of vengeance on individual Protestants, especially those on board *Defiance*.

It was on the night preceding the seventh of *Fructidor* that the planned mutiny was enacted. *Defiance*, having been detached from the main blockading fleet, was sailing close to the Breton shoreline and only 20 miles from Brest. That was the moment for which Lindsey had been waiting. With his fellow mutineers forewarned, each quietly made his way from the lower gun deck where many had been asleep in their hammocks. On the main deck was the officer of the watch and a few loyalist seamen. Quickly the mutineers struck, overpowering the loyalists and the officers with bludgeons and sticks that had been secretly stored in the berths below deck and in the barrels of the guns that lined the ship's upper

PROLOGUE

deck. Others, in having climbed onto the quarterdeck, were able to take from where they were stored boarding pikes normally used to defend the ship against an enemy in battle drawing close and attempting to capture the ship by boarding. These were fearsome weapons, 8ft in length with tapered metal spearpoints and backward-facing hooks. Armed with these, some of the mutineers went wild, slashing and prodding at those attempting to defend the ship, giving no quarter, especially if the man they were about to kill was either a hated Protestant or known to be English.

'Damn and bugger all Protestants,' yelled John Hopkins as he viciously drove a pike into one seaman.

'Damnation to the English,' called out Richard Kennedy. 'Lord Love the United Irish. Eternally bugger the English and send them all to damnation.'

By striking at night when most of the officers were in their cabins and crew loyalists below deck, the taking of the ship was made much easier. Those on the upper deck who had not been killed were soon pushed below, joining the rest of the crew. With exit hatchways held in place by the weight of several cannons removed from their firing positions, some of the mutineers stood guard, ready to fire on any man who might try to escape.

To captain the ship Lindsey appointed John Hopkins, a man of the lower deck and a seaman without any navigational experience. For this reason, before she could make passage into Brest, *Defiance* first anchored off Pointe de Mathieu. This stood 12km west of the Goulet, a treacherous bottleneck of a channel through which *Defiance* would have to pass before she could reach the safety of the roadstead. Contact was made with the French, for here were two gun batteries, with a request made that a pilot be sent from Brest to guide the ship through the Goulet.

This simple manoeuvre was not one with which all the mutineers agreed.

'Any man in the ship can carry her into Brest,' Lindsey claimed.

Others were less certain. Some remembered that only two years earlier a French 'seventy-four' had run aground while attempting to leave Brest.

'Over 600 seamen were drowned,' remarked one of the mutineers. 'And I for one can't swim.'

'He's right enough,' added another. 'She was the "Soggysant", or some such name.'

'*Séduisant*,' offered one of the Irish seamen who had spent time in an Irish seminary before returning to Dublin, where he had been pressed into naval service.

'What use is the taking of the ship if we are all to be drowned? No ship can run the passage without a pilot,' another added.

Finally, although he was not a man who usually listened to those who questioned his orders, Lindsey had to give way. Doubtless he was worried about a resulting loss of time. Just beyond the island of Ushant, and which could just be seen through the early morning mist, was the entire Channel fleet, no less than fifteen ships, some of them even more powerful than *Defiance*. Should the taking of the ship be conveyed to the admiral in charge of that fleet, Alexander Hood, 1st Viscount Bridport, by one of the British frigates constantly patrolling these same coastal waters, then all hell would break loose. *Defiance* would be trapped and outgunned and possibly only those seamen capable of swimming ashore would be saved.

Of course there was the possibility that United Irishmen on board some of those ships, if sent to attack *Defiance*, might themselves take action. Lindsey in particular was aware that the conspiracy that had led to the taking of *Defiance* was part of a much wider plot. On board at least ten ships of the Channel fleet were United Irish emissaries, men who had deliberately volunteered to join the British Navy to lead fellow Irish revolutionaries into the taking of the ships upon which they served.

Another potential risk in anchoring *Defiance* off Pointe de Mathieu was that an over-enthusiastic and inexperienced French artillery officer might order the two batteries mounted on the high cliffs to open fire. This too was possibly running through Lindsey's mind. Fortunately, the sight of a white flag raised on the maintop mast and another at the stern led to the officer commanding the two batteries being rowed out from the shore to investigate. With a megaphone pressed to his lips the officer queried, 'You are surrendering, *oui*?'

'Yes, in the name of Ireland,' came Lindsey's retort. '*Vive la République!*'

'Why are you anchored here?'

'To bring her into Brest.' And referring to the ship's navigating officer Lindsey added, 'The master refuses to help us. We cannot get into Brest without help.'

Perhaps the investigating officer might not have understood all that he was told, but the need for a pilot seemed clear enough. Returning ashore, a messenger was despatched to the naval yard in Brest and within a few hours a pilot, together with twenty or more infantrymen, were rowed from the beach to the ship. Nevertheless, and despite the white flag of surrender now replaced by a *Tricolore* at the stern, the guns at Pointe de Mathieu, together with those positioned either side of the Goulet, were held at readiness. Could this be some trick of *le rostbifs*?

It was now that news of *Defiance*'s arrival began to circulate around Brest and some of the nearby villages. Eventually hundreds, if not thousands, of enthusiastic *citoyens* and *citoyennes* began to line the harbour wall, thrilled as they witnessed the giant British warship enter the roadstead to make her way

PROLOGUE

towards a vacant mooring 50m offshore. On board, the mutineers felt themselves truly welcomed, the strains of *Ça Ira*, a song most of them already knew, could be heard in the distance. However, as the crowd continued to grow, the singing became more raucous, more enthusiastic, with the mutineers, some by this time drunk from over-consumption of wine normally reserved for the officers, wildly chorusing *Ah! Ça Ira, ça ira, ça ira!*

Among the first to board the vessel once she was safely moored was Adjutant General Theobald Wolfe Tone. A founder and leader of the Society of United Irishmen, he had, since his arrival in France two years earlier, worked tirelessly in his efforts to gain French support for the cause of an independent Ireland. To the Directory, *le Directoire*, he had promised that upon a French Army setting foot in Ireland it would be joined by 100,000 United Irishmen ready to fight alongside them. If the French failed to provide the 20,000 soldiers that he felt would be needed, Tone declared that he would join any expedition, even if it consisted only of a corporal's guard.

To encourage crews on other British warships to mutiny and hand each vessel taken to the Republic of France, members of the Directory insisted on an early valuation of *Defiance*, with the value of the warship paid out in equal proportions to all those who could prove to have taken part in the mutiny. Each mutineer would eventually receive a sum of around £400 (£40,000 in today's money). Most were also, on Tone's insistence, offered the chance to serve on board either a French warship or *Defiance* once she had been surveyed and refitted. This same offer, employment on a French warship, was also given to the imprisoned loyalist members of the crew, but with only a few accepting.

Of even greater importance to the French, and serving as a highly useful piece of propaganda, was the need to announce far and wide the arrival of *Defiance* in Brest together with the fact that she had been taken by an Irish crew supported by English and Scottish revolutionary sympathisers. In so doing, the financial benefit that each had received was also broadcast widely. This latter inducement, it was supposed, would encourage other crews to mutiny. Whether Irish radicals or otherwise, all would soon learn of the major rewards on offer should they surrender their ship to the French.

PART 1

Pathway to Mutiny

During 1798, ten ships of the British Navy's Channel fleet are known to have had activists on board who were intent on creating revolutionary cadres for the purpose of leading and directing a recruited echelon of supporters from the lower decks to capture and take each of those ships into an enemy port. Ships serving with either the North Sea or Mediterranean fleets, or detached into the Irish Sea or elsewhere, also saw the formation of similar cadres, with activists attempting to stimulate crews of ships on those stations to also rebel. If those additional ships are included, the number of British warships that saw the formation of revolutionary cadres rises from ten to sixteen, with the strong possibility of cadres formed on a number of other ships of which there can only be supposition. The activists who set about creating those cadres, together with others who committed themselves, were often but not exclusively Irish, for among the rebels were those who were English, Welsh or Scottish by birth. In common, they held republican beliefs and were committed to the ideals of the French Revolution and the creation of a more equal society.

An important stimulus to these shipboard conspiratorial networks was the Society of United Irishmen, an underground revolutionary organisation that was conspiring to end English hegemonic rule over Ireland. It was through links made by the United Irishmen with radical organisations on mainland Britain that also inspired others, though not Irish, to support the cause of Irish independence, believing that if Ireland was successful in breaking from English rule, then the whole structure of governance across the British Isles could also be destroyed. On offer for those who were successful in taking a ship into a French port was not only the delivery of a blow against the British establishment but also an ensured financial reward. As proclaimed by the Society of United Irishmen, upon a ship being brought into a French port, the government of France would not only purchase the ship but the price paid would be distributed among those who had been active in the taking of the ship. It was akin to prize money, the sum paid to British seamen when an enemy merchant vessel or warship was captured and the value of the ship, and any cargo carried, shared among the officers and men of the ships that had made the capture.

Chapter 1

The Ships

The most significant of those ships to see the formation of a cadre or the attempted formation of a cadre of revolutionaries in the Channel fleet was *Queen Charlotte*, a 100-gun first rate three-decker carrying the flag of Admiral Viscount Bridport, the admiral in overall charge of the fleet and whose main duty was blockading Brest. It was the standard practice of the Royal Navy to categorise all three-masted square-rigged warships into one of six rates, and the rate into which a ship fell denoted its size rather than its quality, also determining the number of officers allowed on the ship and the level of pay each would receive. Launched at Chatham naval dockyard in April 1790, *Queen Charlotte* had been completed at an approximate cost of £56,000 and was calculated to be of 2,278 tons. Through her great size she was not the easiest ship to manoeuvre and sail and one of the slowest of the fleet, but she packed a powerful punch. Thirty of her heaviest guns, 32-pounders, were placed on the lower gun deck to ensure the ship's stability at sea. Each of these guns weighed 3 tons and was capable of firing a single 32lb iron shot to a distance of just over 1 mile. On her middle gun deck were twenty-eight 24-pounders, these having the same range as the guns on the lower deck, but through firing a lighter weight shot each was around 10cwt lighter than the 32-pounders on the lower deck. On the upper gun deck were thirty 12-pounders, with the fo'c'sle (the raised deck at the fore-end) and quarterdeck (the upper deck near the stern) housing twelve 12-pounders. In total, when delivering a broadside, the firing of all the guns from one side of the ship, it was possible to direct at an approaching enemy no less than 0.47 metric tonnes of iron shot that could cause inestimable damage to such an unlucky opponent. Furthermore, a skilled gun crew could, and most gun crews on British warships were highly trained in the task of firing their guns, deliver one shot every minute or thereabouts.

While *Queen Charlotte* might have been the largest of the ships of the Channel fleet to witness a mutiny plot, six other line-of-battle ships in the fleet also saw plots being developed, ships that were almost equally as impressive. Three of them, *Captain*, *Glory* and *Neptune*, were second rate three-deckers carrying ninety-eight guns each, while two were two-decked third rates, of which one, *Caesar*, was armed with eighty-four guns, and the second, *Defiance*, with seventy-four guns. As with *Queen Charlotte*, the heaviest guns carried by these ships were a large cluster of 36 pounders on the lower gun deck, with the second rates having an overall layout not dissimilar to *Queen Charlotte*. For the two-deck second rates, *Neptune* had thirty 32-pounders on her gun deck, thirty-two 24-pounders on her upper deck, eighteen 9-pounders on her quarter and eighteen on her fo'c'sle decks. As for *Defiance*, her original armament, as first completed, had consisted of twenty-eight 32-pounders on her lower gun deck, twenty-eight 18-pounders on her upper deck, and eighteen 9-pounders on her quarter and fo'c'sle decks. Further vessels of either the Channel fleet or patrolling off the French Atlantic coastline also witnessed Irish-orchestrated mutiny plots in 1798: the 50-gun fourth rate *Adamant*, the 44-gun fifth rate *Amelia*, and the much smaller *Haughty*, a gunboat of 167 tons armed with two 24-pounders at the bow and ten 18-pounders along her single deck.

One notable feature, common to virtually every ship operating in the Channel fleet, was that of experiencing, between April and May 1797, on-board mutinies, with the crews of virtually every ship refusing to leave when anchored at the fleet's two major anchorages: Spithead and Plymouth Sound. It was at Spithead, a stretch of water lying between Portsmouth and the Isle of Wight, where crews had first refused to perform duty until a number of grievances were resolved, not least of these an increase in pay. Surprisingly, no increase in the pay allowed to the lower deck had been granted since 1653. Admittedly, prices had increased little over much of that period, but the war now being fought against revolutionary France had seen a sudden and dramatic rise in the price of food and other basic necessities. As well as the demand for a wage increase, other grievances crews wished to see redressed were harshness of discipline, poor food and lack of shore leave. Much more akin to an industrial dispute than an all-out mutiny, the seamen at Spithead and the Sound conducted themselves in a peaceful and organised manner, continuing to carry out their everyday duties but refusing the leadership of their officers. One ship playing an especially important role at Spithead was *Queen Charlotte*. The seamen of her lower deck had been among the first to make their demands known, sending in February 1797 a petition for an increase in pay to Admiral Richard Howe, 1st Earl Howe, a former commander-in-chief who had always been popular with his men. This petition, together with those from several other ships, including *Glory* and *Defiance*, were passed by Howe to the Admiralty, with the lords of the Admiralty choosing to ignore them. In the meantime, *Queen Charlotte*, along with other ships of the Channel fleet, had sailed, ordered to continue the blockade of Brest, relieving other units of the fleet that now returned to revictual. In an adopted turn and turn-about procedure,

THE SHIPS

Queen Charlotte and her retinue of ships came back to Spithead at the end of March, replaced on blockade duty by the ships they had previously relieved. On their return, it was learnt that no action had been taken to meet the request for increased pay, resulting in considerable anger among those of the lower deck and talk of mutiny. One report sent to the Admiralty by Vice-Admiral Peter Parker, the port admiral at Portsmouth, stated categorically of *Queen Charlotte* that her crew would 'refuse doing their duty till there *[sic]* wages is increased'. On 16 April, with the order issued for a return to sea, there was a refusal by all crews of the Channel fleet to sail.

At this point, *Queen Charlotte* took on an even more significant role, for in being the flagship of the fleet she now became the parliament ship in a rapidly escalating situation. From her, and other ships, boats were sent out to inform the ships of the immobile fleet that each was to send two delegates to *Queen Charlotte*, with *Defiance* and *Glory* among the seventeen ships that immediately responded. In his log for the afternoon of 16 April, Theophilus Jones, captain of *Defiance*, noted: 'Ships cheering to each other repeatedly.' On the following morning he added: 'Several boats came alongside making mention of raising seaman's wages.' As well as sending delegates to the newly proclaimed parliament ship, oaths of loyalty to the cause were taken by seamen of each ship, the oath on *Defiance* administered by John Saunders and John Husband, her two appointed delegates. Most of *Defiance*'s crew appeared willing to take the oath, although a corporal of marines was twice ducked for refusing and, according to one newspaper, threatened with hanging before he was finally sent ashore following his continued refusal to take the oath. On board *Queen Charlotte*, with the fleet parliament now sitting, rules were drawn up governing conduct and actions to be taken, including the wording of two petitions that were also in the process of being drawn up, one to be sent to the Admiralty and the other to the House of Commons. According to a letter received from Portsmouth dated 18 April and reproduced in several newspapers:

> *They have a ship, which is the* Queen Charlotte, *on board of which everything is regulated; they call her the parliament ship, and 4 seamen from every ship at Spithead go on board in the morning, to consult what measures to pursue, and solemnly take an oath, administered to them with the greatest decorum.*

However, the correspondent of the *Kentish Weekly Post* was incorrect, for in stating each ship appointed four delegates, only two were appointed by each ship. In concluding, this same correspondent added that no ship would go to sea:

> ...*unless their demands are complied with, except the enemy are at sea, and a convoy wanted; and if their demands are not promised, they will convey the ships into Portsmouth harbour on Saturday morning.*

While several crews upon their return to Spithead had sent letters to the Admiralty outlining individual ship grievances as well as the demand for an increase in pay, the petitions drawn up by the delegates on the parliament ship and sent to the Admiralty and House of Commons encompassed only grievances affecting every ship. In addition to the demand for increased pay, these petitions included a call for a fairer dispersal of prize money, better-quality food, including a sufficient quantity of vegetables, improved treatment for the sick and wounded, the provisions allowed them not to be embezzled, granting of shore leave when in harbour, and payment of wages to those wounded in action. However, one final clause was added, a hope that the lords of the Admiralty would redress the grievances of any individual ship as far as lay in their power 'to prevent any further disturbances'.

While awaiting the Admiralty's response, the crews of each ship continued to perform their daily chores as if they were under the charge of their officers, only refusing to put to sea. Some ships were even permitted by the delegates to leave the anchorage for convoy escort duty while *Porcupine* was permitted to sail to Plymouth for a refit at the dockyard. At 8 a.m. and 8 p.m. every day, cheers were given by the seamen of each ship to show their enduring unity while the delegates continued to meet daily on board *Queen Charlotte*, returning to their own ships at night. In London, despite the urgency of the situation, Prime Minister William Pitt delayed bringing the affair before parliament, while the Admiralty offered only an increase in pay with this in turn lacking an assurance that parliament would approve the necessary expenditure. Accompanied by an order that the fleet should put to sea, tension mounted, with some ships, among them the especially militant crew of *Glory*, rolling out their guns and aiming them directly towards Portsmouth. On board *Queen Charlotte*, the delegates stood firm. No ship would sail until all their demands were met.

On the afternoon of 8 May, and again referring to the log kept by Captain Jones, 'a general cheering took place throughout the fleet', this upon news that parliament had at last debated their petition with it agreed that money would be set aside for both an increase in pay and rations and to receive Royal Assent on the following day. In a letter to Bridport, Jones provided a little more detail, informing him that on that day a boat came from *Pompée*, and upon its arrival the crew cheered and rove the yardarm. To help placate the seamen and ensure their

THE SHIPS

return to duty, Howe, the popular former commander-in-chief of the Channel fleet, was instructed by the Admiralty to proceed to Portsmouth to finalise the matter. Arriving on Wednesday 10 May, he boarded *Queen Charlotte* and met with the delegates. While the delegates were generally favourable to a return to normal discipline under the terms given, despite not being granted all their demands, it was required that the grievances of individual ships should be addressed and, in particular, the removal of unpopular officers. Many ships, including *Defiance* and *Glory*, had already despatched some of their officers ashore. Jones of *Defiance* observed on 9 May, 'the ship's company sent on shore one lieutenant, the gunner and two midshipmen' and for reasons which will be returned to shortly, *Glory* sent ashore their first lieutenant, Henry Hicks. With the king having signed a pardon that extended to all serving in the fleet 'who may have been guilty of any act of mutiny', so ensuring that there would be no recriminations against any seaman, the mutiny was brought to an end. In celebration, and on the morning of 15 May:

> Lord Howe passed through the fleet...attended by the boats from each ship here, manned ship and cheered his Lordship. At 11 o'clock the Royal George fired a Royal Salute. Answered the signal to unmoor ship.

Mutiny had also effected a further element of the Channel fleet, twenty ships and their crews in Cawsand Bay, just by the entrance into Plymouth Sound, where they had been originally ordered to revictual. Included among those ships, and demonstrating their support for their fellow seamen at Spithead, were *Caesar*, *Princess Royal* and *St George*, ships all witnessing the plotting of further mutinies in 1798, the latter two when sent out to join the Mediterranean fleet. News of the mutiny at Spithead had been brought to Plymouth by *Porcupine*, the ship permitted by the delegates at Spithead to sail to Plymouth for a refit at the dockyard. Arriving on 26 April, it was *Atlas*, the flagship of Sir John Orde, commander of the Plymouth squadron, that was the first to receive the news and which was soon conveyed to the rest of the ships in the Sound. Either because of the information received from *Porcupine* but more likely the result of prior discussion among crews of the various ships of the Channel fleet, the procedure adopted on ships in the Sound was identical to that enacted at Spithead. A parliament ship, *Atlas*, was declared, with a series of articles drawn up and taken to the rest of the ships. Later, Captain John MacDougall of *Edgar* described in a letter to Orde, receiving on board his ship the paper containing those articles:

> *A boat from His Majesty's Ship the* Atlas *came on board this ship from the Sound this morning with a person having the appearance of a petty officer, he immediately ran down betwixt Decks, and in a few minutes the whole ship's company came after and requested that he might be allowed to read a paper (a copy of which I enclose). On my endeavouring to appease them a number of men run on the poop and took possession of the Armed Chests, while others were placed as Sentinels over the Magazines; I found it in vain to resist the torrent, and dreading the evil consequences which might not only result to this ship, but the service in general, I judged it prudent to yield.*

Mathew Squire, captain of *Atlas*, did make an attempt to regain control of his ship, coming aboard at 7 p.m. But his efforts proved fruitless and he informed Orde accordingly:

> *...on getting on Board I found by the Lieutenants report that the Ship's Company had Cheer'd the other Ships which was return'd by them...I have harangued the Ships Company since I have been on Board & find they have had letters from Portsmouth & from the Edgar, Informing them that if they do not act as the Ships have done at Portsmouth they will treat them very ill when they join.*

The Articles that had accompanied MacDougall's letter to Orde declared that 'every person onboard pay due respect to his Officers as before, and discharge the Duty of the Ship as formerly in every respect' and 'no Person belonging to the Ship be admitted to go on Shore excepting Officers and Boats Crews on Duty'. This orderly behaviour and respect shown to the officers was further confirmed by Captain Squire, who had added in his letter to Orde that those on his ship 'have promised me that they will be Obedient and respectful to every Officer on Board the Ship & execute the Order of every Officer with alertness.' Nevertheless, it was also being made clear that no ship should put to sea until the outcome of the demands made at Spithead were known, and with which there would be willing compliance 'with the Terms, which may be accepted of by them.'

Orde, in having received both these letters and those from other captains, failed to accept that the men of his squadron had probably long been in communication with other ships of the Channel squadron, including those at Spithead, choosing not to believe the actions now being taken to be ones already broadly agreed. Instead, he took the view that the refusal to obey the officers of his squadron were the result of threats from those at Spithead:

THE SHIPS

I had hoped that all the seamen of all the ships here would have remained in perfect obedience, notwithstanding the arts I feared were practised to seduce them; but it seems the latter joined to the threats and persuasions of the crews of H M Ships at Portsmouth (which the Lieut. of the Edgar *sent to me by Capt. McDougall says that Ships company acknowledge they have received and been influenced by) have prevailed, and led them to adopt a conduct, which leaves nothing in my power to do, until I receive the Lordships commands, but by desperate means to endeavour to keep these deluded men within bounds if I should fail in recalling them to their duty, which I think an official recount of all being settled at Portsmouth would much contribute to effect.*

From each of the ships moored in the Sound, delegates boarded *Atlas* on the following day, with a decision taken to charter a boat to send two deputies from each ship to confer with the delegates at Spithead. On the cutter passing *Atlas*, the crew of the parliament ship manned the rigging, yards and bowsprit and saluted them with three cheers. Having agreed that no ship would sail, each remained with their lower yards down and topgallant masts struck. So that all would know the terms of the Articles, these were nailed to the mainmast of each ship, alongside any correspondence received from *Atlas*. Throughout, discipline was maintained as it would have been if the officers had remained in charge. The bringing on board of alcohol was especially prohibited, with any seaman found to be 'intoxicated and behaving in a contemptible Manner' liable to punishment. On board *Atlas*, a woman was 'duck'd' for bringing strong spirits on to the ship, while on *Saturn*, another ship refusing to sail, a woman was put in irons for the same offence.

News that a settlement had been reached at Spithead came to Plymouth on 2 May by way of a letter sent post-haste by the deputies sent to Portsmouth and who were back with the squadron lying at Portsmouth just a few days later. On the letter being received, *Atlas* raised a blue flag at her mizzen peak, a sign that the delegates from each ship were to assemble. The contents of the letter were made known, with the deputies sent to Portsmouth indicating that they were perfectly satisfied with the manner of the settlement and bade their brethren at Plymouth to return to their former obedience and discipline. On this there was no outward demur. The officers regained their former authority and the squadron, upon being ordered to sea, set sail on 15 May.

At the Nore, a naval anchorage in the Thames lying just off the Isle of Grain, where a further mutiny had broken out in support of the men of the Channel fleet, matters would eventually go in a very different direction. As had happened at both Spithead and the Sound, a parliament ship, on this occasion *Sandwich*, the receiving ship for pressed men and volunteers, was established, oaths were sworn by crew members of the ships in mutiny and two delegates from each ship sent to *Sandwich* to determine the rules governing conduct and future actions. On some ships, unpopular officers were removed while four delegates, Charles McCarthy, Matthew Hollister, Thomas Atkinson and Edward Hines, were sent to Spithead to confer with the Channel fleet. For this purpose a collection of £20 was made among the seamen to cover their travelling costs, which included conveyance on the daily passenger coach from Sheerness to London, with an overnight stay in London before boarding the early morning coach from London to Portsmouth.

Arriving in Portsmouth during the second week of May, the four delegates stepped into a town full of celebration, for here matters had now been resolved. Howe, of course, could have had the four men arrested, for they were technically deserters from their ships, but he chose to encourage them to return to the Nore. He considered them to be useful propaganda tools. In allowing them to take back the message of a settlement, he believed those at the Nore would be persuaded to act in a similar manner.

Unlike the ships in Plymouth Sound, the arrival of news brought by McCarthy and Hollister, the other two delegates choosing not to return, failed to result in the mutiny there being brought to an end. Many of the delegates from individual ships were angry that not all of the demands made at Spithead had been met, with no indication that unpopular officers on ships at the Nore would be dismissed. Yet in continuing the mutiny the seamen were taking one almighty risk, for the number of ships in mutiny was considerably smaller than those that had been in mutiny at Spithead. At the Nore, the mutiny was primarily centred on three capital ships supported by a few smaller warships. If attacked by forces loyal to the government, the fleet at Spithead could have defended itself by unleashing a fusillade of devastating cannon-fire. Those at the Nore could muster nothing like that level of firepower. In making the decision to continue the mutiny, there must have been something else going on other than simple anger that all demands had not been met. It is possible that they were influenced by McCarthy and Hollister. After all, these men had talked with their fellow seamen at Spithead, probably learning that many were unhappy with the settlement made and may well have been talking of the possibility of a further mutiny breaking out at Spithead. Hollister, who had formerly served on *Defiance*, might well have gained an even deeper insight from a ship whose crew was so disgruntled that it would mutiny, all be it for the cause of Ireland, just over a year later.

THE SHIPS

On board *Pompée*, one of the most radical ships of the fleet, there was considerable disaffection, more openly surfacing on 1 June while she was at sea, a petition for peace by then circulating within the ship. Eventually signed by just over eighty members of her crew, it called for those signing the petition to agitate among the fleet upon its return to either Plymouth Sound or Spithead for peace, an outcome that would inevitably involve the dismissal of Prime Minister Pitt and a change of government. Upon its discovery, six seamen identified as ringleaders were court-martialled on the pretext of having 'mutinous and treasonable designs'. Two were subsequently executed and the other four given terms of imprisonment. Unfortunately, the full wording of the petition is unknown, but those signing, as revealed at the court martial, were committing themselves to be 'true till death in promoting the cause of Freedom with Equity while any probability of furthering its Progress remained'.

At the end of May the situation at the Nore dramatically changed when the ships in mutiny were reinforced by the arrival of eleven ships from Yarmouth, the revictualling anchorage of the North Sea squadron. This was the command of Admiral Adam Duncan, a popular officer who appears to have had absolutely no knowledge that such was being planned on the ships of his squadron.

Strengthened by the arrival of those ships, the seamen at the Nore now determined on a blockade of London, forcing all ships entering the Thames to anchor. Those carrying perishable items would be allowed to proceed onwards while those carrying non-perishables were ordered to remain. This proved extremely successful. About 100 merchant ships within the first few days of the blockade were unable to reach London. In many ways, though, the plan was too successful. The seamen were unable to find sufficient quantities of food to feed such a large number of merchant crewmen, resulting in the abandonment of the blockade only three days after it had begun. In London, panic set in. Not only was there concern that imports into the metropolis would completely cease but the additional fear that these heavily armed ships would attempt to proceed upriver and bring parts of London within range of their guns. While several of the forts lying alongside the Thames were reinforced with additional cannons, the Common Council in the City of London began to encourage volunteers to join an association for 'preserving the peace', this designed to counter any uprising in support of the seamen.

While those who led the mutiny were fairly radicalised, this did not apply to the vast majority of the lower deck. Often, it is difficult to assess their views, but an interesting glimpse into their thoughts becomes possible from letters intercepted by the Home Office. Still in existence to this day, these letters provide a unique insight into the views of some of the literate personnel present at events unfolding in the Thames. While some may have been leaders, most were not. Instead, they were the passive majority whose views ranged from total support to that of complete opposition. The seamen themselves certainly knew that letters going through official channels were being intercepted, and they attempted to use alternative methods for getting news to their families. As the intercepted letters demonstrate, these alternative methods were not always successful. Wills, a seaman on board *Leopard*, in a letter to his wife stated that he had not sent his letter 'via the boatswain to be franked' but it was still intercepted. Similarly Day, on board *Sandwich*, hoped his letter would arrive when he declared he was sending it 'by long boat by stealth'.

Unable to continue the blockade and increasingly aware that the government was not about to concede to any of their demands, many on those various ships began to re-evaluate their situation. Of particular significance was the role of London newspapers. These were widely circulated throughout the country with statements made by the London press also carried by the various provincial newspapers. In turn, London papers were dependent upon the provincial press for important news stories that took place outside the metropolis with printers of many of the London newspapers carrying directly copied items from a range of provincial newspapers to which they subscribed. In reporting the actions at Spithead, the London press often acted in a neutral way, not only reporting on events taking place but printing letters written by the seamen in defence of their actions. The London *Times*, on 24 April, as just one example, carried two accounts written by the seamen, the first a detailed breakdown of the reasons behind their demands and the second a response to an earlier vilification of their actions that had appeared in another London newspaper, *The Sun*.

Whereas the seamen at Spithead had been helped in gaining public support through favourable newspaper coverage, this had been denied to those at the Nore through a piece of government legislation that made it a felony to either communicate with or be on board a warship named as being in a state of mutiny. This made it virtually impossible for seamen of the Nore to publicise their version of events. From now on, the only accounts available to the press would be based on hearsay or ministry-produced carefully massaged accounts. Furthermore, the seamen on board those ships at the Nore were also reading those same newspaper accounts that told of government intransigence and an increasing amount of military preparation clearly aimed at bringing a violent end to the mutiny.

Isolated from their supporters in London with the government also cutting off their food supplies, an increasing number of seamen began to recognise that surrender was the only avenue open to them. On some ships, fighting was to break out as those who favoured a continuance of the situation clashed with those who were now less certain. First one ship and then another came back to the navy, with all eventually surrendering. But, unlike Spithead, no concessions were made and no royal pardons issued. Instead, an incensed Admiralty determined on retribution with 400 seamen detained for punishment. While the majority were eventually pardoned, fifty-two were condemned to death (of whom twenty-nine were eventually hanged), with a further twenty-nine imprisoned and nine flogged.

The government in preventing the newspapers publishing anything favourable to the striking seamen was clearly very effective. While public support for the seamen at Spithead had been quite considerable and certainly aided by a sympathetic or neutral press, matters were quite different for those seeking a redress of grievances at the Nore. This, in turn, not only undermined the resolution of those at the Nore to remain firm, but it also couched the views of their friends and relatives on shore. While the seamen were writing letters attempting to explain the reason for their actions, they in return received letters from friends and family that pleaded with them to think again. Some of those writers were clearly influenced by newspapers that were no longer permitted to print material emanating from the seamen and providing a defence of their actions. Most definitely affected by what they had read in the press were the parents of William Green, a seaman from Greenland Dock serving on board *Montagu*:

> *We are sorry to hear from the newspapers that you are all in disobedience. We hope that with the blessing of God you will all return to your duty and not to be led away for to come to an untimely end. Pray be careful what you say and keep your mind to yourself.*

Peter Cudlip of Union Street in Deptford, received advice from his brother:

> *Let me beg of you to be true and loyal to your King and Country [this is] a time when every brave and true Briton ought to come forward as one man to resist it and frustrate every attempt of the enemy of this happy island.*

One letter, however, does imply an interest in the wider political context of the age and offers no suggestion that the recipient should break with his fellow seamen. On this occasion Richard Reddy, who had a London address, in writing to Michael Delaney of *Britannia*, informs him of an emerging crisis in Ireland.

However, sympathetic or otherwise, the writer was no activist, indicating his own desire to go to sea, intending to join either the navy or the East India Company. Of matters in Ireland he informed Delaney:

> *Ireland is in proper confusion; and indeed I lately heard from a person come from thence that two delegates had arrived there from France and that the boys of the* Shamrock *had sworn blood that they will join them.*

On *Neptune*, one of the ships of the Channel fleet to witness a mutiny plot in 1798, several Nore mutineers were tried with those condemned both held and hanged on that same ship during the summer of 1797. Richard Parker, who had emerged as 'president' of the Nore ships in mutiny was among them. At the time, *Neptune* had ben moored in Long Reach on the River Thames with Parker charged with 'making and endeavouring to make mutinous assemblies... disobeying the lawful orders of his superior officers and treating his superior officers with disrespect.' In showing that Parker had been the elected president of the delegates, it was given as evidence that he had led the mutiny, a charge that could not be fully sustained, given that he was not an initial leader of events and that it was not him who had instructed some of the ships, led as they were by more politically motivated delegates, to open fire on *Leopard* and *Repulse*, two ships that slipped their cables one night to escape the mutiny. Parker, executed on 30 June, was the first of those held on *Neptune* to be hanged with eighteen others, while awaiting their fate signing a letter dated 3 July and addressed to *Neptune's* captain, Sir Henry Stanhope, praising him for his treatment of them while held on board the ship:

> *SIR, To pay our tribute to a friend to humanity is generally deemed unwarranted flattery, but from us truth only can be looked for. Accept, therefore, Captain Stanhope, our last and grateful acknowledgments of your humanity during our unhappy confinement here; and that our Country may long continue to be benefited by the service of Officers of your disposition, is the fervent wish of the following men under sentence of Death from the Sandwich:– Charles M'Carthy, William Gregory, John Davis, John Lewer, Thomas Appleyard, Joseph Hughes, James Hockless, John Brooks, George Taylor, John Whitely, Charles Chant, George Gainer, James Jones, Thomas Brady, Peter Holding, Charles M'Cann, Henry Wolfe, John Porter.*

THE SHIPS

A further ship witnessing Irish mutiny plots during the summer of 1798 was *Adamant*, which in 1797 had been part of the North Sea squadron but was not one of the eleven ships that sailed into the Thames to join the mutineers at the Nore. Instead, *Adamant* had remained under the command of Admiral Duncan in blockading the enemy port of Texel. Nevertheless, *Adamant's* crew had, just eighteen days before most ships of the North Sea squadron sailed for the Nore, challenged Duncan's authority by giving three cheers in the manner of 'their friends at Spithead'. Seemingly, while a proportion of *Adamant's* crew wished to support the demands being made, a majority had chosen to take no further action when called upon to desert Duncan and sail to the Nore. Doubtless, crews of all ships were similarly split, with those loyal to their officers on most ships either cowed or simply in a minority.

Defiance, a ship that was to play a key role in the Irish mutinies of 1798, at Spithead sent two of her officers ashore, while also having witnessed on board an earlier crew mutiny that had broken out in November 1795 while the ship was moored in Leith Roads. On this occasion, the mutineers had demanded less water in their rum, the ship's cheese to be condemned, and an acting lieutenant to be removed because of his continual drunkenness and ruthlessness. However, the immediate cause had been the refusal of the ship's captain, Sir George Home, to permit shore leave when the captains of other ships were allowing small groups of their own men ashore upon condition that others would only be so permitted upon the return of each shore party. Home, though, was a harsh disciplinarian whose method of controlling the crew was through the frequent use of the cat o' nine tails, often several times a week.

This first *Defiance* mutiny had been highly disorganised, with no prior planning and no clear leadership. While possession of the ship was gained, including access to arms and gunpowder for the firing of the ship's main armament, the mutineers had eventually to concede upon the arrival of a military force that secured the arrest of those deemed to be the leaders. Seventeen were brought to trial, with nine sentenced to be hanged, six to be lashed and two discharged. Of the nine to be hanged, and possibly much to Home's disappointment, four were reprieved. For the safety of the non-mutineers, a number of the crew were transferred to other ships: 180 removed on 24 February 1796 to *Goliath*, three days later ninety-two to the Nore receiving ship *Sandwich*, and later twenty to *Jupiter* with 100 on 18 March to *Director*, whose commander was William Bligh. Among those who went to the latter ship was London-born Matthew Hollister, a 42-year-old gunner's yeoman who was, of course, one of the four delegates sent from the Nore to Spithead in May 1797. He had joined *Defiance* in 1795 from Chester and had been called as a witness at the court martial, providing evidence sufficiently favourable to one of the Leith Roads *Defiance* mutineers, William Parker, that might have helped Parker escape the death penalty, sentenced instead to 300 lashes, of which he received only sixty.

As for the Irish mutinies that broke out in 1798, many of those active in the advancing of those plots were present on those same ships during these earlier mutinies, seeing at first-hand how events had played out at Leith, Spithead, Plymouth Sound, the Nore and Yarmouth. The experience gained was clearly digested and used to underpin the plots that were developed in 1798, aware that a single-ship mutiny would ultimately fail if any ship attempting to mutiny was nestled either between other warships remaining loyal to their officers or within easy reach of a military force on shore. From talk among seamen themselves, they would all have been aware of the mutiny on *Bounty* as captained by William Bligh, successful because *Bounty*, at the time of the mutiny led by Fletcher Christian, was thousands of miles away from any naval ship that might have intervened. Similarly, *Hermione*, of which more will be said later, was taken by her crew following an especially bloody mutiny into the Spanish port of La Guaira (modern-day Venezuela) in September 1797. She also had been a considerable distance from any other British ship. As for lessons learnt from the mutinies of 1797, it was clear that much was possible but only if the crews of numerous ships actively co-operated. But if that unity broke down, so did the mutiny itself. Also essential in achieving success was good organisation co-ordinated by a committee formed of those steadfast to the cause, with the taking of oaths by those who might otherwise be less committed used to ensure long-term support rather than a sudden change of mind. Finally, secrecy was essential, for only if the officers of the ship were totally oblivious to any actions planned by the lower deck, would the plotting of a mutiny flourish.

Chapter 2

The People of the Ships

On ships of the Channel fleet where revolutionaries formed cadres and proceeded to recruit activists and followers, this all went unknown to the officers of the ship for lengthy periods of time. Discovery of the plots usually only coming at the very moment of the onboard mutiny, or more accurately rebellion, was about to be sprung. Yet, among the people of the lower deck, from virtually the first moment of inception, all would have had knowledge of an insurrection being planned. For each mess group, the six or so seamen who cooked and ate together, it would have been a lively topic of conversation, mulled over for weeks on end. Yet it never reached the ears of the officers. While some, especially the Irish and those of a more radical leaning would have been sympathetic to the planned rebellion, others were not. And those who were unsupportive were rarely tempted to take what they knew to the quarterdeck. On the face of it, this seems quite inexplicable. Any man possessing even the slightest knowledge of a mutiny in the planning was, by rule of the Admiralty, culpable, and so faced the possibility of being court-martialled and the death sentence passed upon him. Indeed, such severity of sentence could hardly be doubted, for in planning to take the ship over to the enemy, the United Irish plot was, for those loyal to Britain as ruled from London, nothing less than treason, the worse possible crime imaginable.

A suggested reason for that silence, and one already given, is that those of the crew who opposed the mutiny, while aware of its planning, were afraid of the consequences of reporting it, exposed as they would be to violent retribution. That, however, cannot be seen as the only reason. A number of other factors also came into play. One of particular importance was group loyalty. The people of the lower deck, through working closely alongside each other, often for periods of several years, shared a sense of social identity. Firmly embedded, this shared identity quite naturally created a close bond which, in turn, resulted in an overwhelming distaste to informing on a fellow member of that group. Only at the last minute, when the mutiny was on the verge of being actioned and the long-delayed reality of having to choose sides, did one or two of the lower deck finally break ranks, sometimes anonymously but always discreetly, with an officer informed that mutiny was about to break out. With this information taken to the captain, those named or thought to be among the mutineers were swiftly apprehended and securely held on board or transferred to another ship of the fleet.

To gain a full understanding of the complexities of the situation, the most useful starting point is to consider the gulf that existed between the officers who commanded from the quarterdeck and the people of the lower deck. In simple terms, those of the lower deck were drawn from the lower strata of society and those of the quarterdeck were drawn primarily from a landed background or were sons of professional or commercial fathers. With social hierarchy of huge importance during the late eighteenth century, those drawn from such diverse classes had limited understanding of each other. For those committed to the United Irish cause, the gap was even greater as, from their point of view, the officers of the ship, the 'quality' or 'nobs' as often referred to by the lower deck, were, through birth and privilege, very much part of the governing elite and, as such, seen by those who were plotting as their true enemy. As for contact between officers and men, this was at its closest only during times of inspection. The men mustered on deck two or three times a week for the officers to examine the cleanliness of each man and the clothing he wore. A man discovered to be insufficiently clean or his clothes found to be damp or dirty would face certain punishment. While of benefit to the crew in general, these inspections were simply to ensure the fighting efficiency of the ship, with officers showing only limited interest in the wellbeing of the men. To uncover the real sense of feeling or opinions held by the people of the lower deck would have required a much closer understanding to have developed between the officers and the lower deck.

Terms of service also differed greatly between the men of these two very different social strata. For the officers, their arrival at sea, if not the ship upon which they were serving, was by way of choice. An officer could hand in his commission at any time or, upon appointment to the rank of captain, could even reach the very pinnacle of his profession. This sharply contrasted with any man serving on the lower deck. While some were volunteers, others, possibly the majority, had been forced to serve, with promotion to anything more than petty officer rank while not impossible was entirely dependent upon the favour of a captain offering his patronage. Among those forced to serve were those who were brought on board naval ships by press gangs, small parties of seamen led by a junior officer. These gangs were legally allowed to detain any man seen as suitable for service on a seagoing warship. Legal restrictions did exist. Under the Navy Act of 1740, it had been laid down that those liable for impressment should be seafarers aged between 18 and 55. In addition, they should be British citizens, foreigners married to British women, or foreign nationals who had served for a minimum of two years on a British ship. Landsmen, apprentices and 'gentlemen' were excluded, as were those carrying certificates of exemption – such as men employed in naval dockyards. At certain times, usually when war was newly declared and the Admiralty in desperate need to get ships out to sea, the Act did allow the declaration of a 'hot press', which meant that many of those restrictions could be ignored.

If not caught by a press gang sent out by a captain of a particular ship, a man might also be ensnared by the Naval Impress Service, a permanent organisation within the structure of the navy. As with individual ship recruiting parties, they also sent out gangs to recruit seamen, but the difference was that these were men permanently employed in the duty and paid both additional travel money (3d per mile for officers and 1d for men) and anything up to 10s for every man pressed. An additional duty performed was that of seeking out deserters and, for this purpose, gangs of seamen working for the impress service would often position themselves on the roads leading away from shorelines close to ports where a man might have escaped from a warship at its moorings.

While the muster books of all naval warships distinguished between those who volunteered and those who were 'press'd', these books do not provide a true indication of how a man came to serve. On being brought on board a naval ship, a pressed man was given the chance to sign up as a volunteer, receiving as a reward both an advance of two months' wages and an additional payment known as conduct money. Both were supposed to be paid only to those who volunteered but were usually given to any man prepared to deny that he had been pressed. As a result, only the most stubborn, or those with a strong belief that they could gain release, would choose to be mustered as a pressed man. In 1776, to give one example, a total of 250 men were reported to have been pressed in London but, according to a newspaper report, on being brought on board a naval tender lying off the Tower of London, all but a few were entered as volunteers. A clue as to the true level of impressment comes from a survey conducted by the Admiralty between 1803-5, which revealed that of 11,600 men recruited in thirty-two ports around mainland Britain, but excluding London, forty-eight per cent were pressed. In the late 1750s, following a request from the House of Commons, the Navy Office produced figures showing that almost half the men entering the navy during this wartime period, and who had entered the navy from the shore as opposed to already being at sea, were pressed. This, of course, does not apply to the entire wartime navy. A great many serving on the lower deck were also carried over from earlier peace-time recruitment or had joined from merchant ships already at sea. However, it is suggestive of the navy being heavily dependent on the impressment of men, with this quite naturally creating on any warship a considerable degree of resentment among the people of the lower deck. This resentment was inevitably directed towards the officers, so increasing the unwillingness of any man to report to an officer a fellow seaman guilty of mutinous or subversive talk.

Another means of forced entry into the navy was by way of the law courts, judges and magistrates, by the Navy Act of 1795 authorised to offer convicted felons the choice of a prison sentence or entry into the navy. Given the harsh condition of prisons and the fact that in joining the navy a wage would also be paid, many accepted this option. In particular, the Act listed 'rogues, vagabonds, smugglers, embezzlers of naval stores' as eligible for the navy, alongside 'other able-bodied, idle and disorderly persons exercising no lawful employment'. The result was that men with little or no connection with the sea were entered onto the books of naval warships, unable to offer any of the essential skills needed on board while proving difficult to discipline. However, there was one group of convicted felons that when directed into the navy by local magistrates ultimately proved even more troublesome. These were men from Ireland, especially those found guilty by magistrates of rebellious acts against the Crown. Seemingly, the Admiralty was unaware of the danger this particular group of Irish recruits posed, at best ensuring that many, to reduce the potential for them to mutiny, were placed on either small vessels or in ships serving on more distant stations. A warning of the danger did, however, come from Sir Edward Newenham, an ultra-protestant loyalist and a member of parliament for Dublin. In April 1797, he wrote to Earl Spencer, the First Lord of the Admiralty, asking him to accept no more of these rebels into the fleet, 'for one of them would poison 700 men'. He cited as evidence a conversation he had with friends who had conversed with several United Irish rebels sentenced to be put on board ship. Their common declaration, he informed Spencer, was that they would be of more service to the cause on board a man-of-war, ambitious to form rebel clubs wherein each man would swear 'to be true to each other in the cause of Irish freedom'.

It is certainly the case that United Irishmen often displayed joy when learning that the sentence given to them when found guilty of rebellious acts was to serve in the fleet. Furthermore, it fitted in nicely with the direction pursued by the leadership of the Society of United Irishmen who were actively encouraging members of the society to enlist into the navy for the purpose of subversion. By September 1796, one of their agents, Christopher Carey, was reported to be travelling through south-west England accompanied by a French agent. One particular success was the establishment of a United Irish club in Portsmouth, which may have played a part in the mutinies that broke out in 1797. However, neither mutiny at the Nore or Spithead was orchestrated by Irish radicals, although much evidence exists that, at the Nore, Irish radicals dominated several of the ships' committees and were an influence on decisions being taken. In a somewhat belated effort to support the mutineers of 1797, funds were raised at fairs held in Ireland and from subscriptions among members of the United Irishmen. But by the time such monies were available, the mutinies at both Spithead and the Nore had ended. It was also planned that William Duckett, a United Irish emissary, would travel to Portsmouth to make contact with Irish seamen on board some of the ships in mutiny, but he too never arrived. Nevertheless, aware of the continuance of underlying seething discontent, efforts to send more United Irishmen into the navy intensified, with a possible 1,200 United Irish sympathisers reported to have joined the navy by July of that year.

A further method of naval recruitment came about in 1795 when the government under William Pitt adopted a quota system whereby each county provided an allocated number of men for naval service. The number required of each county depended on the size of its population and the number of sea ports within its boundary. London, as a case in point, had to provide 5,704 quota men while Bristol had to provide 666. To induce men to sign up, county magistrates usually offered a bounty, while those sent into the navy by magistrates could also be included as part of the quota. Given the more extensive trawling for recruits through the quota system, those who entered the navy were often better educated and frequently politically aware, their number including tradesmen, attorneys, teachers and clerks. As such, they helped enhance the political and philosophical awareness of those serving on the lower deck, described by one writer 'as a fractional but sinister and important new strain of navy chattels'. Through their superior education, and according to one lower deck commentator, the addition of considerable guile and cunning, they were no asset to the navy, bringing to the fleet their notions of justice and the works of the nation's leading radical, Thomas Paine.

Naval officers themselves frequently viewed quota men as troublesome, believing such men to often be the dregs of society, men who the parishes wished to off-load into the navy. Cuthbert Collingwood, Nelson's second-in-command at Trafalgar, accused the newly arriving quota men as responsible for inciting the fleet mutinies of 1797. Such questioning of the value of quota men to the navy persisted into the twentieth century, with Michael Lewis, in a social history of the navy, castigating them as 'gaolbirds, ne'er do wells and starvelings', further describing them as 'social misfits and outcasts'. Similarly, Kindleberger described the Quota Acts, for others followed in 1796 and 1805, as degenerating into the means of 'clearing out the jails, delivering tramps, idlers, poachers, beggars, minor thieves and pickpockets' into the navy. Nick

Slope, in a more recent account, takes a more considered view. In examining records of a number of Royal Navy frigates for the period 1796 to 1803, he found little supporting evidence that quota men made poor and troublesome sailors. According to his finding, quota men, while suffering higher rates of sickness and death through sickness, 'deserted less, were flogged less and developed into competent sailors'. However, Slope did admit the need for further research, with greater consideration given to local county and sea port records alongside the tracing of the subsequent naval service of the quota men associated with the ships whose records he examined.

Once brought on board a ship of war, each man was entered into the ship's muster book, an entry next to his name indicating whether he was an 'able' or 'ordinary' seaman, or a 'landsman'. These grades, always ultimately determined by the captain, were a reflection of seamanship skills (or lack of) that a man already possessed, with the pay to be received reflecting those skills. To be rated 'able', a man would need to be familiar with the various duties of seamanship, competent to 'hand, reef and steer' – that is, a seaman capable of handling a sail, and working the masts and sails as a 'topman'. This was the most demanding of work on board a ship, requiring a high level of skill backed by quickness and dexterity. An able seaman would also be expected to take over as the main helmsman, keeping the ship on course, with some also receiving minor responsibilities that might include sail handling in one area of the ship. This was reflected in being accorded the informal title of captain of the maintop, captain of the foretop, or captain of the mizzen top. A man rated 'ordinary', however, was a seaman of less experience, possibly having only two years of sea service, but one who might after time be raised to that of 'able'. To put it another way, a man rated 'ordinary' was someone who had a degree of usefulness but was not as yet an expert sailor. The least experienced were 'landsmen', men with no experience of sea but after one year could be raised to the rank of 'ordinary'. A common duty assigned to 'landsmen' was that of forming part of the gun crew, as firing a naval cannon mostly required a great amount of labour, with the firing of a broadside involving as many as fifty guns on the largest ships.

Within each warship, crews were divided into administrative divisions, a system first introduced during the mid-eighteenth century. Placed at the head of each division for the purpose of ensuring efficiency and the wellbeing of the men was a lieutenant with the assistance of an inferior officer, usually a midshipman. In turn, the men of the lower deck were divided into those smaller units of around six men known as messes, taking their meals together. For this purpose they would be seated around a small table slung between the guns of the lower decks. Self-selecting, each man chose the mess he would join if accepted by those of that mess. As such, those who constituted each group were closely tied to each other, normally holding shared beliefs and other matters in common. While of value for creating unity within a ship, they might equally be quite divisive, with many seamen choosing to join groups reflecting their own ethnicity, with values, such as those of many Irish seamen, differing from their fellow shipmates.

As for the number of Irishmen actually serving in the Channel fleet, and therefore potentially supportive of any plot to take a ship into a French port, this was something that the Admiralty itself endeavoured to discover. Aware that there was talk of such a possibility but unaware of any real detail upon which action could be taken, the captain of each ship under Bridport's command was asked to provide a return of the number of Irish on board and to give an estimate of the number who might be 'evil disposed'. These returns indicated a total of 1,517 Irish seamen serving in the Channel fleet alongside 460 Irish marines, with some ships having as many as thirteen per cent of the crew born in Ireland and others less than five per cent. Of the total number of Irish serving under Bridport, 328 seamen and eighty-three marines were classified as to be of an evil disposition. Obviously, the decision to regard an Irishman as evilly disposed was doubtless based on a high degree of subjectivity, tinged by possible prejudice, and offers nothing in the form of accuracy. Not taken into account in that survey was that the Irish rebels were supported by English, Scots and Welsh revolutionaries. These men were often as equally committed to the taking of British ships into French ports as some of their Irish shipmates.

While the divisiveness of the mess system is something that will be returned to later, it is worth noting that the Irish were one particular group that favoured messing by national identity, but so too did other ethnic groups, whether Scots, English, Welsh or those from the many other nationalities serving on board British warships. However, for Irish seamen it was a choice made more vital by many being of the Catholic faith and a frequent desire to see Ireland freed of English rule. Often discriminated against and treated badly by other members of the crew and officers, there was an understandable desire that they spend their off-duty time with those who would, when needed, come to their defence. John Nicol, himself a Scot serving on the frigate *Surprise* during the American Revolutionary War (1775-83), in a later account of his service at sea wrote of Irish seamen being frequently subjected to ferocious attacks, telling of one incident that followed upon the distribution of prize money:

> *We came upon deck; the crew were all fighting through amongst each other in their drink, English against Irish, the officers mostly on shore, and those on board looking on. I meant to take no share*

in the quarrel, when an Irish-man came staggering up, crying, 'Erin go bragh!' [Ireland Forever] and made a blow at me. My Scottish blood rose in a moment at this provocation, and I was as throng as the rest. How it ended I hardly recollect. I got a blow that stupefied me, and all was quiet when I came to myself, the liquor having evaporated from the others, and the passion from me.

It was this same messing system, with seamen able to choose with whom they messed, that greatly facilitated the development of the mutiny plots in 1798. The Irish, with occasional sympathisers among the more radically minded members of a crew, were able to form exclusive units unfettered by the presence of potential loyalist members of the crew who would argue against such an action being taken.

It was in the Channel fleet, especially if a comparison is made with the Mediterranean fleet, that the officers took least interest in the wellbeing of the men who they commanded, inclined to see them as mere cogs in a machine. For those officers, the outcome was a failure to understand the grievances that resulted from impressment and the endless chores inflicted upon them while at sea. It was a situation that not only accounted for mutinous talk to flourish, but with the majority of the lower deck, whether loyalist or otherwise, harbouring a grievance against the officers, such talk rarely reaching the ears of the officers. Certainly the Irish dissidents in the Channel fleet felt safe in developing their plans, but would not have been if the officers who commanded them had shown greater vigilance and a greater understanding of the men they commanded. Even knowing the names of the men they commanded seemed beyond the capability of some officers, relying heavily on petty officers, who themselves were drawn from the lower deck, to oversee the general running of the ship.

In the Mediterranean, where a sizeable element of the British Navy was also present, a very different regime prevailed, and one that greatly hindered the ability of Irish and other republican rebels to develop similar plans. In 1798, the fleet here was under the command of Admiral John Jervis, 1st Earl of St Vincent, a future First Lord of the Admiralty, and a man noted for the harsh enforcement of discipline but one who was couched by his attentiveness to the reasonable demands of those under him. Mercilessly quelling the slightest sign of insubordination, St Vincent sought to anticipate any grievance of the lower deck through watchfulness and sympathetic foresight. In doing so, he endeavoured to pass on these characteristics to the officers who were under his command, ensuring that they too enforced discipline and efficiently performed their duties. To one captain he wrote, 'the very disorderly state of His Majesty's ship under your command, obliges me to require that neither yourself nor any of your officers are to go on shore on what is called pleasure.' In the Mediterranean fleet, captains of vessels were not only subject to his strict regulation as to their personal proceedings, but were compelled to sleep on board, even in home ports with duties customarily left to subordinates also assigned to them by St Vincent.

Under Lord Bridport, the Channel fleet saw the prevalence of a much more relaxed atmosphere, with captains feeling less compulsion to attend to the needs of the men under their command or the enforcement of discipline when the men were below deck, so ensuring that Irish rebels were secure from officers discovering what they were about. St Vincent himself commented on the laxity that prevailed within the Channel fleet, noting of those officers serving in the Channel fleet that few were 'qualified to command ships of the line'. Indeed, it was the poorest officers, whom St Vincent described as 'old women in the guise of young men', who clung to the Channel fleet because of that lax discipline. In 1800, when it was first learnt that St Vincent was himself to take command of the Channel fleet, a toast was drunk at Bridport's table. 'May the discipline of the Mediterranean never be introduced into the Channel.' A captain's wife, wrathful that her husband was kept from her side by the admiral's regulations, is said to have proclaimed of St Vincent, 'May his next glass of wine choke the wretch.'

The want of discipline among the ships of the Channel fleet was something that greatly shocked those who commanded ships in the Mediterranean, a point highlighted during the summer of 1797 when the frigate *Thames*, fresh out of Portsmouth and escorting a large West India convoy, arrived at Madeira. Here also were ships under St Vincent's command, the crews of which were aware of what had taken place at Spithead and the concessions gained. While discipline was fully maintained on those ships under the command of St Vincent, this was not so on *Thames*, 'the men doing exactly what they pleased and the officers being absolutely afraid to control them.' It was also learnt that this situation was not peculiar to this one ship, but prevalent among all the ships of the Channel fleet, where the people of the lower deck 'did exactly what they pleased'. On arrival at Madeira, and making contact with crews of the Mediterranean fleet, they attempted to get them to behave in a similar fashion, telling them to turn out all the officers they disliked. While this may have had an impact on some, the arrival of inflammatory papers brought over to one of the ships of the Mediterranean fleet, *Minerve*, were immediately brought to the attention of her captain.

The question that needs to be asked is why the men of *Minerve* immediately reported the coming on board of papers calling for a mutiny, while on board those ships of the Channel fleet when at their moorings in home waters to revictual there was no attempt by any man to report the arrival of similar material. In command of *Minerve* was George Cockburn, an officer whose approach to command replicated that of St Vincent in that he was a firm disciplinarian but one who took an interest in the welfare of his men, rewarding those who performed well but never ignoring those who defaulted, with severe punishments often inflicted. Through showing an interest in his men and their welfare, a bond was created between Cockburn and the men of the lower deck, which ensured that he was trusted and liked. He made certain that money owed to his men was always paid, representing individuals or small numbers of individuals who had claims from service or bounty money from other ships, making personal approaches to the captains of those ships on behalf of the men. To those injured or incapable of continued service, he recommended them to the Greenwich Hospital to receive pensions or a lodging within the establishment. Those who served him well were recommended for promotion, and to protect the health of those he commanded he often supplied them with fresh vegetables and fruit obtained ashore. It was this bond so created that led the men of *Minerve* to reject the idea of mutiny, and quickly inform the captain of what was afoot, with Cockburn writing a month later to Horatio Nelson, then also serving under St Vincent:

> *Indeed, I had every reason to be very much pleased with the conduct of the majority of our ship's company (in the midst of temptation) who, on my turning them up on account of some suspicion about them, assured me of their firm attachment to their government and officers and offered to prove it by going alongside either of the other frigates that should behave improperly.*

Nelson was also a commander who held firm to discipline while showing an interest in the welfare of his men. In the Mediterranean, he always ensured the ships under his command were well supplied with victuals and the conditions on board were never unsanitary. As a captain and a later commander of the Mediterranean fleet, Thomas Hardy, famed as Nelson's flag captain at Trafalgar, also took great pains to ensure the health and wellbeing of those he commanded. While there appears to be a prevalence of such commanders in the Mediterranean, in the Channel fleet during the late 1790s they were a rarity, with a bond between officers and the lower deck missing.

That lack of discipline in the Channel fleet, compared with the Mediterranean fleet, reached a new low point following the mutinies of 1797. The disinterest of the officers in both the welfare of the men and their conduct below decks was reinforced by a dread of further outbreaks of mutiny, with officers fearful of entering the lower deck for the reception they might receive. Most striking was

Richard Worsley, commander of *Calypso*, a ship-sloop in the North Sea fleet. He became so afraid of his own crew that, according to one naval historian, Niklas Frykman, he turned the vessel into 'an armed camp', posting marines around the ship, these armed 'with drawn swords and loaded pistols' with orders to 'shoot and kill'. In addition:

> *He also barred the crew from accessing the main deck without reason, unshipped several ladders, ordered grates laid down, and for long periods of time kept them confined below.*

In response, the crew refused to undertake work when ordered, forcing Worsley to finally leave the ship.

Among the officers of the Channel fleet a belief emerged that if left to their own devices the men below deck would be less troublesome. While at sea, the men of the Channel fleet continued to be worked hard throughout the day, as was also the case in the Mediterranean fleet, and given, when no other work existed, meaningless tasks such as the holy-stoning of the deck (the rubbing of the deck with a stone and sand to ensure it was clear of all dirt and stains) or drilling, with maintenance work set aside for the afternoon. It was work designed to keep the men occupied and to prevent them from reflecting on their grievances or behaving in a disorderly fashion. Apart from floggings and other punishments, it was a useful tool of social control and which the men, while disliking the work, came to accept. Once at anchor, such concerns within the Channel fleet appear to have evaporated, it being assumed that the men would be happy with a rest. When at anchor, the regime of the day was forgotten, the men given lengthy periods of rest, while the officers abandoned the ship, leaving the men to their own devices. On board *Defiance*, her captain since 1796, Theophilus Jones, on each occasion his ship came to anchor in Cawsand Bay to revictual, chose to leave the ship to live ashore, allowing his officers to do likewise. Consequently, there was no attempt at supervising the crew, with the people of the lower deck knowing that their meetings were completely secure from the sudden and unexpected arrival of an officer. A more efficient captain, one aware of the prevailing attitudes among a proportion of his crew, would not have left his ship. Instead he would have been attentive to the overseeing of the crew.

Richard Kempenfelt (1718-82), a particularly innovative officer who rose to the rank of rear admiral, had identified a decade earlier the likely problems befalling a ship if a captain should absent himself when arriving in port or at an anchorage. He pointed to the greater chance of men in this situation having time to compare their conditions with life ashore, and cursing the officers for the situation in which they found themselves. In a letter written in September 1779 and addressed to fellow naval officer Charles Middleton, the future 1st Lord Barham, Kempenfelt advised that captains 'should not be absent from their ships' when they were in port. In his view, if there are no officers on board, the men will become 'riotous and licentious' with some taking the opportunity to desert, adding 'the men must be constantly employed to keep them orderly.'

In December 1779, Kempenfelt addressed a further letter to Middleton on his thinking as to the duties that should fall on an officer appointed to a naval warship. His assessment was that these were easier to perform than that of army officers, as unlike ordinary soldiers, seamen on board a warship were confined to narrow limits as defined by a ship. Soldiers, when off duty, had much greater freedom, able to frequent tap houses away from the barracks, or might even be quartered in local inns when barrack space was not available. In either case, they were well removed from the attentions of even the most conscientious officers. According to Kempenfelt:

> *Certainly, the situation of a ship's crew is more favourable to sustain order and regularity than that of a corps ashore, confined within narrow limits, without tippling houses to debauch in, and under the constant eye of their officers. But if six, seven, or eight hundred men are left in a mass together, without divisions, and the officers assigned no particular charge over any part of them, who only give orders from the quarterdeck or gangways – such a crew must remain a disorderly mob, business will be done awkwardly and tumultuously, without order or despatch, and the raw men put into no train of improvement.*

His solution, and one certainly not adopted by any of those who commanded a ship of the Channel, was that of dividing and subdividing the crew, and over each division an officer or midshipman to be appointed to inspect into and regulate conduct and to discipline the men as necessary:

> *Let the ship's crew be divided into as many companies as there are lieutenants, except the first lieutenant, whose care should extend over the whole. These companies to be subdivided, and put under the charge of mates or midshipmen; and besides this, every twenty-five men to have a foreman to assist in the care of the men, as a sergeant or corporal in the army. Each lieutenant's company should be formed of the men who are under his command at quarters for*

action. These companies should be reviewed every day by their lieutenants, when the men are to appear tight and clean.

As for the captain, he should review the entire crew at least once a week.

This, of course, is something that Theophilus Jones was not doing. While, of course, Jones was not the only captain failing to attend to his crew, his inadequacies were recognised, for despite a shortage of sea-going officers once the war was renewed with France in 1803, he never again received command.

In a letter to First Lord Spencer at the Admiralty, following the transfer to the Mediterranean in May 1798 of a squadron from the Channel fleet under Rear Admiral Sir Roger Curtis, St Vincent clearly expressed his views with regard to the indiscipline he witnessed upon the arrival of that squadron:

The squadron your Lordship has sent me under the orders of Rear Admiral Sir Roger Curtis exhibits a lamentable specimen of the state of your fleet at home...unless your admirals and captains are compelled to sleep on board their ships and keep all their officers tightly to their duty when at Spithead, Plymouth Sound and Cawsand Bay your navy will be ruined past redemption. There is a dreadful licentiousness in the conversation of the officers which is very soon conveyed to the men and I attribute in a great degree the disgraces which have befallen your fleet at home to this decay of discipline and unless you have an officer at the head who has vigour and disposition to lay the axe to the root of this evil and you give him the most unequivocal support there will very soon be an end to all activity or energy in the natural defence of the country.

Perhaps the most telling evidence as to how little officers of the Channel fleet generally knew of their men was the outbreak of mutiny at Spithead in 1797. Seemingly, not one officer was aware of the impending event, with crews on numerous ships not only discussing among themselves their refusal to obey orders, but making regular contact while in port with crews of other ships. First Lord Spencer writing to Admiral Sir John Jervis, the future Earl of St Vincent, in May of that year and referring to the mutiny at Spithead wrote:

The extraordinary part of the business is the secrecy with which it was conducted; not an officer in the whole Channel fleet appears to have had a suspicion of anything of the kind having been in

> agitation, and yet when the mutiny broke out at Spithead there had evidently been much concert and communication among the several ships.

However, this lack of awareness on the part of the officers was not one that was restricted only to the Channel fleet. As noted already, Admiral Adam Duncan, the commander-in-chief of the North Sea squadron, in writing to Spencer on three occasions in May 1797, informed him that the men of the lower deck on all his ships were 'perfectly satisfied and quiet'. Yet, within a few weeks of him making those remarks, the majority of the ships of the North Sea squadron had broken away, sailing independently to the Nore to join up with the ships already in mutiny at that anchorage, accepting the command of Richard Parker over that of Adam Duncan.

In theory, an intermediary between the quarterdeck and lower deck was provided by the petty officers of the ship, seamen of the lower deck who had been promoted from among those who had shown both a willingness to command and a determination to see the work of their department well performed. The vast majority of petty officers were assigned to a watch, as were all of the lower deck, with each watch working a set number of hours while the ship was at sea or in the process of taking on stores. On board the ships of the Channel fleet a two-watch system was followed, with the day divided into seven watches, four watches of four hours and two watches of two hours, with each watch working a turn-and-turnabout system that gave each man at most a four-hour break below deck. At the head of each watch was an officer (a lieutenant, midshipman or master's mate) who would then be dependent on the various petty officers within the watch to ensure work was efficiently performed. Among the most important of the petty officers were quartermasters, gunner's mates, captains of the forecastle and captains of the tops, but with those appointed receiving no supplement to their wage. It was the quartermasters who supervised the steering of the ship, overseeing the man at the wheel and reporting on his competence while captains of the forecastle and tops oversaw the men working respectively the sails in the forecastle and top masts. Some petty officers, however, possessed important skills necessary to keep the ship afloat and were themselves also accorded an assistant, known as a mate, who held junior petty officer status, among them the ropemaker, caulker and sailmaker. Among the people of the lower deck, the most unpopular of the petty officers was the boatswain's mate, a junior petty officer whose duties included flogging a man condemned by the ship's captain.

While petty officers might be expected to keep officers informed of any activities on the lower deck that might endanger the ship, they rarely chose to do so, for in also living among the men of the lower deck, their lives would be unbearable if they were seen as an officer's toady. John Wetherell, a British seaman impressed into the Royal Navy, provides a rare account of life at sea during this period, writing of one such petty officer, a captain of the tops who he refers to as a 'Judas'. Because of his constant willingness to inform on any man's indiscretion, the men had constantly to be on their guard 'in dread of giving him the smallest offence'. To this it needs adding that petty officers also had their grievances directed against the officers, for they too were often pressed men. Some would have served for many years on merchant ships, pressed into naval service from a ship returning to a home port. In being forced into the navy, they not only lost their freedom to choose the ship upon which they might next sail, but forfeited a much higher wage than the one paid by the Royal Navy. Nor, despite their assumed seniority among the men, were they necessarily treated well by the officers, Wetherell telling of how, when chasing a Swedish merchantman, the top stud sail boom went overboard, resulting in the captain having all of the main topmen of the watch, including the captain of the top, stripped and flogged.

PART 2

Liberty and Revolution

The cause, or *raison d'etre,* of the planned mutinies on board several ships of the Channel fleet and elsewhere in 1798 was nothing less than the total freeing of Ireland from English governance. To achieve this, the assistance of revolutionary France had been called upon. With these calls not in vain, the Directory in Paris sent into Ireland two military expeditions. Of course, if victory had been achieved, France would have required a payback in the form of using Ireland as the point from which an invasion of England could be mounted. After all, Ireland was the back-door into England. It was relatively easy for the French to amass hundreds of troops around Boulogne and Calais, but the English Channel, over which they would need to pass, was an insurmountable obstacle. While the distance between England and France at the narrowest point of the Channel is only around 20 miles, it was a seaway totally controlled by the Royal Navy. Any invading force attempting to cross the Channel would have little chance of success, likely to be intercepted by an overwhelming force of British warships. Admittedly, if a landing had been achieved, the defences of the Kent and Essex coastline were, at that time, very weak, but a force, if not already destroyed by the Royal Navy, would have been so enfeebled that it would have been unlikely to achieve a meaningful foothold.

Ireland, on the other hand, offered something very different. The distance across the Irish sea to the British mainland was, at its shortest, no more than 10 miles, with a possible landing anywhere from Campbeltown in Scotland to Milford Haven in Wales, a length of coast in excess of 250 miles. Consequently, ships of the Royal Navy brought into the Irish Sea would have been hard pressed to make contact with an invading force making a surprise attack somewhere along such an extensive coastal area. Even if sufficiently forewarned, the British Navy's other difficulty would have been that of assembling a force of ships of sufficient size to take on a French fleet entering the Irish Sea. Already the Admiralty was over-committed, a great many of its ships assigned elsewhere, and unavailable for defending the Irish Sea. If nothing else, the blockade of the French Atlantic sea ports had to be continued with a second fleet having to be kept in the North Sea, maintaining a watch on Texel. From any of these ports, should a suitable opportunity arise, an additional expeditionary force might just be successful in making it to the shores of Britain, especially if the Channel and North Sea fleets were reduced of available ships. Such a landing, if co-ordinated with a landing from Ireland, would result in Britain fighting a defensive war on two fronts.

Chapter 3

Harsh Laws and Discrimination

Memories are long in Ireland and history of inestimable importance. Without doubt, Irish seamen serving on British warships during the eighteenth century would certainly have had some understanding of their nation's past – an understanding that heavily influenced their attitude to England and its hegemonic control over Ireland. Even for those with the most partial knowledge of historical times, an awareness would have existed of Ireland having once been divided into several kingdoms ruled over by a high king. In knowing this, some might also have been aware as to when this independence was lost, telling their shipmates that it was during the twelfth century that Norman knights from England along with King Henry II stole great swathes of territory from the original Irish landowners. In doing so, Henry declared those parts of Ireland conquered by England to be a 'lordship', which during the reign of his son King John was brought under direct English governance. Here then lies the genesis of the rebellion of 1798, the desire to wrest back control of Ireland that had been lost for 500 years. Admittedly, in 1297 an Irish parliament had been established, but it was a parliament with no real authority other than that of approving taxes to fund Dublin Castle, the seat of Irish administration.

It was stories like these, and tales of several unsuccessful rebellions against English rule, with each of those rebellions followed by bloody retribution, that helped bind many of the Irish serving on naval ships to the rebel cause, while to each man, with maybe a few exceptions, detailed knowledge of these events would have been hazy or just plain inaccurate. But in truth they were part of the national psyche. Learning of the nation's history was something that all strived to attain, the importance of learning about Ireland's past not being something to be brushed aside. Naturally, stories of English misdeeds, made worse by a string of anti-Catholic discriminatory laws, would have been a regular topic of discussion, not only with their mess mates but previously within their families and at the village ale houses. Also, for private reading, there were numerous political tracts ready to be purchased from itinerant sellers that also delved into past events that showed England to be a treacherous ruler and responsible for many past crimes –

the underlying ingredient that ensured those born and bred in Ireland, especially in the Catholic faith, were receptive to the rebel call, united as one in a suspicion, if not a venomous hatred, of the English as rulers of their country. Outside the family, and before gaining general entry into the male bonding regime of the ale house, children, again mostly those of Roman Catholic families, received a more carefully structured introduction to what Ireland was and ideas of what it might be through lessons given in what were commonly known as hedge schools. Illegal institutions, for no Catholic prior to 1782 was permitted to either teach or be taught. There were by the end of the eighteenth century around 9,000 of these schools, attended, it has been estimated, by as many as 400,000 pupils.

It was in hedge schools that the children of the rural workforce, which at the time were among the poorest in Europe, received an education. Between each and every school the subjects and the way things were taught varied considerably. But of one thing that is most certain, these schools were very much part of the communities that they served and the teaching was only what the community demanded. Given that Catholic communities already possessed a desire to free themselves in some way from English oppression, stories of past injustices found their way into the nature of what was taught.

And what material these teachers had to draw upon!

From the injustices of land stolen by Norman knights, they could move on to the wrongs of the reformation and Oliver Cromwell's claim of doing 'God's work' when he wrote in his diary of Irish Catholics being not human and putting to the sword hundreds of thousands. From there it was easy to move onto the ousting of the Catholic King James II and battles fought in Ireland during the Williamite War (1688-91) in favour of the Jacobites, whose intention was restoration of the house of Stuart.

While there can be no certainty as to how any teacher represented the past, for of that there are no records nor copies of any syllabus, there is certainly evidence of English rule being questioned within the hedge schools. William Carleton, an Irish writer and novelist, while critical of the political message being taught, affirmed that politics and history did enter into the classroom:

> *The matter placed in their hands [the children of these schools] was of a most inflammatory and pernicious nature, as regarded politics; and as far as religion and morality were concerned, nothing could be more gross and superstitious than the books which circulated among them.*

He refers to pupils being encouraged to read books on the Williamite Wars, others with a hatred of the Protestant religion, including *The Downfall of the*

Protestant Establishment and the Exaltation of the Roman Church. In continuing he declared:

> *Political and religious ballads of the vilest doggerel, miraculous legends of holy friars persecuted by Protestants, and of signal vengeance inflicted by their divine power on their persecutors, were in the hands of young and old, and, of course, fixed in their credulity.*

William Shaw Mason, while admittedly writing in 1819, refers to the existence in those schools of a 'pernicious little book' entitled *Articles of Limerick*, and which he claimed would be 'impossible for children to read, without imbibing a spirit of disloyalty to the government, and hatred of the present royal family and English connection.' In 1825, the commissioners of the board of education reported that in at least one school, a copy of *A Sketch of Irish History by Way of Question and Answer for the Use of Schools* was found, a book they saw as uncompromisingly demonstrating a clear bitterness towards the English governance of Ireland.

Despite the name suggesting that teaching took place in an open field close to a hedgerow, this was only true of some hedge schools, most housed in mud huts, barns, and maybe even the home of the teacher. Although illegal, the authorities made little effort to prevent the continuance of any of these schools, a fact that explains why the English social reformer John Howard, when touring Ireland in 1782, had little difficulty in visiting several, and making a few remarks on how they were run:

> *The lower class of people in Ireland are now by no means averse to the improvement of their children. At the cabins on the roadside I saw several schools in which, for the payment of 3s. 3d. (Irish) per quarter, children were instructed in reading, writing and accounts. Some of these I examined as to their proficiency, and found them much forwarder than those of the same age in the Charter Schools.*

Reinforcing the importance of these schools was Thomas Rawson in his *Statistical Survey of Kildare* published in 1807 but written immediately after the rebellion of 1798, in which he stated:

> *All over the county are numbers of schools, where the lower orders have their children instructed in writing, arithmetic and reading; scarcely a peasant who can muster a crown after tithe and priest's dues, but is emulous to expend it on his little boy's education.*

The scholars who undertook the work of teaching must be much admired, for the payment they received was but a poor remuneration and often regarded as a voluntary payment. While Howard does refer to the teaching of only reading, writing and accounts, most taught a much wider range of subjects, of which Latin, Greek, History and Mathematics often featured. Being completely free of state control, for the schools were owned by the scholars who provided the teaching, they were certainly regarded by officialdom as a threat to the status quo. But it was not until 1831 that any real effort was made to bring about an end to hedge school scholarship. In that year the multi-denominational national school system was established by the British government, these under the full control of the state, and through the setting up of a national board of education controlled both what was taught and who did the teaching. Not that hedge schools disappeared, but their position was certainly undermined. In the hedge schools of the late eighteenth century, most of the Irish rebels in the British Navy would have been schooled, their teachers unrestricted in what they might teach but undoubtedly, if only in a small way, espousing the nationalist cause. From these schools they gained that certain grounding in Irish history that gave them a lust to fight the English supported by a belief that Ireland once again should be free of English rule.

In those hedge schools, religious doctrine was the cement that held everything together, its teaching both supported and led by a priest who, at the very least, approved of the teacher who would be teaching the young of the community. Dowling, in a fairly detailed history of the hedge schools, refers to teachers covering religious doctrine but that it was not left to the teacher alone, the priest having final responsibility, although both parent and priest were entrusting the children's spiritual welfare to the teacher.

For the Irish seamen of the lower deck, especially those who came to support the scheme to take ships into French ports, religion was undoubtedly an important factor. Most, but not all, were Catholic. In part this was because the vast majority of the poorer sections of the Irish population adhered to the Catholic faith and in so doing were at the forefront of numerous penal laws, a series of laws designed to force Irish Catholics to accept the established Church of Ireland. It was not just in education that Catholics were excluded, but in most areas of civil life. With both England and much of Scotland during the reformation of the sixteenth century turning against Catholicism, those adhering to the old faith had now been seen as potential enemies. In Ireland, the vast majority, including many wealthy families of Norman descent and virtually the entire native population, in choosing to remain true to the pope in Rome, were treated as if they might be enemies. A sort of self-fulfilling prophecy. The worst of those penal laws

HARSH LAWS AND DISCRIMINATION

were introduced following the Williamite War of 1688-91 when the Protestant King William III of England overcame the Irish Jacobite forces intent upon the return of the deposed Catholic James II. Again, it was one of those flash points in history that bonded the Catholic community in its hatred of the English Protestant ascendancy and helped motivate the rebel cause on both land and sea during 1798.

Following the Williamite victory, one of the first laws passed by Dublin's English-controlled parliament was the banning of all Catholic clergy within the country. In turn, this was followed by a torrent of vicious discriminatory laws that simply intensified the hatred held by many Catholics towards their Protestant masters. Among those laws was that of excluding Catholics from public office, so denying them from becoming judges, members of parliament, solicitors, jurists, barristers or civil servants. On top of that, no Catholic was allowed to vote, own land or lease land for more than thirty-one years. These last two measures ensured that by 1778, only five per cent of land in Ireland was Catholic-owned. Catholics were also barred from the armed forces, not allowed to marry Protestants, and denied the right to establish their own schools or to send their children abroad for education. In addition, Catholics had to pay tithes to the Protestant Church of Ireland, this causing further resentment. While there were ways that Catholics subverted these laws, and some, such as the ban on Catholics having their own schools, was generally unenforced, it was quite clear that Catholics, in a land dominated by Catholics, were simply not welcome.

Also victimised by the penal laws that discriminated against Catholics were Protestant non-conformists who renounced membership of the Church of Ireland. Among those non-conformists, and by far and away the most numerous, were Presbyterians who had begun settling in Ireland during the reign of James II. Of Scottish descent, they settled mainly in Ulster and upon land once held by Catholics but which, following a long drawn-out uprising against English authority, had been confiscated. On these lands they had established plantations that were not just owned by Presbyterians, but the tenants and labourers who worked the land were also Scottish Presbyterians. As with Catholics, dissenters, regardless of property possessed, were entirely excluded from involvement in public affairs and, as with Catholics, had to pay tithes to the Church of Ireland, a church to which they had no allegiance.

This long-time legal discrimination against Catholics and dissenters had seen a degree of alleviation towards the end of the eighteenth century, a series of relief Acts introduced that began to reverse some of the most pernicious of the penal laws. In 1760, Catholics were offered the hitherto denied privilege of serving in the army and navy, but with this right restricted to non-commissioned ranks.

The Papists Act, passed in 1778, allowed Roman Catholics to own property and to inherit land, but only providing they took an oath renouncing Stuart claims to the throne and the civil jurisdiction of the pope. This was followed in 1782 by an Act that permitted the founding of Roman Catholic schools, but with teachers in these schools having to take an oath of allegiance and gaining a license from the local Church of Ireland bishop. The British Roman Catholic Relief Act, passed in England in 1791 and adopted by the Irish parliament in 1793, permitted Catholics entry into the legal profession, universities and the lower ranks of the army. In addition, it removed the disqualification of Catholics from the franchise, one at the time largely determined by property, so giving votes to Roman Catholics holding land with a rental value of £2 a year.

Nevertheless, none of these relief Acts altered the relationship between Dublin Castle and the British parliament in Westminster, with Dublin Castle continuing to be no more than a conduit of English authority. As for the Irish parliament, this did nothing more than the bidding of Westminster. As in England, it was a parliament that consisted of two chambers that were also styled the House of Commons and House of Lords. The former, while directly elected, was based on a very limited franchise, and prior to adoption of the British Roman Catholic Relief Act in 1793, those eligible to vote had to be both a member of the Church of Ireland and in possession of extensive property. As for the Irish House of Lords, in common with its counterpart at Westminster, this was also not elected, formed of Irish peers and Church of Ireland bishops.

A substantial population increase during the latter part of the eighteenth century was adding to the general list of grievances pressing down on the poorer elements of Irish society, bringing about increased impoverishment due to resulting pressures on land. In the south of Ireland in particular, the value of land had rapidly escalated with landlords frequently attempting to expel existing tenants so as to replace them with other tenants who were prepared to pay a higher rent. Through the institutional bias of the Irish judicial system, redress of this and other grievances was, through the constituted legal process, impossible to achieve with the rural poor increasingly taking the law into their own hands through the formation of numerous secret agrarian societies. Among them were the Steelboys, Rockites, Rightboys and Hearts of Steel, but most well-known were the Whiteboys, named after the white smocks worn by members when carrying out night-time raids upon designated targets. These secret societies frequently threatened or took violent action to keep tenants already in possession of a farm holding from being evicted by landlords attempting to gain a higher rent. Landlords might be attacked or a new tenant threatened with violence if the property was not immediately relinquished. As well as supporting tenants in the retaining of their lands, these secret societies protested the level of wages paid to labourers, and opposed landowners who turned arable land over to grazing and which in turn reduced the number of labourers employed.

The formation of these Catholic societies gave rise to the formation of Protestant gangs, such as the 'Peep o' Day Boys', which attacked Catholic homes in retaliation, using the pretext of claiming to be confiscating arms which, under the terms of the penal laws, Catholics were prohibited from possessing. It was the failure of the authorities to take action against the Peep o' Day Boys and their persistent attacks on Catholics that led to the creation of another significant rural secret society formed by Catholics, that of the 'Defenders'. Originating during the 1780s in Armagh, a county where, through being the most densely populated in Ireland, competition for land was particularly fierce, Defenders and Defenderism had, by the 1790s, spread far beyond the borders of Armagh.

Undoubtedly, these Irish Catholic societies also had a powerful influence on the Irish of the lower deck, teaching of the need to support and stand by all other Irish Catholics serving in the fleet and ready to threaten violence at the slightest provocation. Of this, the English and Protestants of the lower deck were aware. While forming the majority on any warship, they simply did not have that culture of violence and unity as fostered by those secret societies and which permeated Irish society, leading them to fear crossing them in any way. This led to those who did not wish to mutiny to think twice before they reported such matters to an officer. With a strong element of truth, Dennis Mahoney, an Irish rebel serving on *Glory* and sentenced to receive 200 lashes and a year's confinement in the Marshalsea Prison, declared to one fellow shipmate what would happen if he was molested by any Protestant crew member:

> *I would in one minute raise fifty or sixty men who would go through the ship. I am the captain of the gang.*

Chapter 4

The Society of United Irishmen

With the rural poor taking the law into their own hands through the formation of long-standing secret societies such as the Protestant Peep o' Day Boys and the Catholic Defenders, Ireland was ripe for revolution. All that was needed was some kind of flashpoint, and in June 1789 just such a flashpoint occurred. This was news from Paris that the Bastille had fallen and the country had overturned its government. How this must have reverberated in a country where a large number of the population had nothing but contempt for those ruling over them. Of course, not all were favourable to the ideas encompassed in the well-publicised slogan of *liberté, égalité, fraternité*. Much depended on the individual, their position in society and what they might lose if Irish society was transformed in the same way. Protestants were the least likely to benefit and saw little reason to support such massive alteration to the fabric of a society that brought to them considerable advantage. Similarly, Catholic landowners saw nothing advantageous in the imitation of society where most of their land would be redistributed and the possibility that some of their number would be executed under the blade of a guillotine. They were already committed to a reform of the existing system, and just four years after the fall of the Bastille would see their own authority greatly enhanced when, once again, they were allowed to vote in elections.

Another group within the Catholic community who viewed the possibility of a revolution in Ireland with nothing but fear was the Catholic clergy. In France, following the revolution, the Catholic church saw heavy persecution that included the mass imprisonment and execution of the clergy, church property stolen, and the church turned into a subordinate arm of the secular French government. At no time under the Protestant ascendancy had the penal laws that discriminated against Catholics gone to those extremes. In recognition of this, Catholic bishops regularly spoke out against the 'fascinating illusions' of French principles, urging Catholics to remain loyal to the government.

Catholic agricultural labourers, a significant portion of the Irish population, were one group especially attracted to the actions if not the ideals of the French Revolution, were supportive of a redistribution of land that would bring an end

THE SOCIETY OF UNITED IRISHMEN

to the many hardships they suffered. Also positively attracted to the ideals of the French Revolution were a small number of merchants and artisans. How far many of these were prepared to go in support of revolution was questionable, but many agreed that a break from England, either partial or complete was a cause worth supporting. In Ulster, where such thinking was strongest, several of that class came together in the autumn of 1791 to form the Society of United Irishmen, a society with a reform agenda that looked to move power away from Westminster and given instead to the Dublin Castle Executive. It was a society that also wished to see Protestants and Catholics working alongside each other in unity. Theobald Wolfe Tone, a youthful Protestant barrister who was later to travel to France as a United Irish representative, argued in 1791 of the need for Anglicans, nonconformists and Catholics to work alongside each other as all would benefit from constitutional reform. In doing so, and concentrating on the need for Catholic support, he eschewed a frequent argument put forward by supporters of the ruling hegemony that 'Catholics are ignorant and therefore incapable of liberty'. Instead, he claimed that what had made Catholics ignorant was 'the cruel injustice of Protestant bigotry', which denied Catholics education and the means by which to better themselves.

The agenda to be pursued by the Society of United Irishmen called not only for the rescinding of all the remaining laws that penalised Catholics and non-conformists, but the establishment of a parliament in which 'all the people' would have 'an equal representation'. The total rejection of such ideas, both by parliament in Westminster and moderate reformers, eventually saw the society prescribed by an increasingly repressive government, fearing any individual or group that called for radical reform during a time when a desperate war was being fought against revolutionary France. The effect was that of driving out of the society its more moderate members while those of a more revolutionary persuasion were able to take control.

Helping to increase the support base of the Society of United Irishmen was an alliance formed with the Defenders, with Defender cells sometimes transformed into United Irish cells, a move aided by United Irish propagandists travelling the country and making the necessary links. As well as talking with local leaders of Defender cells, they also carried copies of the *Northern Star*, the newspaper of the Society of United Irishmen and the most widely read of all Irish newspapers. Helping in the process of linking the two bodies was that the Defenders as an organisation was not only widespread but had developed a centralised structure headed by a grand master. While this made a fusion between the two societies relatively easy, much more important was the development by the Defenders of a radical political agenda that far exceeded that of preceding and more localised rural Catholic secret societies whose concerns were traditional rural grievances.

Defenderism, while encompassing those same rural grievances, was much more subversive, avowedly anti-English and anti-Protestant, believing not only in the removal of all remaining anti-Catholic penal laws but also a redistribution of land through confiscation of large Protestant-owned estates. As to the extent to which Catholic labourers and peasants appreciated this radical agenda, it is difficult to assess with much of the available evidence on peasant attitudes in Ireland derived only from those generally unsympathetic to the peasantry. According to R.B. McDowell writing in 1943, the peasants' policy might be described simply as a determination to lessen all the burdens that pressed directly on their own backs. Thomas Pelham, Ireland's chief secretary, was informed by one correspondent that the peasants had a list of grievances, including 'price of lands, unequal taxation, illegal fees, tithes, non-residence of clergy and landlords and the whole of the revenue laws as they now stand'.

To undermine the United Irishmen and their radical agenda, in April 1793 the government in London pushed through the relief measure that was to grant Catholics in Ireland the same voting rights as Protestants. It was a measure that did little more than annoy both the ultra-loyalists who had opposed it in the Irish parliament and the Catholics who now gained the vote, but questioned why, in having the vote, they did not gain the right of representation in parliament. Rather than continuing to move forward with a further raft of reforms, fear of the influence of revolutionary France, with which Britain was now at war, led instead to the opening shots of a war upon those who sought reform, and which included the banning of political assemblies and laws allowing prosecution of those found spreading seditious libel. Eventually, the society was to be prescribed by an increasingly repressive government, fearing any individual group that called for reform during a time when a desperate war was being fought against revolutionary France.

This increasing government repression and the eventual outlawing of the society saw the emergence within its ranks of a group that favoured the use of physical force to achieve reform, with this of necessity to be supported by French military intervention. Such would be a legitimate right, it was argued, for the constitution upon which Ireland was ruled was one that resulted from the revolution of 1688 in which William III had taken the kingdom of Ireland through military might and not by right. Declarations were frequently made that resistance to unlawful rules was a natural right, with resistance, when tyrannical violence was to be opposed, seen as the principle of patriotism. Reference was frequently made to the USA, Switzerland and the Netherlands, all of which were nations that had overcome oppressive governments, 'drubbing them soundly and forcing them to an act of justice at the point of a bayonet'.

Of this increasing radicalism, the Earl of Westmoreland, Lord Lieutenant of Ireland, informed the prime minister, William Pitt, in 1791 that the Defenders were frequently heard to declare 'that the king was not the Catholic king' and 'English settlers' were 'not of their nation'. The Irish historian Thomas Bartlett suggests the existence of circumstantial evidence indicating that, as early as 1792, the Defenders were in touch with the French authorities with a view to obtaining military aid from that quarter, with the French toying with the idea of using them in an Irish *Chouannerie* against the English. Within the United Irishmen, Tone had adopted a revolutionary approach by 1794, conceding the need to work alongside the French. In the early part of that year he had a meeting in Dublin with the Reverend William Jackson, a French agent, Tone providing Jackson with a letter to be sent to France requesting military aid. The letter, in being sent through the public postal system, was intercepted and both Tone and Jackson arrested. Jackson eventually faced trial, but one where he, on the day he was brought into court to have judgement passed, succumbed to a deadly poison that had probably been brought to him earlier that morning by his wife. Tone was dealt with much less severely, friends in high places ensuring that he avoided both imprisonment and execution, banished instead from all British territories.

The government in London must have come to regret the mild sentence given to Tone for upon his banishment from Britain he travelled to the United States where he continued to work for the cause of Irish independence. Before leaving he agreed, in a meeting held with leading members of the United Irishmen, to seek out while in America representatives of the French government and hopefully gain French assistance for the cause of Irish freedom. It was a meeting that concluded with all present taking the solemn oath that they were, 'never to desist in our efforts until we had subverted the authority of England over our country and asserted her independence'.

True to the oath taken, Tone, upon his arrival in America, or Philadelphia to be exact, sought Citizen Adet, the French minister to the United States, supplying him with a written outline of the situation in Ireland and the value to which French assistance could be put. Adet promised to forward the appeal as written by Tone to the government in Paris. However, Tone appears to have come away with the impression that Adet was little enthused by Tone's appeal, performing no more than the basic duty of any administrator. Tone had even offered to travel to France and personally present his plans to the Directory, but to this the French minister had refused. Possibly Adet was merely erring on the side of caution, for he had reminded Tone that the British stopped and carried indiscriminately into their ports all American vessels bound for France, leading to the likelihood of Tone's arrest and certain imprisonment if not execution.

Matters, though, changed dramatically several months later when Tone received letters from Ireland informing him that opinion in Ireland was rapidly shifting, with increasing numbers unhappy at English rule that had become progressively more repressive following the outbreak of the war with France. Many more were now favouring a complete elimination of England's authority in Ireland and looked to France as a model upon which an Irish Republic could be established. With these letters in hand, Tone once again sought out the French minister, finding Adet to now be more willing to offer assistance. This time he agreed on Tone taking passage to France, providing him with letters of introduction that strongly recommended the Irish cause as worthy of French support. Unhesitatingly, Tone settled his affairs in America, taking passage on board the ship *Jersey* that departed Sandy Hook on 1 January 1796. It was a crossing of the Atlantic that was to last exactly one month and, apart from numerous storms, proved surprisingly uneventful. According to Tone in his own account of the passage:

> *We did not meet a single vessel of force, either French or English; we passed three or four Americans, bound mostly, like ourselves, to France. On the 27th we were in soundings at 85 fathoms; on the 25th we made Lizard and, at length, on the 1st February, we landed in safety at Havre le Grace, having met with not the smallest accident during our voyage.*

It was Tone's presence in France, alongside other members of the society, that was to persuade the French to mount an expedition to Ireland that departed Brest on 15 December 1796. On his arrival in Paris earlier in the year, Tone had first met with Delacroix, the minister of foreign affairs, in an initial step in a long process that was to see Tone repeatedly visiting the Luxembourg palace that housed the French legislature, the War Office, and the Ministry of Foreign Affairs, pressing not only for an invasion but for an invasion of adequate scale. In outlining the defensive forces that would oppose the landing in Ireland, Tone estimated it to be of around 30,000, but assured the French that only 12,000 were of any real quality, some of the best troops having been sent to the West Indies and the remaining 18,000 militia who were likely to desert to the French should they invade in sufficient number.

For Tone, who accompanied the expedition as Adjutant-General Smith, it was to prove a tortuous affair, not only because the fleet, despite reaching Bantry Bay, failed to land the invading force, but the voyage to Ireland had been full of peril. As a passenger on board *Indomptable*, a ship of eighty guns, he records in his diary that on the night of the 16/17th, while passing through the Raz de Sein, they came 'within an inch of running on a sunken rock, where we must every soul [on board] have inevitably perished.' Describing the Raz as 'a most dangerous and difficult pass', Tone went on to add that 'ours is the first squadron that has passed through the Raz, which even single ships avoid unless in case of necessity'. It was later learned that the 74-gun *Séduisant*, which belonged to the squadron, had run onto hidden rocks in the Raz with the loss of 680 lives. Throughout the voyage the winds were either slack or totally against them, leading to the constant fear of being set upon by a superior British fleet.

The failed expedition of December 1796 and the planned transporting of troops to Ireland by a Dutch fleet in 1798 offered clear proof to those of a radical persuasion in Ireland that French support was for the taking. Such an invasion was now seen as a key to both an independent Ireland, one allied to France, and the means by which a French victory in the war against the British could be achieved. In turn, however, this threat to the Protestant hegemony in Ireland greatly intensified the brutality of repression, with floggings, house burnings and mass arrests becoming almost common place. With much of the United Irish leadership under arrest, and more arrests likely to follow, the organisation was on the point of crumbling, forcing the launching of an uprising before it was too late.

The organisers of the rebellion initially planned to capture Dublin Castle, the centre of British administration in Ireland, with further uprisings in the nearby counties that would help protect Dublin from being retaken by government forces. Captured papers and weapons alerted the authorities to the planned attack, with forces loyal to the government occupying rebel assembly points from which the uprising was to have been mounted, preventing the rebellion in Dublin before it could commence. Elsewhere in the country the rising went ahead as planned, with the first clashes between rebels and the military taking place on 24 May 1798. Despite some early successes, most markedly in County Wexford, a series of rebel defeats brought the rebellion to an end. The total death toll numbered somewhere between 10,000 and 50,000.

According to one account, provided by a Home Office informer, the leaders of the United Irishmen had grown apprehensive of any immediate French support as 'they had been deceived often by them before'. But such apprehension was disabused four weeks after the final crushing of the rebellion when, on 22 August, just over 1,000 French troops under Jean Joseph Humbert landed at Kilcummin Harbour. While they were far too late to support the main uprising, the French were joined by 5,000 local rebels. A few early successes were gained, with British forces defeated at Castlebar (27 August 1798) and Collooney (5 September 1798). At Castlebar, County Mayo, the French troops and their Irish compatriots routed a force of 6,000, and at Collooney, County Sligo, following a minor battle, troops from the British garrison of Sligo town were forced to retreat, leaving 120 dead and 100 taken prisoner. A short-lived 'Irish Republic', lasting just twelve days, was also declared, this in the province of Connacht. Finally, on 23 September, French and Irish forces were defeated at Killala, and while the surrendering French troops were repatriated to France, the Irish who were captured were mostly executed. In October a second landing by the French was attempted, but this proved even less successful. Nine French warships carrying 3,000 troops were intercepted and dispersed by the Royal Navy off Tory Island, County Donegal, with seven ships eventually captured. Among those taken from the captured ships was Wolfe Tone who, despite holding a commission in the French Army, was treated as a rebel and sentenced to be publicly hanged on Monday 12 November 1798. It was an appointment he was not to keep as in the early hours of that morning he cut his throat with a pen knife, partly severing his windpipe. While a military surgeon successfully closed the wound, it was considered inadvisable to move him to the gallows as, in all likelihood, he would not survive the journey. Instead, he remained under guard in Prevot Prison, Dublin Barracks, where he died on 19 November and was buried a few days later in the churchyard of Bordentown, where his grandfather was also buried.

Chapter 5

'Mankind are naturally friends to each other'

While it was seamen of Irish birth who were the primary organisers in many of the ships where rebel cadres were created, it was by no means an exclusively Irish plot. The Society of United Irishmen had become a revolutionary organisation committed to the ideals of the French Revolution, as had similar societies in England and Scotland. To begin with, the most important of those societies on mainland Britain had sought to achieve by peaceful means a more democratic society through the reform of parliament and the voting system. As with the Society of United Irishmen, which had also at first adopted a peaceful approach to bringing about reform, they had been confronted by government intransigence and brutal repression. This created a much more hostile environment with increasing numbers who had once supported reform turning instead to thoughts of insurrection as the only means by which change would be brought about. During the early months of 1794, the government suspended *habeas corpus*, an action that permitted the unlawful detention and imprisonment of leading reformers, while later that same year the Seditious Meetings Act and the Treasonable Practices Act, known as 'The Two Acts', forbade the holding of public meetings of fifty or more persons (unless a magistrate's licence had been granted), and extended the laws of treason to include both the written and the spoken word. In turn, these pieces of repressive legislation were followed by attacks on the press, whereby magistrates were encouraged, through giving them increased powers, to act against newspapers that could be claimed as printing items deemed blasphemous or seditious. To ensure that the net was cast as wide as possible during what can be termed 'the English reign of terror', but from which Scotland was not excluded, radical leaders not held under arrest were carefully monitored. Letters sent and received by them through the postal service were intercepted, with government informers paid to infiltrate reform society meetings, reporting all that they saw and heard to the Home Office.

THE NAVAL MUTINIES OF 1798

During the early years of the war against France, and before much of the repressive legislation had taken effect, one society in England, the London Corresponding Society (LCS), had proved particularly influential. Formed in January 1792, it gained in only four years a membership in excess of 10,000, its rallying cry that of 'universal suffrage'. In a more reasonable age, the LCS, through being centred in the capital, might well have turned itself into a national campaigning organisation unimpeded by fear of reprisal. Standing in its way, however, even before the full onset of the reign of terror, was an already existing law banning the formation of national organisations. Instead, the political activists of London resorted to alternative means of maintaining links with the rest of the country and which was, as the name of the society suggests, through correspondence. Outside London, numerous reform societies were also established, their numbers spiralling as the notion of campaigning for universal suffrage gained impetus from events in France. As each was created, a link was made through correspondence with the LCS, each of these new societies adding the words 'corresponding' or 'united corresponding' to the town or towns to which they belonged.

Among those provincial corresponding societies were several formed in various naval towns and where direct contact could be made with the people of the lower deck. During the fleet mutinies of 1797 and the Irish mutinies of the following year, it will be noted that those with connections to the corresponding societies had certainly an involvement, an involvement that was to become especially crucial during the second of those two years. There is even a hint that the more radical elements of the LCS had already determined upon a plan that would help ensure a successful overthrow of the government through a naval mutiny that would help safeguard the unimpeded arrival of military support sent from France. Why, otherwise, would two of the most prominent LCS activists, John Gale Jones and John Binns, choose two of the nation's greatest naval towns as objects of their most important speaking tours?

In February 1796, just over a year before the fleet mutinies at the Spithead and Nore anchorages, John Gale Jones and John Binns were found promoting the cause of the LCS in the two major naval towns nearest to those anchorages, Jones travelling to Chatham and Binns to Portsmouth. Both were men who, in their own minds, had already decided upon insurrection to overthrow the existing government, convinced that this was the only way of achieving universal suffrage along with bringing an end to the war with France, which they viewed as unjust. At Chatham, Jones even made a point of meeting with French prisoners-of-war, at that time held on hulks moored in the River Medway, telling them of his admiration and respect for the French Republic, declaring, '*Je suis Anglois, mais je suis un Citoyen.*' To that he was to add, '*J'aime votre Patrie,*' and '*je souhaite qu'elle seroit libre.*'

Binns, an Irish-born artisan plumber, was later to show his support for a French military expedition for, while remaining in the LCS, he also joined the United Britons, a revolutionary organisation with just such an ambition, and the London United Irishmen. E.P. Thompson, in his seminal work *The Making of the English Working Class*, suggests that the decision to send these two men to Portsmouth and Chatham may not have been unconnected with a desire to achieve an English Republic. According to Thompson, it casts doubt on a later denial made by one member of the society, himself opposed to the use of violent tactics, that no member of the LCS had looked upon 'the formation of a republic by the assistance of France'.

While involvement in the organisation of fleet mutinies by the LCS or any of its allied corresponding societies can in no way be substantiated, it is known that seditious handbills were distributed among the seamen in mutiny at both Spithead and the Nore. Also, it is clear that the chairman of the LCS, Alexander Galloway, made contact with the seamen in mutiny at the Nore, but little more is known of the outcome of these meetings. Aaron Graham, a London magistrate tasked with examining the extent to which the radical societies had possibly incited those mutinies, while failing to find a close connection, a not unsurprising conclusion given the secrecy under which such organisations were forced to operate, did confirm a degree of involvement when he concluded:

> ...*several whose mischievous dispositions would lead them to the farthest corner of the kingdom in hopes of continuing a disturbance once begun have been in company with the delegates on shore, and have also (some of them) visited ships at the Nore, and using inflammatory language endeavoured to spirit on the sailors to a continuance of the mutiny*...

In noting the work of radical societies such as the LCS, the much respected naval historian Nicholas Rogers voices the view that it would be 'fanciful to believe such political aspirations' as those put forward by the LCS 'had not penetrated the fleet'.

A possible direct impact that the political radicals might have had on those naval mutinies was that of the seamen at the Nore continuing to stand out when those at Spithead had reached an agreement to return to their seagoing duties. It is known that Cork-born Charles McCarthy, during his overnight stopover on the outward journey from Sheerness to Portsmouth, had met with several political contacts at a tavern in Leman Street and later with an attorney of law in Goodman Street. The latter, in particular, was a rather mysterious character known only as Fitzgerald who, on meeting with McCarthy, as well as the other three delegates that accompanied McCarthy, had kept them waiting 'for some notes which Mr Fitzgerald was writing for them to take to Portsmouth'. Later, Fitzgerald was known to have met with other Irish delegates from the Nore, it being rumoured in the Whitechapel area of London, where these meetings took place, that 'Fitzgerald always made a point of going into town previous to giving them an answer'.

On his return, and then only accompanied by Matthew Hollister, McCarthy again remained overnight in London, giving sufficient opportunity, prior to the departure for Sheerness of the morning coach, to discuss with others the developments that had taken place at Portsmouth. It is these meetings that might well explain why, and despite the expectations of Admiral Howe, the mutiny at the Nore was not brought to an end. Possibly also, the delegates at the Nore, through connections with the LCS or the Society of United Irishmen, were more responsive to an action that might embarrass the government. For unlike those at Spithead, those at the Nore, especially the men elected to some of the shipboard committees, appear to have had links with various political groupings. At his court martial it was evidenced that James Smart, a pressed landsman and an elected seaman delegate serving on board the naval store ship *Grampus*, had not only been a member of the LCS but had regularly vented his views at political meetings held in London. James Lewin, the secretary to the committee that met on board *Sandwich*, appears to have been working towards some sort of union with revolutionary France, requesting that James Bray, a fellow seaman, be supplied with a hat as he was 'about to go on an embassy to France'. Later, Lewin was heard to say, when told that the ship was short of food supplies, 'we shall go cruize on the coast of France, and there shall get provisions enough.' Thomas Jephson, another leading name, was in London immediately before the mutiny and returned with quantities of literature that called upon Irish seamen to work for the cause of their homeland. As a bandsman he had also refused to play the national anthem, reputedly calling it 'an old stale tune' and adding, 'I care nothing for kings or queens – bad luck to the whole of them.'

In Scotland a similar development had also occurred, various repressive measures leading to one-time reformers gaining an increased willingness to consider insurrection as a means of achieving reform. Change through peaceful campaigning had been the aim of several societies, including the Glasgow Society for Burgh Reform (established in 1783), the Associated Friends of the Constitution and of the People (established in July 1792), and the Society of the Friends of the Constitution (established in September 1792). However, as

'MANKIND ARE NATURALLY FRIENDS TO EACH OTHER'

in England, the suspension of *habeas corpus*, passing the Two Acts, and the presence of government spies, led to the reform movement going underground. For this purpose, a new clandestine body, the United Scotsmen, was formed, a body that looked single-mindedly towards a violent insurrection as the only means of achieving significant political change. From the outset, this new body had close links with the Society of United Irishmen, with one member of the United Scotsmen, when under examination, suggesting that 'persons from Ireland...were the original founders of the Society of United Scotsmen,' this possibly a reference to Joseph Cuthbert and Thomas Potts who had been sent to Scotland from Belfast to seek out an alliance with political revolutionaries. Cuthbert and Potts brought with them to Scotland a copy of the constitution of the United Irishmen, which, apart from the name of the society, was adopted in full by the United Scotsmen. These links were to continue over the following years with the United Scotsmen, in one resolution as expressed in their constitution, declaring that 'Mankind are naturally friends to each other' and professed the United Scotsmen 'friends to mankind, of whatever nation or religion'.

As with the United Irish, the United Scots also looked to France to aid their cause which was, as one member proclaimed, a cause founded on 'French principles and French rules'. To this end, emissaries with a revolutionary agenda also travelled between France and Scotland, the ultimate purpose being that of a French invasion supported by Scottish republicans.

Another society far more radical than that of the LCS or the societies corresponding with the LCS emerged south of the border following the passing of the Two Acts. Within the LCS it is known that serious internal divisions occurred over future tactics to be adopted, with a sizeable number favouring the overthrow of the government through outright rebellion. To specifically serve that objective, and working in collaboration with agents sent into England by the Society of United Irishmen, this new society, formed in 1796, took the name United Englishmen. Again it adopted a constitution close or identical to the United Irish, with its earliest sections centred around Manchester. Soon, however, it spread much further afield. Sizeable divisions formed in Leicester, Nottingham, Wolverhampton and Birmingham. In Lancashire, it was reported that during the summer of 1797 there were around 900 United Englishmen while in Stockport, a government spy indicated the number of United Englishmen to be increasing 'very fast every week', with some 'six or seven hundred' thirsting for 'revolution as soon as they should be able'. In London further divisions were formed, sometimes known as the True Britons or the United Britons, many of whom had been members of the LCS, among them, as already noted, John Binns, the delegate sent to Portsmouth in February 1796.

Through the close links developed between the various revolutionary groupings existing in Ireland, England and Scotland, those seamen serving on board a naval warship and who had been members or supporters of one or other of these societies, naturally gravitated towards each other. As on land, through this already formed bond, a similar alliance was formed at sea for the purpose of supporting political change. Those at sea also came to believe that the nature of change they desired could only be achieved with French military aid.

On this, one other important point needs to be made. While those who were brought to trial for the crime of either leading or being one of the chief activists in the organisation of one or other of those on-board ship mutinies were invariably Irish by birth, this does not necessarily reflect accurately the true state of play on any warship. Among naval officers, the Irish were always seen as more troublesome, leading to the greater likelihood of an accusation against an Irish crew member being taken as more truthful than one against an English or Scottish member of the crew. The minutes of the *Defiance* court martial certainly reveal the involvement of English and Scots radicals in the mutiny plot, with one witness indicating the smoking club had several English members but did not name them, while other witnesses named Thomas Goldsmith and Jack Crow as members. The latter in particular is a surprising omission from those who Jones chose to prosecute, Crow being the armourer's mate who had agreed to supply arms and other materials to aid the taking of the ship. Furthermore, in gathering evidence against rebel crew members apprehended for mutiny and awaiting trial, some were offered the chance of not facing a court martial if they gave evidence against their co-accused. On board *Defiance*, at least ten accepted this offer given to them by Jones, appearing as witnesses, and to avoid later retribution from the still remaining Irish of the lower deck, offered a discharge from the navy, with most taking this opportunity, which allowed them to immediately leave the ship. It is also possible that evidence was gathered from others who were not called as actual witnesses but offered the same immunity from prosecution. There are few clues to the factors determining who would be offered such a lifeline against a probable sentence of death. The choice was a matter left to each ship's captain and any personal prejudices that they possessed. All that can be said is that most of the witnesses who took advantage of such an offer were invariably English by birth, suggesting that ethnicity could well have been a major reason for the decision taken.

However, Jones did draw in some Irish who were to act as witnesses against others placed on trial, among them Daniel Lynch, who would certainly have been condemned to death if he had not agreed to be called as a witness for the prosecution. The impression given by Lynch according to evidence that he gave is that he was a political radical, but one who became desperate to avoid facing a court martial. Following the detaining of the various prisoners, Lynch, through some unexplained arrangement, was brought to the captain's cabin where he appears to have been offered an amnesty and a discharge if he was prepared to return to the coal hole and remain with the prisoners, reporting back to Jones all that he overheard. But the prisoners in the coal hole suspected that Lynch was now acting as a spy, ostracising Lynch accordingly.

'I was put there for the purpose of hearing what they had to say,' Lynch told the court. 'They used to gather in the starboard side of the coal hole and they would not let me hear then what they said.'

Threats, of course, were made against him, with Lynch responding in a similarly violent manner. 'Any man who puts a finger in my eye I will put three in theirs.'

'You've now got a rod to whip your own arse,' he snarled at David Reed, the man he blamed for his original incarceration in the coal hole.

Through William Lindsey, one of the key conspirators on *Defiance* believing, rightly or wrongly, that Lynch was favourable to the Jacobin cause, he unwisely put a great deal of trust in him, providing Lynch with details of the planned mutiny, all or some of which Lynch later produced as evidence against those of *Defiance* accused of mutiny at the time of their court-martialling.

In all, of the thirty-five witnesses produced by Jones, at least five can clearly be identified as members of the smoking club and would therefore have been liable to being court-martialled if an arrangement had not been struck with Jones, whereby they received an amnesty from prosecution. Almost certainly other witnesses were also regular attenders of the smoking club and had faced the possibility of trial by court martial if they had not agreed to becoming prosecution witnesses. In addition, a further nine *Defiance* crew members were named by witnesses as conspirators, against whom Jones had chosen to take no action. Among those witnesses called by Jones, and who would have been a key player in the mutiny, was Laurence Carroll. He was the first to be called, immediately implicating all twenty-five as conspirators, most of whom he had observed having taken the United Irish oath of loyalty administered by Lindsey. Carroll had also taken the oath, a potential for the passing of a death sentence if he had been on trial. But like Lynch he had been offered an amnesty and a discharge. Again, how this arrangement emerged is unknown. On the first day of the court martial Carroll stated that following the discovery of the plot, he was 'kept separate'.

PART 3

Ushant: The Key to Irish Independence

The island of Ushant, or to the French, Ouessant, lies at the head of the Iroise channel leading into Brest, the most important of the French naval bases that faced into the Atlantic. It was from Brest that military operations against England were usually initiated, the town not only the home of an important naval base but the location of various military facilities that included barracks, artillery stores and powder magazines. Throughout each successive war fought against France during the eighteenth century, the British Navy had attempted to keep a close watch on the port through the stationing, whenever possible, of a large squadron of warships off Ushant, these to keep the French fleet trapped inside the port. It was a strategy that dated back to the reign of William III and a time when France, rather than the Dutch Republic, had emerged as Britain's major enemy. In carrying out this blockade, the line of battle ships of the British Navy's Channel fleet would lie 20, 30 or even 40 miles out at sea to give plenty of room against Atlantic gales coming in from the west. Within sight of the French coast would be an additional line of frigates, these in constant communication with the main fleet, keeping the admiral acting as commander-in-chief fully informed of enemy activities in and around the port of Brest.

While it was always possible that in sailing out of Brest the French fleet might be used to support an invasion of England's south coast, the British government by the end of the eighteenth century was fearful that Ireland was the more likely target. In 1798, when Ireland was in a full state of rebellion, the landing of a sizeable French force would not only have led to a likely rebel victory but would also have placed Ireland in lock-step with Britain's sworn enemy – revolutionary France. Thus the necessity of preventing an invasion force sailing out of Brest or any other port. But if it did, the hope was that it would be defeated in a battle at sea before reaching the coast of Ireland.

Chapter 6

The Blockade of Brest

According to Admiral Sir Cloudesley Shovell, writing in 1702, the position to be taken by ships of the Channel fleet when blockading Brest was between the Lizard and the coast of France, but more specifically '20 to 40 leagues S.W. to W.S.W. from [the island of] Ushant'. The positioning of a fleet at such a location was supported in 1755 by Lord Anson when he wrote to Sir Edward Hawke that:

> ...the best defence for our colonies, as well as our coasts, is to have a squadron always to the westward as may in all probability either keep the French in port or give them battle with advantage if they come out.

Nevertheless, a degree of dissent existed among the leading sea officers of the age as to the value of keeping a fleet constantly at sea, given the wear and tear it inflicted on ships. The alternative was to hold in full readiness a British battle fleet within the anchorages of Spithead or Plymouth Sound so that they could immediately sail and meet in force any French fleet breaking out of Brest.

A critic of the close blockade strategy was Admiral Edward Vernon who, in 1745, suggested that a fleet positioned close to Brest, and lying off the island of Ushant, would:

> ...leave all Ireland, the western coasts of this island and even the Bristol Channel and all our East and West Indian trade expected home, open to them [the French] to do what they please. [Instead] a western squadron formed as strong as we can make it...and got speedily out into the Soundings, might face their united force, cover both Great Britain and Ireland and be in condition to pursue them wherever they went and be at hand to secure the safe return of our homeward bound trade from the East and West Indies.

Lord Howe, in 1784, also opposed the idea of a close blockade, although his reasoning was different, for him:

> *[The] stationing [of] a large fleet off the coast of France was a very improper and hazardous measure. The ships, particularly the large ones, were liable to receive great damage, the crews get sickly... he could affirm from his own knowledge that a station off Brest was a dangerous station, and should never be taken but upon great emergencies.*

Despite the reasoning of those who opposed the close blockade, it was the constant stationing of a large fleet of ships to the west of Brittany, and usually in close proximity to the island of Ushant, that had become the adopted British naval strategy since the outbreak of war with revolutionary France in 1793. Helping determine the continuation of that policy was the British Navy, at the time having a sufficient number of ships to ensure that those on station could be regularly relieved by others on a turn-and-turnabout principal. Once in home waters, ships returning would normally remain for a brief period, usually three or four weeks, during which time food and other essentials would be taken on board. If showing signs of wear and tear or suffering substantial damage at sea, a ship could remain out of service for a much longer period, placed into the hands of a dockyard, usually Portsmouth or Plymouth, for repair and a complete examination of the hull. For the task of revictualling – the taking on of food, water and other essentials – this was a much more straightforward task, with ships of the Channel fleet required to moor or take-up an anchorage off Portsmouth or in Cawsand Bay.

It was Spithead that was the main anchorage of the Channel fleet and where it over-wintered, but this was far from being an ideal location for the blockading of Brest. Lying 200 miles from the island of Ushant and to reach it from Spithead, a wind blowing from the south-east was the one most sought as this allowed for an easy sailing down the English Channel. Yet such a wind also created difficulty for the heavy and cumbersome three-deck battleships when they attempted to leave this anchorage. These bigger ships were unable to tack their way out in the fashion of the smaller and nimbler ships of the fleet. The Sound, by contrast, presented far fewer problems. Much closer to Ushant, it also required a less complex pattern of weather, making it easier for larger ships to both leave this anchorage and sail for Ushant. Eventually the Sound, especially the sheltered waters of Cawsand Bay that lay close to the entrance of the Sound, would become a more important anchorage for the revictualling of ships on blockade duty.

THE BLOCKADE OF BREST

However, despite Plymouth having a major dockyard for the repair and maintenance of ships, a ship in poor condition brought into Cawsand Bay might not always be permitted to enter the dockyard. Instead, the need for her to make an instant return to Ushant should a French force come out of Brest was seen as far more essential. Any ship placed in dockyard hands was unlikely to be available for a return to the rendezvous point off Ushant for at least two or three months. *Mars*, for instance, in December 1798, despite being in need of considerable repairs to her rigging and masts, was held in Cawsand Bay in a constant state of readiness. At no point were artificers from the dockyard allowed to come on board to remedy those defects, leaving her in a perilous condition when she did finally put back to sea in April of the following year.

A not infrequent strategy, and one that eliminated the keeping of a fleet constantly at sea on blockade duties, was to mount a seaborne raid on an enemy port for the purpose of capturing or destroying the vast majority of ships lying within that harbour. Such occurred in Toulon, the home of the French Mediterranean fleet, when in 1793 Admiral Hood successfully destroyed by fire forty-two French ships. Similarly, in the Indian Ocean, the tactic of destroying an enemy navy while in harbour was successfully used. On this occasion the enemy was the state of Mysore where, under its father and son rulers, Haidar Ali and Tipu Sultan, a substantial navy had been created, and one that if allowed to prosper could well have brought about the expulsion of Britain from India. By precipitating the destruction of several Mysorean dockyards and ships both in harbour and on the building slips, the threat of Mysore at sea was completely eliminated.

At Brest such a tactic was, at the very least, problematic due to its geographical location and the strength of its defences. The naval base, together with the city, lay on the north side of a large open stretch of water, the Rade de Brest, one of the largest roadsteads in the world. Here, ships preparing for sea would be held at various mooring points awaiting a suitable time to sail. Leading into the Rade de Brest from the north, with the dockyard on its west side, together with other naval and military facilities on both banks, was the Penfeld River. Of significance for any attempted raid on the naval base was that at the mouth of the Penfeld was located both a castle, the Chateau de Brest, and a defensive tower, Tour Tanguy. Between them they not only controlled the entrance to the river but a sizeable swathe of the Rade.

For a fleet commander contemplating a direct attack on the naval facilities in and around the Penfeld, there was not just a matter of avoiding significant damage from guns mounted on the chateau and the tower. There was the even greater problem of gaining access into the Rade. This could only be achieved by way of a narrow 1.9-mile-long strait, the Goulet de Brest. On both its north and south shores the Goulet was heavily fortified, several forts and batteries sited along its length, with ships forced to pass close alongside these fortifications due to the Goulet having at its centre and running the entire length of the strait a line of rocks. Further hindering a safe passage by an enemy fleet was the danger of being caught by a foul wind, for while a south-westerly wind would take a sailing ship through the Goulet, a north-easterly was required for a speedy return. Essential also was a favourable current, as on each receding tide water ran out of the roadstead at a force of 4 to 5 knots, with water again flowing in at a similar speed on a rising tide.

While a fleet of ships attempting to enter the Rade would find this an impossible task, it was nevertheless feasible to spy out and assess the readiness of the French fleet in Brest and the Rade through the use of frigates that might sail close to the entrance of the Goulet. For this purpose the Channel fleet, under Admiral Bridport, had attached to it a squadron of frigates, these under Commodore John Borlase Warren. Closing in upon the Breton coastline to gain information on what was happening ashore was a regular task of Warren's frigates. Some frigates even ventured into the Goulet before being fired upon by the numerous guns of the forts and batteries mounted along its entire length.

Chapter 7

Bantry Bay

Bantry Bay, in County Cork, lies on the south-west coast of Ireland running into the Atlantic Ocean and for a French invasion force leaving from Brest, it provided the nearest safe haven in Ireland for a landing. Its distance from Brest is 340 miles, a distance that could be covered with a favourable wind from the south-east in less than a week. The bay itself has a length of 22 miles and at its entrance is 6.2 miles wide and a depth at its centre of 40m, making navigation through the bay a relatively easy task for ships carrying a large invasion force. It was a bay familiar to the French Navy, for in supporting James II following the loss of his throne to William III, a large French naval force had entered the bay in May 1689, landing 1,500 men together with money, arms and ammunition. Possibly the only disadvantage to the French choosing, once again, to land an invasion force in Bantry Bay in December 1796 was that it was such an obvious point of landing, given the ease by which it could be approached from Brest.

That expedition to Ireland in 1796 had long been expected, the frigates of the Channel fleet constantly reporting on a fleet in preparation. Finally, a large convoy of troopships departed the Rade on 16 December. Its destination Bantry Bay. Consisting of forty-three sail that included seventeen ships of the line and thirteen frigates, it did not escape detection by the in-shore frigates, with *Indefatigable*, under the command of Edward Pellew, shadowing the French while two other frigates were sent in search of the main blockading force. Fortuitously for the French, heavy winds had recently blown the British fleet much further to the west, with Vice-Admiral Sir John Colpoys (*c.*1742-1821), then commanding the blockading fleet, not aware of the breakout until the 18th. Although commanding fourteen ships of the line, he appears to have made no attempt to chase the French, returning with seven of his ships to Spithead where the Channel fleet under Bridport had been brought in to serve out the winter. Possibly, to put the best light on Colpoys' unusual decision, was that of him being confused, claiming that, according to one widely circulated newspaper report 'he had received certain intelligence [that] the French fleet [had] been dispersed in a gale of wind.' While, indeed, the French had been so dispersed, the bulk of the expedition still remained on course, with Colpoys' failure to act leaving Ireland vulnerable to the French making a successful landing.

Pellew also sent news of the breakout to Bridport, with Bridport sending ships to search for the enemy fleet. Through having no absolute certainty as to where the French might be bound, Bridport kept some ships in the Channel while also sending part of his fleet south, to ensure that the breakout was not intended for the Mediterranean. When news was finally received that the French fleet had arrived off Bantry Bay, the Channel fleet was so dispersed that it was not until 3 January that it finally sailed out of Spithead to meet the French, the Admiralty having insisted that Bridport order it to sail irrespective of whether ships had a full proportion of stores and water on board. As for the French, and despite having entered Bantry Bay, no attempt was made at a landing, the fleet was battered by storms, the worst in living memory, and against which even the sheltered waters of Bantry Bay gave little protection. Instead, a decision was taken to return to France, with many of its ships entering Brest well before Bridport finally departed Spithead. Now all that was possible was for Bridport, under new instructions issued by the Admiralty, 'to proceed off Brest' where he was to intercept 'any of the enemy's ships of war or transports' that might still be at sea and attempting to enter Brest or any French port on the Atlantic seaboard.

The arrival of the French expeditionary force in Bantry Bay that December came as a surprise not just to the British Admiralty, but also to those in Ireland who had been hoping for just such an eventuality. Preparations, admittedly in a very early stage, were in hand, for an uprising timed to coincide with just such an invasion. With communication between the rebel leaders in Ireland and the government in Paris difficult to maintain, this lack of awareness on the part of those who would have led the uprising, meant that there was no supportive action in Ireland. At this point in time, such an uprising, unsupported by an eventual landing by the French, would have been a complete disaster for those potential rebels, a disaster just as great as the similarly unsupported uprising that occurred just under two years later. However, the fact of the French having brought into Irish waters an invading army did encourage the rebel movement, with the idea also emerging of using the Irish seamen of the British Navy to overpower their officers and take the ships on which they served into French ports.

The following year saw a further planned invasion of Ireland, this to be mounted not from Brest but from Texel in Holland. Here, since 1795 and a successful intervention by French revolutionary forces, the Directory in Paris had gained a close ally. Now renamed the Batavian Republic, and acting as a client state, the French had acquired use of Dutch warships for both the mounting of attacks on British merchant shipping and an invasion of Ireland. To counter such activities, the British Navy was forced to operate a second blockading force, this under the command of Admiral Adam Duncan (1731-1804). While the number of ships in his squadron was considerably smaller than those available to Bridport, it had the welcome addition of a number of Russian ships forming a separate squadron under the command of Vice-Admiral Hanickoff. At that time Britain and Russia were in close alliance, a friendship that dated back to the reign of Peter the Great (r.1682-1725). The ships assembled at Texel for an invasion of Ireland might well have sailed during the early part of the year, but for much of that time were trapped in port by adverse winds. For the British government, this proved especially fortuitous as should the Dutch invasion force have sailed during May it could not have been prevented by Duncan, the crews on board eleven of his ships having joined the mutineers at the Nore and leaving Duncan blockading Texel with just two British ships of the line and two frigates, with the Russian squadron providing three ships-of-the line.

Similarly, at Brest, if a French fleet had been ready to sail in April or early May it too would have been unopposed at sea, the Channel fleet being also in mutiny. Admittedly the seamen at both Spithead and the Sound had agreed among themselves that if news of the French fleet sailing was received they would immediately return to duty. But of course by that time the French would not only have departed Brest but could be well on course for landing an invasion force in Ireland or elsewhere on the British coastline. Indeed, the Channel fleet, despite orders to Bridport from the Admiralty, did not immediately sail upon the men receiving communication of the concessions made by parliament and the arrival of the royal pardon. Instead, Bridport determined on adopting a much more cautious approach, believing that efforts must be made to understand why the crews of so many ships had acted in the way they did. In a private letter to Prime Minister Pitt, he explained that he 'considered peevish words and hasty orders' to be detrimental to the wellbeing of the fleet. In particular, he was concerned that some crews were still in a mood of defiance, and that if those ships sailed with the fleet the disaffection on those ships might once again spread to the rest of the fleet. For First Lord Spencer at the Admiralty the answer was simple: 'Leave some of the most refractory [ships] behind.' But for Bridport this was no solution, for if he failed to order those ships to join the fleet in sailing to take up blockade duties off Ushant, a supposition might be made on ships not ordered to sea that they were being singled out for retributional punishment.

Bridport also had a second reason for not being able to immediately put to sea. A lack of officers resulting from a demand by many of the crews that unpopular officers should be removed and to which Howe had reluctantly agreed, with a total of 114 officers removed from their ships. While not all were immediately essential to replace, Bridport considered it impossible to sail 'as twenty-one lieutenants are wanted to fill the vacancies of officers passed on shore' alongside 'one master, three captains of marines and three lieutenants, two surgeons and a greater number of quarterdeck gentlemen.' To make good, Bridport was encouraged to avail himself 'of the services of any captains or other officers belonging to ships in a state of refitting or on half pay who may be proper for the purpose and within reach.'

It was not until 17 May that Bridport entered the Channel with fifteen ships of the line, his main concern being a further military expedition sailing for Ireland, with news brought by the *Triton* frigate confirming this to be a very real possibility. On 24 July, having intercepted two Danish merchantmen sailing in ballast from Brest to Bordeaux, the officer carrying out the examination was told by the master of one of the ships that in Brest and in perfect readiness, other than for a shortage of seamen, were nineteen sail of the line and seven frigates, all of which were bound for Ireland upon the expected arrival of 40,000 soldiers. Helping confirm this news as accurate was a British seaman who had been captured by the French and held at Brest, but had escaped and gained passage on one of the Danish merchantmen. Apart from confirming that there were, indeed, nineteen sail of the line in the harbour at Brest, he indicated that each ship had on board an Irish pilot and that the invasion fleet was expected to once again rendezvous in Bantry Bay.

The fleet preparing in Brest for a suspected descent on Ireland during the summer of 1797 never sailed, while defeat of the Dutch-Batavian Navy at the Battle of Camperdown on 11 October destroyed any hopes of an invasion of Ireland from Texel. Nevertheless, there were indications that the French had far from abandoned plans for a landing in Ireland. During the early spring of 1798, Wolfe Tone, in acting as the society's envoy in Paris, reaffirmed in a letter to its executive committee in Dublin that it was the intention of France to send another expedition. Tone also included a request that an agent be sent to update the Directory on the state of affairs in Ireland, with the executive committee sending William MacNeven, a member of the committee, to undertake this task. Travelling by way of Yarmouth and Hamburg, MacNeven was to inform the Directory that across Ireland, both the poor and middling classes were fully committed to the radical cause through a venomous hatred of the English government and its increasing despotism. A request was to be made for a French invasion force of between 5,000 and 10,000 men, together with a large quantity of arms, ammunition and artillery for the emerging rebel army. However, the Directory was, on the instructions of the executive committee in Dublin, to be clearly informed that Ireland was not to become in any way under the domination of France, but the committee was prepared to ensure that the expenses of the expedition would be met out of future Irish taxation once victory had been achieved.

From informers within the ranks of the United Irishmen, it was soon learnt in London that certain sections of Irish society were openly speaking that year of a French landing. Bridport warned of this and instructed that he should keep the ships under his command 'in as complete a state of readiness for sea as possible', and totally prepared for a change of wind that would allow the fleet in Brest to 'push out'. To meet any French ships that did manage to break out into the seas around Ireland, a line of battleships was stationed off Cape Clear on the south-west coast of County Cork, and well positioned to guard the entrance to Bantry Bay. Clearly, it was believed that Bantry would be the most likely point of landing, for Bridport not only kept patrols operating in the waters through which the French would pass if making for the entrance to the bay, but he also took part of his fleet into Bantry Bay for the purpose of meeting the French on their projected arrival. Off the Breton coast, frigates continued to indicate the presence of a sizeable force of ships in near readiness within the Rade de Brest, and other French ports also appeared active in preparing ships that might be intended for an attack on Ireland. One considered possibility was that a fleet under preparation in Toulon was also intended for Ireland, and to counter this eventuality, eight ships of the line taken from the Channel fleet and placed under the command of Rear Admiral Sir Roger Curtis were transferred to the Mediterranean.

In the event, the naval force preparing at Toulon, a total of sixty-five warships and 280 transports, were not intended for Ireland, sailing for Egypt in May to extract French forces trapped there since Buonaparte's invasion the previous year. Despite the hope given out to the United Irish by the letter received from Tone, the French government was now much more reserved in its thoughts upon mounting a further invasion of Ireland, given that the failed expedition to Bantry Bay in 1796 had resulted in the loss of 5,000 men and eleven ships. With French forces heavily engaged in campaigns not only in Egypt but also in Central Europe and Italy, thought of a further expedition to Ireland was now given a very low priority. Nevertheless, upon news reaching Paris of a large-scale rebellion in Ireland breaking out in the spring of 1798, orders were issued for the immediate sailing to Ireland of an expeditionary force. Hastily cobbled together from whatever resources that were available, a small number of warships and merchantmen bound for Ireland sailed out of Rochefort on 6 August. The use of this port, which lies on the Charente estuary 237 miles south of Brest, took Bridport and the Channel fleet by surprise, given that the main blockading force was stationed off Ushant, expecting any real force of size to depart from Brest.

Unsighted on its departure, and the ships lying off Cape Clear receiving no advance warning, the expeditionary force out of Rochefort successfully landed 1,500 troops on the west coast of Ireland, not this time at Bantry Bay, but further north at Kilcummin Harbour, County Mayo, on 22 August.

A further expeditionary force might have sailed from Rochefort, alongside one from Texel if resources had been available, but only from Brest would a subsidiary force eventually sail. Bridport, upon receiving news from his reconnoitring frigates that such a force was close to readiness, kept every ship available to him, granting only a minimum amount of time for any ship to revictual in either Cawsand Bay or Spithead. With the fleet at Brest not having sailed by the end of August, the Admiralty, in a letter to Bridport, were happy to confide their 'great satisfaction' in the actions he had taken in the blockading of Brest, and which had, in their words, 'effectually prevented the sailing of any part of the squadron destined, as supposed, to carry troops to Ireland.' However, an intelligence report received just a few days later, quickly quelled this earlier confidence, for it reported that on the night of 14/15 September, and unseen by Bridport's in-shore frigates, six frigates had sailed from Brest with the intention of landing troops in Killala Bay. In fact it was nine French warships carrying 3,000 troops that had left Brest, but on this occasion they were to be intercepted and dispersed by British naval warships off Tory Island, County Donegal, with seven of those ships eventually captured.

On board a number of the British warships that had been serving in home waters for the purpose of preventing a breakout from Brest or any other of the Atlantic sea ports where ships of the French Navy or their allies were to be found, sections of the Irish crew and other revolutionaries who manned those ships watched and waited. Their interest was that of taking the ships upon which they served into a French port for the purpose of placing these ships into the hands of the French Navy. In doing so, it was their intention to do whatever they could to bring triumph to the French invasion forces. If successful, the entire course of the war might well have been altered, with Ireland gaining its independence courtesy of the French. If this had been achieved, the French would then have turned their attention to mainland Britain, where a second invasion would attempt to bring about in England and Scotland a French-style republic. Admittedly, though, the landing of French forces in Kilcummin Harbour on 11 August had not gone well, for despite a few early successes, the French invasion force under General Lazare Hoche was forced to surrender to the British at Killala on 23 September. All might have been different if the second force that had landed in September had, through the addition of several British warships brought in by their Irish crews, sailed a few weeks earlier, and in a position to outflank the English forces that had defeated Hoche.

PART 4

The Diabolical Spirit of Mutiny

In the way that the shipboard mutinies of 1798 unfolded, in the form of a series of single ship mutinies, outwardly it might appear as one without co-ordination or leadership in sharp contrast to events played out during the previous year at Spithead and the Nore. Here, at both anchorages, clear leadership had emerged. At Spithead, where eighty ships manned by around 10,000 men refused to sail, Valentine Joyce, a quartermaster's mate on the 100-gun first rate *Royal George* emerged as the leading spokesmen, and as such conferred with members of the Admiralty sent to Portsmouth to bring the affair to an end. At the Nore, while the Admiralty made no attempt to meet with the delegates, Richard Parker was the named leader through being elected president. He chaired the meetings of delegates held on *Sandwich*, the parliament ship, but his actual position was no more than that of a figurehead with a number of more powerful individuals standing in the shadows. That leaders emerged in 1797, whether as spokesmen or as figureheads at both Spithead and the Nore, was because the mutiny was rooted in shipboard grievances to which it was expected the Admiralty would be forced to agree. Whether such negotiations came about or not, it did require a man to be named to represent the seamen. In 1798, however, the men who planned to mutiny were not looking to negotiate or gain concessions for grievances they hoped would be redressed by the Admiralty. Instead, their objective was the taking of British warships to the enemy, with every man involved fully aware that any hint of their plan becoming discovered by the authorities would be self-defeating, with the Admiralty inflicting upon any known leader the ultimate penalty: hanging him from the yardarm.

Chapter 8

Amelia, Haughty and *Adamant*

As the year 1797 gradually gave way to a new year, those who enjoyed the luxury of a newspaper had probably concluded that the spate of naval mutinies that had once seemed to threaten Britain's mastery of the sea were now a thing of the past. Admittedly, a further fleet mutiny was being widely reported on ships stationed at the Cape of Good Hope, which had broken out in December. Accompanying this news, however, was an assurance that matters there had been quickly resolved, the ringleaders apprehended, and several already executed. As for the most threatening of all mutinies that had taken place at the Nore, it was still in the news but only because some of those who had been court-martialled were still on board a prison ship on the Thames and were to be hanged from the yardarm of the 74-gun *Cambridge*. This would take place in January, with newspapers eager to report the scene of execution and any last words muttered as the men stood with nooses about to be placed around their necks.

If anything, the outbreak of mutiny at the Cape and the speed in which it had been brought to an end could well have brought comfort to many who might otherwise have been alarmed at the thought of the new year heralding another spate of mutinies. Crews on several ships moored in Table Bay had refused to obey orders, unhappy at the harshness of treatment by some of their officers. Earlier, in October, the people on board the naval flagship at the Cape, the 74-gun *Tremendous*, had confined their officers and threatened to try her captain, George Hopewell Stephens, on charges of cruelty and misconduct. This mutiny was also quickly suppressed, with a free pardon granted to all connected. That a second and more dangerous mutiny had occurred in December resulted from the crew of *Tremendous* perceiving a further injustice when one of them was ordered into confinement for a month on a charge of drunkenness. On shore, a council was held in which the governor at the Cape, Lord Macartney, together with Lieutenant General Francis Dundas and Rear Admiral Thomas Pringle, the two senior commanders, resolved to use force and severely punish the ringleaders. Amsterdam Battery, built by the Dutch East India Company to protect Table Bay, with upwards of 100 pieces of cannon, was put on alert, with these pointing at the flagship that was well in range. Furnaces within the battery were heated and red-hot balls made ready to pour into and sink *Tremendous* should the mutineers refuse to deliver up the ringleaders and return to obedience. With everything ready to begin the onslaught, a proclamation was issued at seven o'clock in the morning allowing two hours for the crew to determine whether they would submit. Ten minutes before the ultimatum expired, finding they had no alternative but to be sunk or surrender, the mutineers hoisted the signal of submission. The leaders were given up, some of whom were hanged while others were flogged through the fleet, with good order speedily restored.

While the news of this large-scale fleet mutiny being so quickly suppressed would have given relief to many a newspaper reader, for Irish radicals it further confirmed a lesson already learnt. This concerned the strategy now pursued by the United Irishmen and those British mainland radicals with whom the United Irish were in contact: planning a series of mutinies that were only to be launched when ships were at sea and close to an enemy port of refuge. To do otherwise, as shown at the Nore and subsequently Table Bay, risked the crushing of any shipboard-planned insurrection by the overwhelming fire power of either shore batteries or by nearby ships with crews loyal to the British government. Indeed, this was what made the planned Irish mutinies so different from any other mutiny conceived within the British Navy. Each ship, through co-ordination by agents on shore, would stage a mutiny, but only when the conditions for the success of the mutiny were in place. Whether several ships mutinied in concert or as individual units would be determined by circumstances and the existing strength of support on each ship.

For the newspaper-reading public, but more so for the Admiralty, news of one further attempted mutiny, right on the outset of the new year, must have come as a severe shock. More so because the ringleaders were Irish and the intention had been to take the ship into Brest. As such, it was the first attempt by members of a radical Irish crew to carry out the plans now effectively finalised by the Society of United Irishmen and their emissary in France, Theobald Wolfe Tone. The ship, with some of her crew planning this mutiny, was the 44-gun frigate *Amelia*. The plot came to the attention of her captain, Charles Herbert, when she lay close to the French shoreline and within easy reach of the Goulet that would take her into the Rade de Brest. If ever there was an opportunity for an Irish-inspired mutiny to meet with success, this had certainly been one that could well have been achieved.

Amelia, although by then serving as a British warship, was French-built, constructed for the navy of the *Ancien Régime* and launched at Brest in 1785. A Hebe-class frigate, she had been armed in the French Navy to carry thirty-eight guns and had then sailed under the name *Proserpine*. Upon the outset of the French Revolutionary War she had, through having excellent sailing qualities, been given the role of commerce raider, and it was in commerce raiding that she was captured by the British frigate *Dryad*, following a lengthy chase. Taken into the service of the British Navy, she was renamed *Amelia* in honour of Princess Amelia, the youngest daughter of George III. Refitted in the Plymouth naval dockyard, she was classified as a fifth rate with changes to her design allowing her to carry a greater number of guns, but this affected her overall sailing performance. Following this refit at Plymouth she was placed under the command of Herbert, an officer of relatively little experience, having seen, through the influence of his father, Henry Herbert, 1st Earl of Carnarvon, a meteoric rise through the promotion lists from being a midshipman in 1790 to that of post-captain only five years later. Nevertheless, he proved himself an able commander, frequently taking *Amelia* close in-shore and successfully capturing a number of French merchantmen.

The opportunity to spring the mutiny came during the first week of February when *Amelia*, detached from the main fleet, sailed close in-shore while chasing a French merchantman attempting to reach the safety of Brest. In an effort to escape, *Amelia*'s quarry had run close in-shore, seeking the protection of one of the batteries that defended the entry into the Goulet. In doing so she ran aground, with *Amelia*, over the next few days, remaining within visual distance, her captain hoping to catch other merchant shipping. Close to enemy shore batteries, but just out of range, Herbert ordered a guard boat to constantly row around the vessel to prevent the French sending over a boarding party.

The leading mutineer, from accounts given at his court martial, was Robert Larken, a Dubliner fully committed to radical republicanism. While his trial did not reveal a direct association with the United Irishmen, the fact of him demanding that 'every officer' be thrown 'overboard' and which would be followed by the vessel having to seek the safety of an enemy port reflected very much his embracing of United Irish sentiments. Moreover, among those mustered to *Amelia*, some 250, around thirty per cent were Irish. If Larken himself, through having previously served as an able seaman in the Caribbean, was not initially aware of the intentions of the United Irishmen to take British ships into enemy ports, he would certainly have been aware of the fate of *Hermione*.

That Larken had returned to England following naval service in the Caribbean was the result of a discharge from the navy through injury at sea. Awarded a small pension by the Navy Office, he had also been given a sick ticket giving him protection against being pressed back onto a warship. Therefore thinking himself safe from any press gang he might encounter, for he wisely carried with him the sick ticket at all times, he took to the streets of Plymouth on Christmas Eve. But he failed to consider that a devious captain such as Herbert, with an urgent resolve to get his ship back to sea but desperately short of men, would simply ignore a legitimate document of protection, claiming it to be forged. Falling into the clutches of the press gang sent out from *Amelia* and led by Mr Austin, *Amelia*'s master gunner, Larken was first beaten into semi-consciousness when he attempted to resist before he was taken on board and thrown into the ship's hold.

Once mustered to *Amelia* as a press'd man, Larken discovered he was in the company of others who were angry at having been taken by the press gang, with some also espousing political opposition to the war. Among them were men of Irish descent but others were English and Scottish radicals. One especially unified group of radically minded seamen had once served on *Saturn*, a ship that had mutinied at Spithead but whose crew were less than satisfied with the final outcome. Once at sea they had opposed their officers, with the committee of delegates elected by the ship's crew at Spithead gradually acquiring greater power. Eventually, the authority of the officers was entirely substituted by that committee, and its members issuing the day-to-day orders that kept the ship at sea. Any punishment threatened by the officers was immediately negated by the committee, with the committee taking on the sole right to determine who and for what crime any man might be punished. It was a brave effort at creating a democratic regime on board a ship of war, but one that would certainly not be condoned upon the ship's return to Cawsand Bay to revictual, a decision taken without any official approval. Many on board realised that the Admiralty would take some sort of revenge, despite no attempt to run the ship into an enemy port. However, reports were circulated in newspapers suggesting that some of the crew were considering the possibility of blowing up the ship 'before she came into Plymouth', but were prevented from doing so 'by the fortitude of a common seaman'. Of course, it is not impossible that this is a mis-reporting of an attempt by those supporting the delegate committee to not blow up the ship but an attempt to take the ship into an enemy port, albeit with the ship to be blown up if the taking of the ship failed. In the event, and at a subsequent court martial, eight men were sentenced to be hanged and three imprisoned. As for the remainder of the crew, many were dispersed into other ships with Herbert, in his desperation for men, taking twenty to join the crew of *Amelia*. Later, Herbert was to claim that it was these men from *Saturn* who had 'carried this diabolical spirit [of mutiny] with them, which they by degrees had since distributed through the sailors of the ship.'

Another group of men, around a dozen in number, who had reasons to be sympathetic to Larken's call for action, were those who had formerly served on *Artois*, a frigate that had sunk off the Île de Ré, not far from La Rochelle, in July. Following a successful rescue operation, all were brought back to Plymouth but then unceremoniously, and without shore leave or replacement of much that they had lost in the wrecked *Artois*, immediately ordered to join other ships, a dozen taken by Herbert.

With such a mix of men holding strong grievances and others with experience of mutiny, *Amelia* was a veritable tinder box. The men from *Saturn* clearly played their part, organising subversive clubs that were supportive of Larken, who became their figurehead. He made it clear that he was at one with them. They had endeavoured, through maintaining their delegate committee on board *Saturn*, to keep the spirit of the Spithead mutiny alive, dismissive of those ships' crews that had reneged on those principals and were now accepting all that the Admiralty threw at them.

'We must kill every bugger of an officer in the ship,' Larken declared to one packed meeting of the lower deck club. These meetings were held in the galley and between decks.

'I'm for the same. I'm for the same,' was the response to such demands frequently made by Larken.

In these meetings Larken was joined by fellow Irishman Dennis Broughall, who, alongside Larken, would eventually be court-martialled on a charge of sedition and mutiny with both later hanged at the yardarm. Broughall, for his part, had been present at Spithead during the mutiny, and was highly contemptuous of the outcome that he felt had brought very little real difference to the lives of those serving on the lower deck.

'If everyone was of the same mind as me or as willing as me,' Broughall was heard to say, 'we would extricate ourselves from slavery and bondage.'

'I'm for the same. I'm for the same,' came calls from the club.

'The cowardly buggers at Spithead,' Larken responded. 'We must free ourselves.'

'The ship might go to hell as we care nothing about it,' both Larken and Broughall were often heard to add.

Such was the regular routine of club meetings, with those attending imbibing large quantities of alcohol that had been brought to the ship by local ale sellers whose boats regularly tied up alongside *Amelia* as she lay in the Sound.

For Larken, his main target was the master gunner, the petty officer who had led the press gang that had so blatantly ignored his sick ticket.

'That bugger of a gunner who has taken me,' he declared. 'I will be even with him, for I am an invalid, and none of the buggers have any business with me.'

'There's not a ship's company in the navy so cruelly dealt with as we are,' came Broughall's supporting rejoinder. 'We must free ourselves of this tyranny.'

Sailing for the French coast towards the end of January, the taking of French prisoners from ships captured by *Amelia* added a new dimension to all that Larken and his supporters were hoping to achieve. Not only could these prisoners help take the ship, but they knew the waters around the coast of Brest, to where *Amelia* had been assigned, and would help steer her into the Rade. A chance meeting with a small French trading vessel, a *chasse-marée*, tied up alongside *Amelia*, allowed the leading mutineers to make contact with the shore while also smuggling on board from the *chasse-marée* a goodly quantity of additional liquor.

News of a mutiny in the planning, and so openly talked about, soon came to the attention of the petty officers through their closeness to the people of the lower deck, and this news was eventually passed on to one of the ship's lieutenants by the quartermaster. Herbert did not take immediate action, delaying his response for several weeks until he had collected sufficient evidence that could be used to sustain a charge against Larken and Broughall. Finally making his move towards the end of February, and with the assistance of the marine guard, he had Larken and Broughall, together with eighteen others against whom he held suspicion, confined in irons.

Seemingly, all had gone well for Herbert with his apprehension of the twenty suspected mutineers undertaken without opposition from the crew. Yet newspapers, in a series of widely circulated reports, suggested otherwise. Not only were they writing that many of the crew had formed a resolution to murder all the officers but also that Herbert feared that the marine guard had been ready to support the mutineers. For this reason, it was reported, Herbert had armed his officers and threatened to open fire on the marines, putting as many of them to death as possible if they did not obey his instructions. Following this threat, and assured that the marine guard would support him, Herbert ordered the ship's company to assemble, declaring that unless, within a given number of minutes, they gave up the ringleaders, he would order the marines to pour a volley in amongst them. As these newspapers then reported, 'This had the desired effect, and the men now in irons were given up.' To what extent the newspaper reports were correct is difficult to say, although Herbert did claim this version of events to be totally untrue, writing in a letter to one morning newspaper of these being 'very erroneous and exaggerated reports'. He also took exception to further reports that *Amelia* was 'laying in the Sound, [still] in a state of mutiny [and] under guard of two 74-gun warships.'

Admiralty vengeance was swift, although not as brutal as some might have expected. Between 15 and 17 March 1798, a court martial was held in the Hamoaze on board *Cambridge*, the Plymouth flagship. Both Broughall and Larken were placed on trial and sentenced to be hanged, their fate eagerly reported by various newspapers across the country:

> *This morning [Wednesday 21 March], at eight o'clock, the yellow flag, as a signal for punishment, was hoisted on board the* Cambridge, *the port admiral's ship, and was immediately repeated by the* Amelia, *in consequence of which the boats from all the ships in the Sound, Cawsand Bay, and Hamoaze, together with a number of gunboats, assembled about the* Amelia, *to witness the execution of the two unfortunate seamen. The platforms were then prepared on the forecastle of that ship, and ropes received at the fore-yardarms, and about ten minutes after eleven o'clock they were both launched into eternity. They both behaved in a very penitent manner, and have addressed a letter to their brother seamen, exhorting them to take warning by their untimely end. After hanging one hour, they were lowered down into their coffins, in a boat alongside the ship; the boats which attended the execution then all returned to their respective ships, and thus ended the very awful scene.*

A third man, Harris, had been placed on trial for involvement in the planning of the mutiny, and on being found guilty was sentenced to two years' confinement in the Marshalsea, a prison in London usually reserved for crimes at sea. This was a relatively light sentence. Harris was extremely fortunate, for normally any man associated with mutiny at sea might also have been hanged. Others may have been tried, for twenty were suspected by Herbert of involvement, but through lack of evidence all charges were dropped. As for the remainder of the crew, they went some way to proving their loyalty, each voluntarily giving a month's pay to the government as a donation towards funding the war against revolutionary France. For some, this money given was to avoid suspicion. To do otherwise might have led to a closer examination as to any part they played in the mutiny.

Four months later, on *Haughty*, the 167-ton gunboat, a second Irish mutiny plot was uncovered. Under the command of Lieutenant Matthew Smith, *Haughty* was part of Sir Edward Pellew's in-shore squadron, serving in an area of water that lay between Jersey and Normandy. With news of rebellion breaking out in Ireland, William Timmings, an Irish Catholic and the recently appointed gun-captain of *Haughty*'s foremost guns, was determined to give what support he could to the United Irish cause. Whether or not he was part of the wider plot will never be known, but he was certainly following a similar trajectory, planning on taking *Haughty* into a French port, possibly Cherbourg or another of the ports on the east coast of the nearby Cotentin Peninsula. His support for the republican cause and the freedom of Ireland was unquestioning and absolute.

'I would like to be soaking my arms in some of their English blood,' he confessed to one seaman who he attempted to recruit. To another he added, 'I will kill two or three of the officers of the ship and then let them hang me.'

As a committed republican, Timmings looked to France as the means to free Ireland from English rule, speaking enthusiastically of life in France since the revolution.

'In France I tell you,' he declared, speaking to those he hoped would soon be joining him in his endeavours. 'In France people live very happy since the present mode of government.'

One who provided him with unquestioning support was James Cormick. 'I will cure two or three of them [the ship's officers] of the itch,' Cormick was once heard to say. The 'itch' being slang for the pox or venereal disease, and his meaning was that it would be a permanent cure, one brought about by the murder of the officers.

Among those Timmings attempted to recruit was William Paul Gilbert, one of many French men serving in the Royal Navy, some volunteering because of having sympathies with the *Ancien Régime* while others were committed Jacobins who wished no favour upon England. These latter had usually been captured at sea and were only serving in the British Navy upon being offered the choice of incarceration in a prison hulk or service with pay on board a warship, seeing the Royal Navy as the better option. Gilbert, whether a Royalist or a Jacobin, was seen by Timmings as a potential asset, a man who would have knowledge of the coastline and could safely steer *Haughty* into a French port. In this, however, Timmings was to be disappointed, for Gilbert, while a native of Cap La Hogue on the Cotentin Peninsula, had only ever sailed to the west of the peninsula and not to the east where Timmings planned to take the ship. Gilbert would later testify against both Timmings and Cormick, recalling one conversation he had with Timmings in May 1798. *Haughty* was lying off the Isle of Wight, taking on fresh victuals. Doubtless Gilbert, in a recitation presented to the court, chose his words carefully, not wishing to implicate himself as a mutineer and supporter of what was being planned. In a thick French accent, and occasionally slipping into his native syntax, he told the court that he had attempted to dissuade Timmings from taking matters any further. In doing so, he iterated the dangers to be confronted and which would he believed lead to Timmings and Cormick facing the long drop.

'I told him that perhaps he would speak to a wrong person,' Gilbert told the court. 'I told him that if he spoke to a wrong person, he would be watched by and by and would then be found out.'

'I told him,' Gilbert continued, 'that it was the greatest impossibility to take such a vessel as the *Haughty*, there being so many hatchways.'

He went on to remind Timmings that to guard the various hatchways he had not the numbers, as ten would be needed for this task alone while another ten would be needed to work the vessel. One must assume, therefore, that Timmings had only recruited a very small number, possibly no more than ten in total. Turning to a second problem, Gilbert pointed to the tiller ropes running through the ship to connect the steering wheel on deck to the rudder at the stern. At one point they passed through the bread room on the lower deck and it was on the lower deck where Timmings planned to imprison the officers. This would give the officers unrestricted access into the bread room, and it was likely they would cut these ropes.

'If they cut the tiller ropes required,' Gilbert elaborated, 'our vessel would have no command at sea, and would lie exposed and easily taken by an enemy or one of His Majesty's cruisers.'

Timmings also asked Gilbert as to the likely reception *Haughty* would receive if taken into a French port. Again, Gilbert tried to dampen Timmings' enthusiasm.

'I gave him but poor encouragement,' he informed the court. 'I told him he would not get more than half the value of the vessel and afterwards he would be looked on by the French as a scoundrel.'

Unphased by all that was being told, Timmings simply informed Gilbert that he had a definite plan and that he would be taking the ship by surprise while she was at sea.

'I will seize the lieutenant on deck and by which he will see me as the principal man.' After that, Gilbert informed the court, Timmings thought it would be much easier to go through with the taking of the ship.

'When we lie as close to the French coast as we do to the English,' Cormick informed one shipmate, 'we will make a brush.' By brush he meant making a clean sweep of the officers by trapping them below or killing them.

Another seaman Timmings attempted to recruit was William Campbell, but he too refused to co-operate, with Campbell also giving evidence at the trial against the two would-be mutineers. It had been assumed by Timmings that Campbell, through being Irish, would grab at the chance of supporting the ongoing rebellion in Ireland. Furthermore, Campbell had occasional possession of the key to the arms chest and could have provided the rebels with small arms, cutlasses and ammunition. But Campbell was having none of it, with Timmings, in frustration, angrily shouting at Campbell, 'You have been too long in England, ever to be good to your own country!' Later to Gilbert, in mentioning his failure to recruit Campbell, he told him that Campbell was 'a villain and a scoundrel'.

As with so many of the Irish plots, the conspiracy was given away by a crew member loyal to the captain, a move made easier on a smaller ship where informal contact between officers and those on the lower deck was much more frequent. Through the information he received, Captain Smith, on 24 June, while *Haughty* was off the coast of Guernsey, took action. Timmings and Cormick were both put in irons, alongside several others suspected of being part of the plot. A message was then sent by Smith to Robert Barlow, captain of the frigate *Phoebe*, requesting that these men be tried as soon as possible. *Sea Gull*, a brig sloop, was detailed by Barlow to escort *Haughty* to Portsmouth with orders for a court martial to be put in motion. At their trial, held on board *Royal William* during the second week of July, both Timmings and Cormick were found guilty and sentenced to be executed.

A further mutiny was uncovered in June, again on board one of the ships of a detached squadron belonging to the Channel fleet, the 50-gun *Adamant*. Under the overall command of Sir Richard Strachan, this was a detachment patrolling off Le Havre, with the conspiracy uncovered during her temporary return to Spithead for revictualling when it was reported to the ship's captain, Henry Hotham, that John Mullins was causing a disturbance among 'the people below deck'. He, and several others of the lower deck were demanding both 'a new ship and new officers', but with the likelihood that if the ship was taken to sea, Mullins and others of the crew who were Irish would aim to take the ship into a French port, most probably Le Havre. When warned he might be hanged, Mullins was quite fearless, proclaiming, 'We will all be hung together and I will be hanged the first.'

At a subsequent court-martial held on board *Royal William* moored off Portsmouth during the first week of July, guilty verdicts and a sentence of execution were passed on Mullins and another seaman, John Stevens. Also sentenced to be executed was Cornelius Keally, but he was reprieved on the grounds of him being considered by Hotham 'a stupid ignorant Irishman'. Given that many captains, when considering who to prosecute out of a large number who could be indicted on charges of mutiny, chose only to bring forward those known to be of Irish birth, and with the full expectation they would be executed, Keally therefore was, if on somewhat dubious and prejudicial grounds, most peculiarly fortunate.

In making reference to the court's verdict, Vice-Admiral William Waldegrave, the president of the court, presented the view of the establishment, an unapologetic requirement that all seamen serving in the navy, however acquired and from wherever they came, should be totally committed to the war against revolutionary France and, in turn, support the British government irrespective of any discrimination they suffered and despite a denial of their right to suffrage. Those who willingly rebelled Waldegrave charged with being guilty of the blackest and most heinous of crimes. He saw the French as 'the common enemy of all mankind, an enemy whose system now clearly appears to be that of subverting all the governments of Europe.'

Given that this was what the Irish revolutionaries and English and Scottish radicals were seeking, it was a speech that might go down well with the elite but not those he was attempting to influence. Furthermore, it demonstrated the wide gulf between those seeking to change society and, through the introduction of a range of repressive measures, had forced those seeking democracy, to look to France for their salvation.

'Do not, lads,' Waldegrave continued, directly addressing the three prisoners, 'suffer yourselves any longer deluded the deceitful sounds of Liberty and Equality. These are only held forth to deceive and betray you into the sacrifice of all the real blessings and comforts you now enjoy.'

Of one other point demonstrated by the trial, and as also pointed out by Waldegrave, was that England still stood in great danger from these continuing plots. Waldegrave, as an admiral, hoped that the hanging of these two men, alongside the earlier hanging of Broughall and Larken, combined with a court martial soon to try Timmings and Cormick of *Haughty*, would so unnerve the revolutionary activists of the lower deck as to bring all future plots to an end:

> *Did not this trial but too clearly prove that these atrocious schemes are still carrying on, I had hoped from their having so often failed, and their iniquity being discovered, that they had been entirely at an end; but truly sorry I am to see that they still exist.*

Knowing that his message would be relayed to the crews of all ships of the Channel fleet, alongside many of those same men of the lower deck witnessing the hanging of these men, Waldegrave pressed home his point.

'However, let us hope and trust that the sad example now before our eyes, and the two others which are at hand,' referring not just to Broughall and Larken but the soon to be held trial of Timmings and Cormick, 'will be the last that we shall have occasion to make.'

In optimism, Waldegrave concluded:

At all events, if any vile miscreants should hereafter be discovered amongst us who have been mercenary or abandoned as to endeavour to betray their king and their country in order to make us become the slaves of France, I am confident that there is scarcely a man in our whole fleet but would readily step forward to seize the traitor as I would myself.

But Waldegrave's hopes would soon be dashed, for the reluctance of crews to report acts of mutiny amongst their fellow shipmates continued. Even more dangerous was that rebellion was spreading to the capital ships – the vessels most vital to the safety of England and its continuing hegemony over Ireland. These ships, not to be the target of a few disorganised mutineers attempting to form isolated rebel cadres, were now the target of a sophisticated co-ordinated plan that involved not just the Society of United Irishmen but revolutionary and radical clubs formed on the mainland alongside French agents who were operating in and around British naval ports.

Chapter 9

All Not Well Within the Fleet

While the fleet mutinies at Spithead, Plymouth Sound and the Nore had long since seen crews returning to duty, leading to a sense of relief among those who were determined upon the defeat of revolutionary France, the Admiralty, for its part, had become increasingly aware of widespread discontent still raging within the fleet. Events on board *Saturn*, *Amelia* and, to a lesser extent, *Adamant* were certainly proof of this, as was the fleet mutiny at the Cape. Another clear warning that all was not well was given by master and commander John Eaton, who was given temporary command of the 74-gun third rate *Marlborough*, one of the more troublesome ships to have mutinied at Spithead. It was a warning Eaton was to give in the most bizarre of circumstances, blurted out at the very moment of a self-inflicted death, words only heard by those around him as he lay prostrate on the floor of Admiralty House with the spirit of life flowing out of his body. It was for him a tragic moment, a moment made worse for, should he have lived for just a few hours longer, he would have learnt of his promotion to the coveted rank of post-captain.

Marlborough, despite the settlement agreed between Admiral Howe and the appointed delegates, had continued to see among her crew a seething rage of discontentment that led to her being the very last ship to return to sea following the fleet mutiny at Spithead. Such fundamental issues as the right to shore leave, forced impressment and limits on the number of years a man should serve, issues not touched upon in that final settlement, still rankled among the seamen of *Marlborough*'s lower deck. Although it must be admitted that before returning to sea *Marlborough* was one of several ships that benefited from one important concession reluctantly given by Howe, the admiral, agreeing to remove unpopular officers, realising that this was the only way a number of ships would depart Spithead and return to blockade duties off Ushant. Henry Nicholls, *Marlborough*'s captain, and by all accounts a man who treated his crew with considerable brutality, was one who was dismissed alongside three other officers of the ship: her first lieutenant, her surgeon and her master's mate. These officers were sent ashore alongside the captains of seven other ships, a further twenty-eight lieutenants and more than seventy more junior officers and petty officers. In objecting to Nicholls continuing to command the ship, the 'Marlboroughs' had specifically accused him of chastising mates who appeared too lenient when beating seamen and punishing a sick man who should have been under the care of the surgeon. Nicholls was also accused of regularly using his fists, telescope and speaking trumpet to beat members of the crew, with the speaking trumpet used so violently that the mouthpiece broke and was replaced by a double sheet of tin and an iron ring, making it more effective when used as a tool of punishment.

In having dismissed so many officers in such a short period of time, no less than eight captains for instance, the Admiralty found itself in a difficult position when finding replacements. It was for this reason that John Eaton was appointed to *Marlborough*, a post he would never have otherwise received. Of very junior rank Eaton, who had no prior experience of commanding a large ship, transferred to *Marlborough* from the frigate *Medusa*. Given the high level of discontent that continued to permeate *Marlborough*, and which was known to the Admiralty, a man of much greater experience should have been appointed. At sea, during the short period of Eaton being in temporary command, he proved himself a weak character who failed to gain the respect of the lower deck as well as the junior officers.

On returning from blockade duty on 30 June, *Marlborough* put into Plymouth where Eaton learnt he was to be replaced by Joseph Ellison, previously the commander of a fourth rate. Ordered to report to the Admiralty in London, Eaton was to be offered a new but smaller ship and raised to the rank of captain. Seemingly, though, his experience on *Marlborough* had unsettled him, for upon arriving at the Admiralty, and while in the lieutenant's waiting room prior to being called before the board, he mortally stabbed himself. Death being not instantaneous, with a fellow captain attempting to staunch the flow of blood, Eaton muttered 'there are traitors on board *Marlborough*…the country is ruined.' Nobody could get more out of him, and so it was never clear as to what or to whom he referred. But clearly, as was already known, all was not well on *Marlborough*, a ship that was to witness the plotting of a further mutiny less than a year later.

Doubtless adding to the Admiralty's uncertainty as to the absolute loyalty of the people of the lower deck were continued high rates of desertion, with seamen, if and when the opportunity arose, taking refuge in France and even serving on board enemy warships. Seven seamen who had been elected delegates at the Nore were discovered in February 1798 to be serving on *Lynx*, a French privateer, with other British subjects who had deserted the Royal Navy regularly coming before the courts when French ships to which they had subsequently given their allegiance were captured and brought into a British port. Recognition that so many British seamen, often Irish, were serving on French ships was given at the Old Bailey in May 1799 when three seamen taken off a French privateer were sentenced to death. One of those seamen, Irish by birth, gave as his defence that he had just come out of a French prison, was starving, and thought he was going onto a neutral ship when put on board the Frenchman. The jury hesitating on determining a verdict were told by the judge, 'If you admit the excuse of the prisoner, you will have all the French privateers manned by British subjects, and your commerce will then be in a miserable situation.'

A further reminder of the unreliability of the lower deck came in February 1798, the same month as the attempted mutiny on *Amelia*. On 3 February, *Raven*, an 18-gun sloop, was wrecked in a gale at the mouth of the Elbe. Her crew, when all hope of saving the ship had been lost, plundered every article of her stores before being rescued and taken ashore. On being landed in Cuxhaven, a great number deserted, with many enlisting on merchant ships at Hamburg. Among them, the Admiralty soon learnt, were five seamen who at the Nore had been elected as delegates. That those former delegates were in Hamburg takes on particular significance as also present in Hamburg was a French agent, Léonard Bourdon, and his Irish secretary, William Duckett. This was the same William Duckett who had been detailed by the executive of the Society of United Irishmen in Dublin to travel to Portsmouth at the time of the Spithead mutiny to make contact with Irish seamen of the Channel fleet. In Hamburg, both Bourdon and Duckett were committed to the possibility that crews on British warships, through sustained discontent, might well continue to mutiny, so reducing the overall effectiveness of the British Navy. On the waterfront of that major port city, they approached British seamen, especially those who had recently served in the navy, attempting to ascertain the attitude of those serving on the lower deck of British warships. It seems highly likely that among those with whom they spoke were some who had deserted from *Raven*, with the former Nore delegates likely to be the ones most prepared to provide an insight into the state of mind of the lower deck. In the report that Bourdon subsequently submitted to the Directory, he made it clear that the level of dissent within the British Navy was extensive, and that officers had failed to regain their full authority following the mutinies of the previous year and had becoming increasingly reliant on draconian levels of punishment. This, in turn, had heightened the resentment among those of the lower deck. Irish seamen, it was confirmed, not only shared that general resentment, but were further embittered by the brutality of English governance in Ireland. According to Bourdon in his report, this combination of overall discontent combined with Irish fury was 'a volcano continuously ready to erupt.'

For Bourdon it was essential that France fully utilise this clear weakness within the British Navy, noting that without French aid those who mutinied, however radical they might be, would simply be struck down time after time. Leaders would be hanged at the yardarm and the less active followers condemned to either imprisonment or transportation. To this end, he emphasised that France must make it clear that those who inspired mutiny and brought their ships into a French harbour would be made most welcome. If a French warship was met at sea, a ship taken by its crew would work with that ship in the spirit of *fraternité*, jointly working towards 'the destruction of that infamous government [they] abhor'. Even before that report was delivered to Paris, two Irishmen had been dispatched from Hamburg to Cork, carrying with them papers that outlined favourable attitudes of the French government to a ship's crew in mutiny and that reliance could be placed on France to provide them with support.

It was following the attempted mutiny on *Amelia* that plans for taking British warships into enemy ports were to be more fully developed. While at sea, those committed to such ideas could only meet with those who served on the same ship, but when ships at sea returned to revictual, most usually at Cawsand Bay or Spithead but occasionally Torbay, it was possible for crews of different ships to intermingle. The normal procedure when on blockade duties was for about ten ships of the line to be stationed off Ushant, with other units of the fleet relieving them on a turn-and-turnabout arrangement. This relieving of ships occurred about once every four or five weeks and once having moored in one of those three locations the crews were left very much to their own devices, with some visiting friends and acquaintances on other ships of the returning squadron or even entertaining on board people from ashore. Thus, between *Caesar*, *Captain*, *Defiance* and *Neptune*, ships that frequently sailed together, there is much evidence of leading conspirators meeting together while moored in Cawsand Bay. Similarly, with *Glory* and *Queen Charlotte*, ships that frequently relieved *Caesar*, *Captain*, *Defiance* and *Neptune* on the Ushant station, there is also evidence of those conspiring having similar meetings when these ships returned to Cawsand Bay to revictual. Further co-ordinating the conspiracy, and providing a link between ships arriving at ports on different rotas, were agents on shore who not only met with Irish radicals on board numerous warships but who also provided a link with the central committee of the Society of United Irishmen and possibly other radical groups.

PART 5

For the Sake of the United Irishmen

Vice-Admiral William Waldegrave, in addressing the three seamen found guilty of plotting to take *Adamant* into a French port, had hoped that hanging two of them, combined with punishments handed out to Broughall and Larken of *Amelia* and later to Timmings and Cormick of *Haughty,* would bring an end to such plots. In this he was to be disillusioned. Unbeknown to Waldegrave and all other officers of the Royal Navy at the time of him expressing that hope, more plots were being hatched, and these were far more threatening. While the mutineers on board *Adamant, Amelia* and *Haughty* were working in an uncoordinated way towards bringing the relatively small ships upon which they served into an enemy port, the plots soon to be uncovered were designed to bring to the enemy ships of the line the most powerful warships afloat. In the Channel fleet they were to include *Captain, Caesar, Defiance, Glory* and *Neptune* while serving as part of the blockading fleet off Brest, and *Impetueux, Marlborough* and *Queen Charlotte* while in Irish coastal waters. Further plots were hatched in the Mediterranean fleet by rebel seamen on *Ville de Paris*, the flagship of the fleet, and on two second rates, *St George* and *Princess Royal*. In the North Sea, Irish and English republican plots were to be uncovered on the 50-gun, two-deck fourth rate *Diomede*.

Chapter 10

Captain

Plymouth, England, May 1798. John Mckenna, the wardroom steward of the 74-gun third rate *Captain*, on shore leave took a leisurely stroll along North Corner Street. It was there he first became acquainted with Edward Mahaney and Thomas Grumley, seamen also serving on *Captain*. These two men were on a mission to recruit Irish seamen into a club formed on *Captain*, a United Irish club that had begun to hold meetings under the forecastle on the larboard side of the galley. Between them they had so far recruited around fifteen of the lower deck and would eventually recruit fifty or more. In their sights, and seen as a useful addition to the club, was McKenna, for he, like Mahaney and Grumley, was also Irish, and through being a wardroom steward could act on their behalf as a spy, able to listen to what the officers were saying as they relaxed and talked freely among themselves.

North Corner Street was familiar territory for the men of the lower deck. Running alongside the Hamoaze just by the dockyard, it was where ships' boats usually tied up to a jetty, allowing those granted shore leave a chance to break free, if only for a few hours, of the ships in which they were otherwise incarcerated. These were ships that would soon be putting to sea for Ushant and the continuing blockade of Brest. Located along the length of North Corner Street were a large number of tap houses and other drinking dens where, at a price, a 'dolly mop' or two, could also be found.

While a man granted shore leave might attempt to desert, this was most uncommon. A man given shore leave, even if pressed into the navy, knew that if he failed to return, others waiting to go ashore would be punished, not allowed their promised shore leave because of another's desertion. So a man on shore leave was bound by his shipmates to return. Beside which, only those trusted to be on their honour to return would be given such a privilege. Finally, as every seaman knew, all the roads around Plymouth were sealed by press gangs and military patrols. Should they apprehend a deserter, as they frequently did, a bonus payment of five pounds was given out, and for the captured deserter a possible hanging or, at the very least, an appointment with the cat.

'McKenna,' he heard either Mahaney or Grumley call out. This surprised the steward, for he had not noticed either of these men before. Although this is hardly surprising. While *Captain* had been launched back in 1787, she was now fresh out of dry dock. In February of the previous year, under the command of Horatio Nelson, *Captain* had played a key role in the Battle of Cape St Vincent where John Jervis, the admiral commanding the Mediterranean fleet, had gained victory and the capture of four Spanish warships. In that battle, *Captain* had sustained considerable damage and had been sent back to Plymouth for essential repair work. Undocked only a few weeks earlier, she had been assigned to the Channel fleet, taking on an entire new crew.

'McKenna, a word if you please.' The steward paused for a moment. What could these men possibly want? But recognising from their brogue that they were men of Erin, he paused.

'Are you after having a drink with us?' Mahaney asked. 'We have much to tell you.'

Intrigued, he willingly accompanied them. From North Corner Street they slipped down a side street to a more secluded ale house where a third seaman, Irishman Patrick McGee, was waiting for them.

'Come here to me, listen up and lean in,' one of the three suggested after having taken a few sips of strong liquor, liquor that was now beginning to take effect. 'Our ship has many men like you. Good men, loyal to the cause of Ireland. We are United Irishmen, one and all. Join us. We now have one great opportunity.'

If McKenna spoke truthfully as a witness, he was now beginning to feel uncomfortable and wished to depart. He had an inkling of what they were about, although nothing as yet had been said of a planned mutiny, which was their true objective. But was McKenna telling the truth? Not only did he keep this information to himself for a good many weeks, but he was to attend several meetings of the United Irish Club, meetings in which plans for the taking of the ship into Brest were unveiled and agreed. McKenna was later to claim that he only sat in on these meetings to uncover the plot and relate it to the 'quality', one or other of the officers of the quarterdeck. But if so, he was playing a dangerous game. Any man associated with the rebels on board *Captain* faced, if found out, a possible court martial that might end in a one-way journey to the yardarm and a noose tightening around the neck. Only when he had enough evidence against the seamen of the United Irish Club did he come forward. More likely he was a sympathiser, but turned against the club and its objective when he realised the plot would fail and to save his own life. Only then did he report it to Mr Shannon, the ship's master-at-arms, with Shannon informing First Lieutenant William Hannah.

Unable to get away, or so he was to claim, McKenna was forced to accept Mahaney's next suggestion, that they return to a second ale house in North Corner Street for a further round of drinks. One ale house that was always popular with the lower deck was *The Swan*. It still stands to this day. Maybe it was here that more of the doings of the United Irish Club were revealed to McKenna.

'I wish to get off, but they would not let me go,' McKenna stated when giving evidence as a witness when twelve members of the United Irish Club were being court-martialled. Pressed to continue by John Ayling, his ship's captain, and the appointed prosecutor, he explained how he finally took his exit.

'I gave one of them a shilling to pay the reckoning.' That someone was Mahaney and the reckoning was the payment for the drinks. 'To the other, I gave a silk handkerchief to put about his neck as he had lost his.' It was a black silk handkerchief, and meant as a loan, but it was never returned.

'I did not agree to joining the club. I did not like it,' McKenna informed the court as he continued his monologue. 'They [referring to Mahaney and Grumley] told me it was a favourable opportunity to get into the secret of becoming a United Irishman – but I did not like it.'

Once the ship was at sea, the meetings in the galley became regular events. Twenty or more were frequently in attendance. It was Thomas Grumley of the lower deck who often led these meetings. To those assembled, he would proclaim loudly on successes claimed by the rebels and of the strength of the United Irish, both in the Royal Navy and the British Army.

'I have a letter from one ship,' Grumley declared a few days short of 28 May, that being the day *Captain,* in company with several other ships, sailed out of Cawsand Bay.

'The ship I do not know,' McKenna admitted. Present at that meeting, he may genuinely have not known, or just chose not to say. 'The substance of the letter,' he continued, 'was the extent of the number of Irishmen on board that ship [the unnamed ship] and the order in which they were carrying it on.'

McKenna also told the court that Grumley had replied to this letter and was awaiting a response. Once he had received a reply, he expected the United Irish on board *Captain* to act in accordance with the instructions given. It was a letter that could only have come from a ship also anchored at that time in Cawsand Bay, a ship that had an organised revolutionary cadre on board. This would seem to narrow it down to just four possibilities, *Caesar*, *Defiance*, *Glory* or *Neptune*. Those four ships were also with *Captain* when she sailed on 28 May.

'If the United Irishmen stick true to each other, true to their trust that we are the best party,' Grumley stated at another meeting, 'then no doubt we should gain the day and we shall have our ends.'

'It's a just and good cause,' came the retort from several.

'Damn the dog who would not die for it,' from another.

This was an especially raucous meeting, for these remarks were followed by huzzas and cheering before all stood to form a circle and join hands.

Another witness was marine guard John Baker. He was to tell of a conversation he had with Rudder and Gadman, two of the less prominent members of the club, but for all that no less committed. Taking place after a number of the club had been put in irons, Rudder and Gadman were aware that Baker, as a marine, would sometimes be one of the sentries guarding the prisoners. From Baker, the two club members wanted to know when he would next be guarding them, possibly in the hope that he would allow them to talk to those now held in irons. If so, the reason was not disclosed to Baker, but as likely as not it would have been to discuss the plans for the taking of the ship and, of course, the releasing of those shackled. Strange, of course, that they should so openly approach Baker, but for this there must have been a reason. All that can be suggested is Baker was an English radical, someone Rudder and Gadman thought, rightly or wrongly, they could trust. Otherwise they were simply assuming that all those serving on *Captain*, both of the lower deck and marine guard, were discontented and would be favourable to supporting the ambitions of the Irish rebels.

To Baker they went on to explain how the ship was to be taken, this in unison with *Caesar*, *Defiance*, *Glory* and *Neptune*. Before doing this, they asked him a few test questions, especially about his attitude to France. Though his answers, as related to the court, were fairly non-committal, it must be supposed he gave words more favourable to the French republic than what he stated to the court. Leastways, Rudder and Gadman were convinced, following the answers he gave, that Baker could be trusted.

'Have you ever been right abreast of France?' was how the conversation with Rudder and Gadman proceeded.

'I have,' Baker told the court.

'Did you like the land?' was the next question that either Rudder or Gadman threw at him.

'I liked it very well,' Baker informed the court.

'Would you like to go there?'

'I would if I could for two or three hours and then come back again,' was Baker's response, as claimed by him in the courtroom. 'Just to see the place.'

Having passed the test, Baker was told that on board *Captain* were many ready to act and that he would be told more if he agreed not to say anything to any other man. He agreed and, following a five-minute discussion out of his hearing, Rudder and Gadman returned to the larboard side of the ship where they had left him. Baker was now placed in a very dangerous situation. Drawn into the club through being entrusted with details of the ongoing conspiracy, he could be hanged if he did not immediately report to one of the officers what he had been told. Yet he did not report it. For this there can only be two possibilities. Either, as with the suggestion made of McKenna being a sympathiser, Baker was himself also favourable to the planned conspiracy. Or, and just as likely, he was more fearful of retribution from those of the United Irish Club than of facing a court martial. Had anyone from the club found out that he had reported the conversation, then he would have been a dead man walking.

'When the time comes, four men will take the helm and two the signal haul yards abaft. Another two at the main mast head,' either Rudder or Gadman explained. 'Those abaft will raise an English ensign with a French one above and those for'ard will fly red, white and blue signals.'

The use of the signal flags was to inform those conspiring on other ships that they should now take control of their own ships while the flying of the French ensign was to prevent an attack upon them by any French warships they might encounter. Apart from the eight men allocated to the helm and signal yards, a number of others would be standing by the lower deck guns which, at that point, were to be fired at the 'English' ships. In telling Baker all this, Rudder and Gadman claimed that support on other ships of the blockading fleet was considerable. According to Rudder and Gadman, there had been many floggings and there was much discontent in general among their seamen.

'Everything will be more peaceful and quieter, among one another, when we get to our journey's end,' Rudder explained. 'The highest man will be no better than the lowest.'

It was a conversation that lasted for about two hours, with Rudder and Gadman shaking Baker's hand before taking their leave of him.

That several of the rebels were by that time in irons, with more to be taken following the ship returning to sea a few days later, led members of the United Irish Club to question how news of their plans had reached the ears of the officers. At first they suspected a bumboat woman, one of the many who were brought from the shore by a small vessel known as a bumboat and would, while the ship was anchored in Cawsand Bay, stay with any man who offered the price demanded. The woman they suspected and who they knew as 'Corner', a name suggesting she was normally to be found somewhere around North Corner Street, had come on board in July when the ship returned to Cawsand Bay to revictual, spending time in the berths of several of the United Irish. It had been shortly after she had been put ashore and the ship had sailed that the first tranche of rebels had been placed in irons.

'If it had been planned out as Patrick McGee, Thomas Gainer and Thomas Garrety planned it, it would have done very well,' Thomas Sawyer, the ship's butcher, said in relating to the court a conversation he had overheard in August. But he was unable or reluctant to name the speaker.

'I am afraid they let the woman know too much,' Sawyer continued. 'I am afraid there is some bloody rascal in the ship,' he recalled the reply he had given. 'I wish I could find him out, I would soon put an end to him.'

Their suspicions were not entirely misplaced. The woman did speak to others of the crew, including Sawyer, telling him and others of the planned mutiny. However, what really led to the officers learning of the plot was the loudness of their meetings and an assumption that anyone they approached would support them and not share what they knew with an officer. Nevertheless, it was some time before anyone on the lower deck struck up sufficient courage to report what most knew was being discussed during those club meetings. Among the lower deck there was certainly a significant element who would like to bring an end to the scheme being plotted, but would not do so, indicating themselves to be too scared, believing they would be cut down by those who wanted to bring about the mutiny. One who clearly stated this to be his reason for not reporting what he knew was marine guard Fortunatus Harvey, who had heard another of the leading conspirators, John Duggan, declare, 'We will have equality here on board, the same as it is in Ireland.' On being asked, when called as a witness against the twelve, why he had not reported this remark to an officer, Harvey simply replied, 'Because I was rather afraid I might be thrown overboard, I was afraid of the people in the galley.'

Chapter 11

Organisation and Leadership

McGee, Gainer and Garrety were among the twelve to be court-martialled, identified alongside Duggan as leaders of the planned rebellion on *Captain* with the court assembling in Portsmouth Harbour on 5 December. Duggan might even have been the main man, painting himself as such when at one club meeting he proclaimed, 'By and by I will be a great man on this ship and better than the officers.' To this he later added, 'Every dog has his day and it will be ours by and by.' Of the other ships expected by the rebels on *Captain* to sail with them into Brest upon the raising of the blue, red and white signal flags and the firing of lower deck guns, namely *Caesar*, *Defiance*, *Glory* and *Neptune*, leaders can also be identified. On board *Defiance*, the name of William Lindsey comes to the fore alongside John Brady. On *Caesar* the primary organiser was Bartholomew Duff but with a further seven named in court as ringleaders, and on *Glory* everything revolved around William Regan.

Also usefully referred to here is Charles O'Neal, the organiser of an attempted mutiny on *Queen Charlotte*, a unit of the Channel fleet that would revictual in Cawsand Bay when *Caesar*, *Defiance*, *Glory* and *Neptune* were at sea. If O'Neal had contact with those ships, it would have been through a United Irish agent on shore. But if this was so, nothing is known. Off Ushant O'Neal recruited Irish seamen, forming an inner cadre through the gaining of support for the freeing of an Irish seaman who was about to be court-martialled. This may well have been a subterfuge, the idea of releasing an imprisoned fellow shipmate likely to gain more traction than a scheme outwardly proclaiming the taking of the ship into a French port. Such an approach was adopted by Irish activists of the Mediterranean fleet intent upon taking ships into Cadiz. It was a useful ploy, for once a prisoner was released by a mutinous crew, the mutineers would face the certainty of being court-martialled, unless they took the ship upon which they were serving into an enemy port and out of reach of the Admiralty. With the plot little developed, other than O'Neal attempting to gain a few signatures to a paper calling for liberty and justice for Ireland, O'Neal in mid-August was placed in irons to be court-martialled ten weeks later.

ORGANISATION AND LEADERSHIP

In general, little is known of those who were recognised as leaders other than their ages, which averaged around 28, and their places of birth. Most were Irish, with Cork and Dublin the most common places of birth. Bartholomew Duff, for instance, was a 33-year-old Dubliner rated able who had joined *Caesar* one year earlier from the Portsmouth receiving ship *Puissant*. Of Duff, however, it must be added that he was a leading agent of the United Irish executive, having regular contact with Lindsey and Regan of *Glory* as well as those on board other ships anchored in Cawsand Bay at the same time as his own ship. In addition, Regan had contact with agents ashore, these relaying to the ship-borne co-ordinators messages received from the central committee of the United Irishmen. Via one such agent, Regan received a letter from Ireland in early July with enclosed letters from France that offered whatever assistance was needed in the taking of his and other ships to France, adding that Buonaparte would be with them soon.

More can be said of Charles O'Neal. He was *Queen Charlotte*'s ship's barber, a position he could use as a cover for making contact with any man he sought to recruit. Also, in shaving and cutting the hair of the officers he would frequently be present in the wardroom, and as such gain useful intelligence from conversations overheard. In his possession, following him being shackled, were ninety-nine razors. These were viewed at his trial as possible weapons that could be used against any man opposed to taking the ship. As for evidence of his sympathy for the rebels in Ireland, this was also shown by the finding in his sea chest a number of songs he had written, these much in favour of the rebels and described by one witness at O'Neal's court-martial as derogatory to the king. Whether these songs were ever sung by those he recruited was never stated.

John Brady was declared by some witnesses during the *Defiance* court martial as the 'next man of consequence' after Lindsey. Brady first joined *Defiance* on 21 May 1795, rated as a landsman, but four months later appointed, like O'Neal, as the ship's barber. The muster book shows him as one of sixty-six quota men taken on board *Defiance* following the ship leaving Chatham where she had been refitting for sea. Although born in Ireland, Brady was listed as mustered from the port of Hull, and upon agreeing to enter the navy under the quota system would have received a bounty payment from the parish. Why Brady was in Hull is impossible to answer, but he may have been a temporary resident or, if the parish was unable to fulfil its quota, a substitute volunteer from Ireland. This in itself would have been quite normal, as when there was a shortfall of recruits from a parish to fulfil the quota number, a substitute from elsewhere had to be found, with a much higher bounty normally paid. Such substitutes often originated from Ireland but also further afield, including New York, Jamaica and even Milan. It is not impossible that Brady's radicalism stemmed from Hull, a town that possessed a well-organised union of journeymen tailors that had taken strike action in 1795 in protest at the dramatic rise in the price of grain. If not in Hull, Brady might well have been radicalised by his own experiences on *Defiance*, being present in November 1795 when part of her crew mutinied in Leith Roads and again when more or less the entire lower deck stood out at Spithead in 1797. Apparently he was well thought of in his role of ship's barber, with third lieutenant Cheetham, who was called as a character witness, describing him as 'honest' but frequently intoxicated.

It was the role of those leaders to first gain and then hold the support of as large a section of the lower deck as possible. It was Irish Catholic seamen who were primarily targeted, with those who did not give their support regarded as traitors. This was clearly stated of Dennis Callaghan (sometimes spelt Kalihan) of *Queen Charlotte* when he refused to give his support, being called by O'Neal 'a traitor to his God and country'. But none of the leadership echelon in any of the ships relied entirely upon religious or ethnic loyalty. On board most ships, those who joined the rebels were frequently reminded of the financial rewards they would gain through the ship being purchased into the French Navy and the value of the ship distributed equally among those who had participated in taking the ship into an enemy port. Regan on *Glory* not only promised that each man would get the 'value of the ship', but also a 'commission in the French service' to assist in the invasion of Ireland, where they would then be considered 'gentlemen for ever'.

The threat of violence was a feature of the recruiting process, used against any Irish Catholic who refused to support the rebels. James Holvey stated at the trial of the *Defiance* mutineers that the Irish rebels 'carried the sway a great deal in the ship,' and indicated that he would be badly treated if he did not give his support to their plans.

'I did my duty with them,' he stated. 'I feared they would do some injury to me in the night.'

Violence was also used to ensure continued support and unity among the rebels once they had been recruited, with Laurence Carroll, another Irish Catholic on *Defiance*, threatened with being 'knocked down' when it was discovered that he had written a letter to his brother who was in the militia. In that letter Carroll had written, 'I hope the country is quiet and the rebels defeated.' The letter had been torn into pieces by Callaghan. In his defence, when first challenged, Carroll had claimed that the words were simply a reflection of his concern for his brother, and he was sorry he was fighting against the rebels.

It was the leaders on each ship who administered the oath. Lindsey, according to one witness, received the wording of the oath in a letter expressly brought on board *Defiance* for his attention. According to several witnesses when questioned by Jones as prosecutor, it was an oath that required support for the rebellion in Ireland and the taking of the ship into Brest through affirmation given to the following question as read to them by Lindsey:

> *Will you take oath to be true to the Free and United Irishmen, who are fighting your cause against tyrants and oppressors and will you agree to defend their rights to the last drop of your blood; and do you agree to go to Brest the next time the ship looks out a-head at sea, and to kill every officer and man that opposes us, and hoist a green ensign, with a harp in it, and afterwards to kill or destroy the Protestants?*

On *Caesar*, Duff used two separate oaths, one swearing loyalty to the United Irishmen and 'to be their brethren in Ireland', the second a declaration 'to take the *Caesar* into Ireland or any other enemy port'. One witness, William Thomson of *Defiance*, described a seaman of the lower deck, stating that he took the oath 'betwixt the two guns on the main deck before the ladder that goes upon the quarterdeck.' This was during the late afternoon while the vessel was in Cawsand Bay. At the court martial, Thomson claimed that he had said 'no' to taking the oath, but through being drunk, Lindsey 'swore him'. While Thomson took the oath apart from the others, it seems that the earliest recruits were sworn in by Lindsey as a single body, 'a book about the size of a prayer book' placed into the hands of each recruit, with Lindsey reciting the words to each in turn.

Once the oath was taken, those so sworn were then admitted to rebel meetings and given the wording of the pass code, 'Are you Up', which was to be accompanied by the placing of the right hand over the left breast and answered by the other seizing with his left hand the other's right hand. On most ships the rebel meetings were known as clubs, on *Defiance* more specifically as a smoking club, the term 'club' being one frequently adopted by radical and French revolutionary political societies. In itself this would have been a sufficient clue that might have alerted the suspicions of any officer who showed the slightest interest in the activities of the lower deck when the men were not undertaking regular duties. During the time in which the ship was anchored in Cawsand Bay, meetings of these clubs, usually in the galley area of each ship, were held most evenings. Those wishing to use the 'heads', the toilet area at the forepeak, had as a matter of course to pass across the galley and would in so doing have been within close proximity of the club when in session. It was impossible for other crew members not to overhear what was being discussed, especially when voices were raised by those who had a little too much to drink. To reduce the possibility of members of the crew who might be unsympathetic to the conspiracy, the Irish mother-tongue Gaelic would always be spoken when an outsider was perceived to be in close proximity. On *Caesar*, another adopted ploy was that of simply preventing or discouraging others of the lower deck attempting to reach the heads by shouting insults at them or tripping them up as they attempted to pass through. James Mason of *Defiance*, in giving trial evidence, indicated that the English were 'knocked about if they approached the group'. On board *Glory*, where the officers were aware of these club meetings but not what was under discussion, an instruction was issued in July to all hands assembled that no future club meetings were to be allowed, with an added directive 'that no conversations should be held in Irish.'

It was on board *Glory* that the officers seemed especially fearful of the Irish of the lower deck, an ethnic group totalling 110 of a crew of around 700. According to Lieutenant Andrew Brown, who had first joined the ship in October of the previous year, *Glory* had the most insubordinate crew that he had ever witnessed, describing the Irish crew members as 'riotous and disorderly'.

'I never saw so many men in irons,' he informed other officers during the court martial of those suspected of mutiny on *Glory*, 'or so many punishments since I've been an officer as I did on that cruise.'

Indeed, so fearful was Brown of the Irish seamen of the lower deck that when he was officer of the first watch, a watch that was predominantly Irish, he would take with him a pair of loaded pistols, 'for fear that I would be opposed for carrying out the duties of the ship.'

Throughout the early part of 1798 Duff, Duggan, Lindsey and Regan set about propagating the idea of taking their ships into Brest, while encouraging their fellow rebels through disseminating news of victories achieved by the United Irishmen. During that time Duff had successfully administered oaths to forty-five seamen and eleven marines and Regan a slightly smaller number on *Glory*, with it reported at Duff's trial that those he had recruited were 'constantly in Duff's company'. From those he recruited, Duff also formed an inner committee of eight, who were responsible for planning and leading the mutiny.

In disseminating news of victories as achieved by the United Irishmen, the leadership echelon on those ships went a good deal further using information they obtained from agents ashore to strengthen their position of authority. To this end Lindsey on *Defiance* took it upon himself to carefully limit access to information available to the rebel club, highlighting successes of the United Irishmen and downplaying any failures. At the Nore in 1797 control of information had been invaluable, the King's Proclamation not revealed to the crews of the ships until

ORGANISATION AND LEADERSHIP

12 May, even though delegates sent to Spithead had returned with a copy four days earlier. This gave time for the delegate committees of the ships in mutiny to provide their own interpretation of its meaning, changing in part the sense of the document, and resulting in crews losing their initial enthusiasm for the terms laid out. On board *Defiance*, Lindsey ensured that all should know of any positive information from Ireland, broadcasting news of the French landing and reinforcing its significance by joyously shaking hands 'with every one of them round about'. Seemingly, he also appears to have created fictional news, telling of a Spanish landing in Ireland and, on another occasion, that 20,000 French had landed.

On *Glory*, Regan went even further than Lindsey in the creation of false news, telling of having acquired a copy of a newspaper found in the wardroom. Regan claimed he had paid William Moore, the second wardroom steward, four shillings to read the paper, but only given five minutes before it had to be returned. A useful ploy as it meant that nobody else had the opportunity to read the paper. Just as well, as no such paper existed, with Regan reeling off to those he had recruited a series of fictional events that related to two of the ships of the Channel fleet, *Queen Charlotte* and *Ramillies*, which he claimed had mutinied. Both had then been run ashore, *Queen Charlotte* off Dublin and *Ramillies* off Cork, with the crew of the latter hanging her captain and the crews of both ships gifting all weapons and stores to the rebels. In addition, he claimed that the entire crew of *Ramillies* had joined the rebels fighting in Wicklow. Needless to say, none of this was true. But it helped cement Irish seamen on *Glory* to the rebel cause.

Although several names can be put forward as identified leaders through evidence given by witnesses during trials conducted in 1798, other potential leaders may well have lain hidden beneath the surface through a lack of evidence. Indeed, those brought to trial represented, at the most, some twenty to thirty per cent of the total number prepared to support the mutineers on board any one ship, leaving a large number returning to duty but under suspicion. On *Defiance*, for instance, Jones originally incarcerated into the after hold and coal hole some 100 suspected of involvement in the planned mutiny, but of which only twenty-five eventually faced trial. On *Captain*, forty were originally suspected with only twelve court-martialled. Similarly, on board *Caesar*, *Glory* and *Neptune*, far more were initially placed in irons than were court-martialled, this again due to a lack of evidence that would have ensured a successful prosecution.

Chapter 12

Caesar, *Defiance*, *Glory* and *Neptune*

Defiance, *Glory*, *Caesar* and *Neptune* along with *Captain* departed Cawsand Bay on 28 May with the organising leadership on board knowing that a rebellion in Ireland was about to erupt and expecting it to be supported by a French military expedition. What they did not know was that the rebellion was already underway, news not having reached Cawsand Bay by the time of their departure and would not be known to them until returning to Cawsand Bay on 6 June. If it had been known that rebellion had broken out in Ireland, then 9 June would have offered a promising opportunity to take by mutiny one or all of the ships as, during the morning of that day, Bridport led most of his fleet, including *Caesar*, *Captain*, *Defiance*, *Neptune* and *Glory*, ships with rebel cadres, close in-shore to reconnoitre Brest. On approaching Bertheaume Roads, just 9km east of the Goulet, three ships of the line and two frigates were discovered, which immediately put underway, with Bridport ordering three of the fleet, one of which was *Caesar*, to give chase. In coming close to bringing the French flagship into action, Bridport judged it prudent to recall the four ships as, being so close to the shore, they had come under fire from the grand fortress of Bertheaume and nearby shore batteries. This, of course, would have been an ideal opportunity for the rebel crew on *Caesar* to have taken her, for not only was she away from the main fleet but she could have sought protection from the French shore battery by raising either a flag of surrender or the French *Tricolore* over the union flag. Similarly, *Defiance*, *Glory* and *Captain,* although not involved in the chase, were also close in-shore, as Bridport had ordered the rest of the fleet to follow the lead chase ships, and rebel crews might also have attempted the planned taking of these ships and placed one or all of them under the protection of the French shore guns.

Upon *Caesar, Captain, Defiance, Neptune* and *Glory* returning to Cawsand Bay, news of rebellion having broken out in Ireland was quickly learnt through letters sent from Ireland. John Brady of *Defiance* was one such recipient. His brother in Cavan, a captain of the United Irish light horsemen, informed him of a successful action fought against the English in which the Irish lost three men but the enemy lost seventeen. In rounding off this letter, Brady's brother added, 'by and by we will sweep them all out'. Lindsey was another receiving a letter, informing him that 24,000 were encamped in the Bog of Allen (Móin Alúine). Copies of an unnamed Irish newspaper were also circulated on several ships, indicating that the Society of United Irishmen had requested that France send 25,000 troops to Ireland and that the Directory had agreed. On hearing this, Nicholas Ryan of *Defiance* reportedly declared that he liked the French a great deal better than he liked the English.

News of the rebellion in Ireland would have been gleaned from the *Exeter and Plymouth Gazette* as well as newspapers arriving from London. These, however, while reporting several victories gained by loyalist forces, were far from conclusive regarding a rebel defeat, with Irish insurgents of the lower deck remaining confident that a French landing would soon occur and that the rebels, despite reports of their numerous defeats, would soon win through. Such confidence spurred the men on board the several ships of the Channel fleet to continue plotting and planning, the ships upon which they served seen as crucial to the victory that they hoped to gain in their fight against the Protestant Ascendancy.

On *Glory*, the means by which she was to be taken was confided to John McKinnon, an Irish-born marine, by one of the inner group of conspirators, George Norton. These two men appear to have had several conversations, with Norton expecting that McKinnon would be 'as good as the rest of the Irishmen'. According to Norton, who gave evidence on behalf of the prosecution at the later trial by court martial, McKinnon told him the ship would be taken at night during the first watch, the watch that Lieutenant Andrew Brown had especially feared because of it being composed of a particularly high number of Irish. To help incapacitate those who were likely to oppose the mutineers they were to be offered large quantities of rum, this especially accumulated by the conspirators from their own daily ration. At the end of the watch, with rebels of this watch joining with rebels of the next watch, the upper deck was to be quickly secured with the officer of the watch thrown overboard together with any others who attempted to resist. To trap the bulk of the crew below, the ladders to the lower deck would be unshipped, the gratings put in place and armed sentries, using weapons taken from the poop deck arms chest, placed over each hatch. Resistance from the quarterdeck, should there be any, would be quelled through the simple expediency of readying the forecastle guns and moving them to point aft. Should the attempt at taking the ship fail, or if it appeared that she was about to be recaptured by ships remaining loyal to the

British Navy, it was intended that *Glory* would be sunk by firing two of her guns from the waist down the hatchway and so blasting a hole through her underwater hull.

To overpower the loyalist crew on *Defiance*, bludgeons of various sizes had been made readily available, secreted into gun barrels. Another potential weapon that might have been used were boarding pikes stored on the quarterdeck, their availability the subject of discussion among those later placed in the after hold. According to John Garvey, who had been sent by Jones to overhear what the prisoners were saying by placing his ear to the upper seam of the bulkhead, Edward McLaughton stated, 'If we had the boarding pikes that were upon the forecastle and divided them each side we would have done it.' William Hynson, a gunner's mate, was heard to say, 'If they had only got hold of the boarding pikes they would have done well enough.'

According to William Lindsey of *Defiance*, there would be little difficulty once the ship was in rebel hands of steering her into Brest, believing that 'any man in the ship could carry her [*Defiance*] into Brest [as] it was a broad deep water'. For this purpose he appointed John Hopkins, one of the Irish rebels, to steer the ship into Brest. Regan on *Glory* was a little more aware that a problem might exist with the taking of a large warship so close to the French coast, selecting a man who he claimed was competent to act as master. To no one did he ever reveal who this individual might be, but possibly one of several French seamen who were serving on *Glory* at that time.

The mutinies attempted on *Caesar*, *Defiance*, *Glory* and *Neptune* never got beyond the planning stage. The key mutineers were all apprehended and placed in irons prior to any attempt to take control of those ships. On *Caesar* it was the sheer divisiveness of the plot that led to its ultimate failure, a fear pervading among a large section of the crew, the majority of whom were Protestant English, that in the event of the mutiny being sprung, they would be slaughtered. This fear was fostered by remarks heard, in English and emanating from some of the leading Irish rebels, that clearly threatened the continued survival of any Protestant if the ship fell into the hands of the Irish rebels. John Devine, for instance, a 24-year-old seaman rated landsman, and recognised as an influential member of the rebel club, made one such chilling remark. 'I will never die easy till I have washed my hands in Protestant blood.' At another time 34-year-old Dubliner Michael Butler, rated ordinary, another leading *Caesar* mutineer, was heard to remark that he would think no more of putting a Protestant to death than a mad dog and that he would put a knife into all heretics.

CAESAR, DEFIANCE, GLORY AND NEPTUNE

It was at precisely 6.30 p.m. on Sunday 29 July that news of a planned mutiny was first brought to the attention of *Caesar*'s first lieutenant John Frasier. According to the captain's log book, *Caesar* was moored in Cawsand Bay, 'Penlee Point SSW½W' and 'Redding Point NE by E', with a light breeze blowing. The means by which it was brought to Frasier, who was in the wardroom, was somewhat complex, emanating from a seaman of the lower deck who had first informed the corporal of the hold who, in turn, passed what was said to William Oliver, captain of the forecastle, with it finally reaching the first lieutenant, through midshipman Lieutenant Thomas Tidy the officer of the watch. If nothing else this roundabout route by which it eventually reached the wardroom demonstrates the difficulty that a lower deck seaman had in reporting anything they knew of an impending mutiny and the possibility of what he was reporting being realised by a vengeful mutineer who would quickly take action against any informer. On *Glory*, a seaman who wished to report the mutiny to his captain had to wait three hours, during which time he was totally ignored before being called away to attend to his shipboard duties and so never given the opportunity to report such a vital piece of information.

Frasier, convinced there was substance to what he was told by Lieutenant Tidy, who was accompanied by William Oliver, immediately placed the ship in a state of security, sending for Roddam Home, the ship's captain, who was ashore. In his log book, Home simply recorded:

> *After an examination of several witnesses. The officers and such part of the ship's company as to be judged to be well affected were armed and several suspected men secured.*

The following morning, twenty of those suspected were sent to *Cambridge*, the port admiral's flagship, while several more were confined in the afternoon 'on suspicion of being concerned in the said mutiny'.

No further mention of the matter is made in Home's log book for just over two weeks, with the following entry appearing on 16 August:

> *AM at 7 sent twenty-three prisoners belonging to* Caesar *confined on board and in prison ships for the conspiracy discovered on 30 July last to the* Cambridge *in Hamoaze to be tried by court martial.*

In numbers given there is a slight discrepancy, as only twenty-two of the *Caesar* rebels were charged, eight identified as leaders and the other fourteen as assisting. As for the final verdict of the court, this appears in Home's log book dated 23 August:

> *10.30am the court passed sentence of death on Bartholomew Duff, John Diamond, William Cottor, James Mahan, Lawrence Buckley and Michael Butler and sentenced James Cluney and John Devine to be mulcted of all their wages and receive 500 lashes each.*

On *Defiance*, *Glory* and *Neptune*, elements of sectarianism were much less evident, although Richard Kennedy, one of the Irish rebels on *Defiance*, was heard to say, 'Damn and bugger the English into hell in a flame of fire.' However, this can be taken as a wish rather than a direct threat with such remarks toned down if only because of the need to work alongside English-born radicals. It is likely that it was for this reason that on *Caesar* Duff used two oaths, the second relating only to the taking of the ship into Brest and so more palatable to English radicals than the first, which was more specific to supporting the cause of freeing Ireland from mainland England's hegemonic rule.

While on *Defiance* it is unclear how news of the conspiracy reached the officers on both *Glory* and *Neptune*, it was given away by once trusted fellow conspirators who now felt unable to continue providing it with their support. The plot being hatched on *Neptune* was similarly given away, discovered on 16 August when one of the conspirators decided he could no longer support a scheme that included taking the ship into Brest and the possible killing of all the officers. For this reason he dropped a letter on the quarterdeck addressed to the captain containing the full nature and extent of the plot. Picked up by one of the officers, it was duly delivered to the ship's commander. In consequence of which the conspirators were immediately secured, many of them, it was to be reported in several newspapers, were Irish. Indeed, it was claimed that there were 'no less than two hundred on board', a fact not supported by the ship's muster book, which shows that of a total crew borne of just 540, only a maximum fifty-nine (eleven per cent) can be positively identified as Irish serving on the ship during the summer of 1798. If anything, this would indicate *Neptune* to have one of the lowest number of Irish, proportionate to her size, serving on any ship involved in the Irish mutiny conspiracies.

On *Glory*, news of the plot was given to the officers on Sunday 2 September by John McKinnon, an Irish-born marine who had taken the rebel oath but who now chose to renege. In doing so he waited until the very last moment, when the rebels were actually preparing to take the ship. Already, though, the officers did have certain suspicions, and for this reason an earlier order from the quarterdeck had been issued banning the use of the Irish mother tongue and the people of the lower deck from holding meetings. To allay those suspicions, and on the day previous to the planned actioning of the mutiny, the ship's captain, James Brine, had been presented with a declaration of loyalty signed by all Irish seamen and marines of the ship, numbering 110 in total, but with some later claiming that their signatures (or marks) had been forged. It was a document that vigorously disclaimed any thoughts or intention to mutiny, with reference made to the planned mutiny on *Caesar*, as revealed in the court martial held two weeks previous and of which the outcome was common knowledge throughout the Channel fleet:

> *We whose names are hereto annexed, natives of Ireland, with grief and anxiety have heard of a horrid plot or conspiracy having existed in this ship and attributed entirely to us and which the late unhappy disturbances in Ireland and the recent horrid transactions on board the* Caesar *give too great a colour to, and these rumours having been industriously circulated by some designing men for the evident purpose of creating a division and party spirit between the English and the Irish. We do ourselves solemnly swear before Almighty God, whose awful name we would not take in vein [sic], that we do not know of any plot or conspiracy or mutinous assembly in the ship, now or at any other time and that we will to the last moment of our lives, defend our King and glorious constitution against all enemies, foreign and domestic, and that we will to the utmost of our power, bring to condign punishment any person or persons who shall dare stir up any sedition or mutiny...*

Intended for the single purpose of putting the officers off their guard, it seems to have successfully served this purpose. On the following morning Brine, having assembled the entire crew on the main deck, read out to them this declaration of loyalty, with an officer later recalling that a sense of relief then infused the entire ship.

It was on the evening of the day in which Brine had read out the Irish declaration of loyalty that the mutiny was to have been actioned, with McKinnon having been turned out of his hammock for the purpose of joining the other mutineers before they proceeded to the upper deck. Making an excuse that he first wished to satisfy a call of nature, he went instead to his own commanding officer, marine lieutenant Henry Priddle, with the information then passed to the ship's marine captain, Henry Lewis. Because of McKinnon's life being now in peril from likely retribution, he was sent to the wardroom with an armed guard outside standing sentry. In the meantime, a guard was also placed over the arms chest on the poop deck and a marine detachment sent into the lower deck where a number of the conspirators, including Regan, were apprehended and placed in irons. Thus, the last of the major units of the Channel fleet had seen the attempts of Irish and mainland British republicans to take ships into French ports finally quashed, with the planned mutiny on *Captain* brought to the attention of the quarterdeck in June, on *Caesar* at the end of July, and on *Defiance* and *Neptune* towards the end of August.

Illustration 1: Richard Parker, the 'President' of the Nore ships in mutiny, hanged from the yardarm of *Neptune* during the summer of 1797.

Illustration 2: Among those Tone met while in Paris was Ferdinand Dubois de Fosseux, minister of war, who gave his support to the French expedition. De Fosseux was also a prominent citizen of Arras, possessing this stately residence.

Illustration 3: Portsmouth Harbour, the main base of the Channel fleet and where it took refuge during winter. Here was witnessed in 1798 several executions of those found guilty of conspiring to take ships to the enemy, including those identified as leaders of the planned mutinies on *Defiance* and *Haughty*.

Illustration 4: A depiction of those preparing in 1798 to take up arms to free Ireland from English rule. Given that it is drawn by popular early nineteenth century English cartoonist George Cruickshank for a book opposed to the cause of Ireland, it is none too favourable to those who joined the uprising.

Illustration 5: A view across Goulet de Brest with Cornouaille Battery in the foreground. The Cornouaille Battery was one of many strongpoints guarding the entrance to Brest Harbour and could have given protection to British naval warships taken by a crew favourable to the French republic.

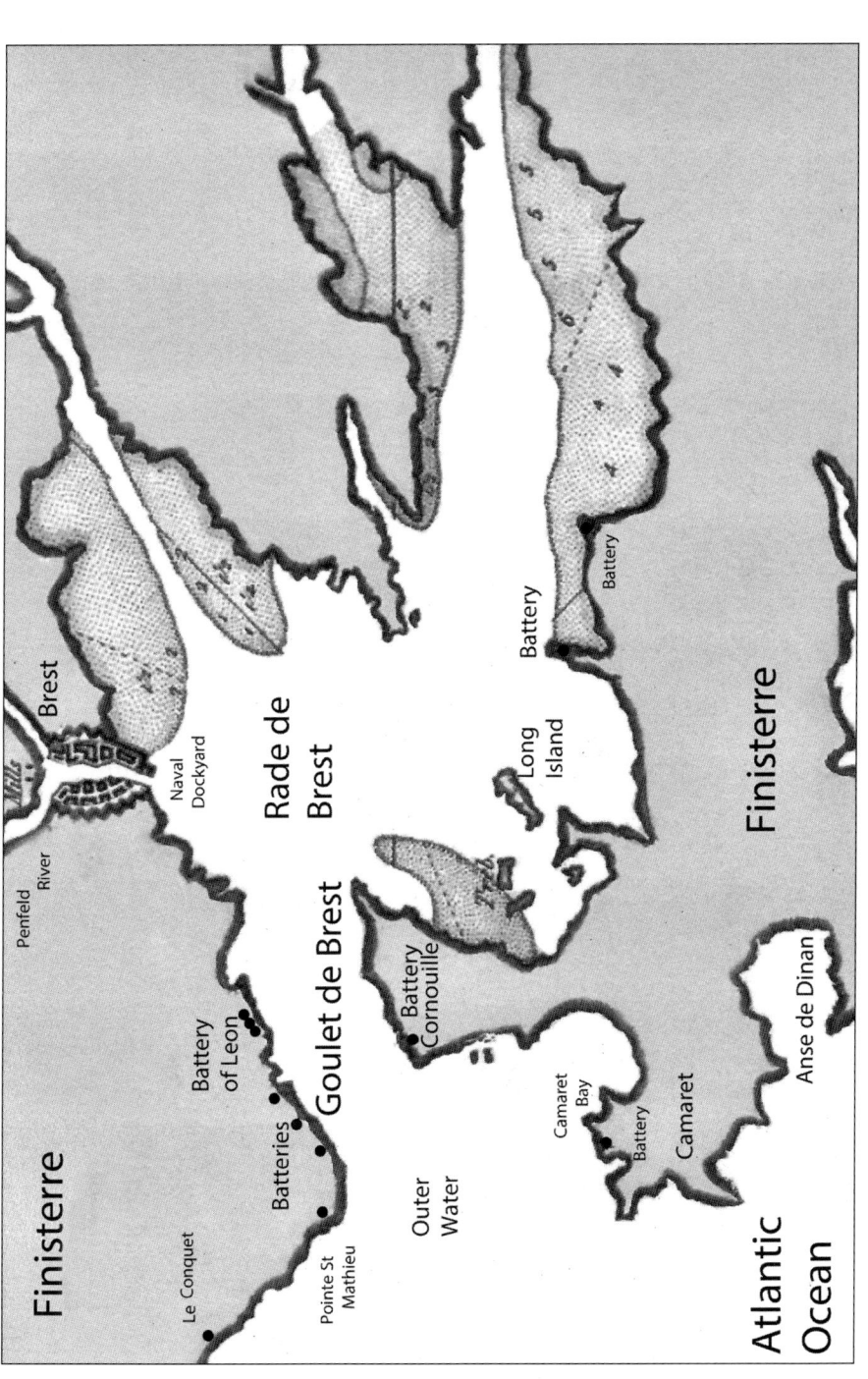

Illustration 6: The Rade de Brest showing the vastness of its protected waters, the position of the naval base and its many outlying fortifications.

Illustration 7: A modern-day view of Brest, the French naval base from which most expeditions set out for an invasion of Ireland.

Illustration 8: Ireland showing Bantry Bay and other important locations connected to the events of 1798.

Right: **Illustration 9**: Admiral Adam Duncan who commanded the North Sea Fleet and who witnessed several of his ships in mutiny during the French Revolutionary War.

Below: **Illustration 10**: Admiralty House, London. Here the Board of Admiralty, the controlling body of the British Navy, met and determined on such matters as strategy to be taken in line with government directives. The board also sanctioned decisions taken by courts martial, including determining the fate of those charged with mutiny and the planning of taking ships into enemy ports.

PART 6

All the Officers Must be Put to Death

The plot orchestrated by the Society of United Irishmen was not restricted to ships of the Royal Navy, although it was on those ships that, if successful, the government of Great Britain stood in greatest danger. In May 1798 a United Irish plot was discovered on an East Indiaman in Simons Bay and several plots were uncovered on board transport ships bound for the penal colony of New South Wales. These last were especially vulnerable to mutiny as they often carried convicted Irish rebels. The transport ship *Lady Shore* was successfully taken in 1797 and brought into the Spanish port of Montevideo in modern-day Uruguay.

Chapter 13

Cadiz! Our Country

John Jervis, 1st Earl of St Vincent, the commander-in-chief of British naval forces in and around the Mediterranean, was also engaged in blockade duties, his ships standing off Toulon and Cadiz. In both ports, enemy fleets were assembling. Toulon, the primary French naval base on the shores of the Mediterranean, had been a threat to English naval power since the opening of the war, but an alliance between France and Spain agreed in August 1796 had seen Cadiz, a naval port on Spain's Atlantic coastline, becoming an equal threat. Much depended on John Jervis, or 'Old Jarvie' as he was known. But since victory at the Battle of Cape St Vincent in February 1797, the 1st Earl of St Vincent ensured that the ships he commanded were keeping bottled into Toulon and Cadiz the maritime forces of France and Spain that were ready to sail, something they managed to do, but not until the following year when they briefly united (see page 122).

For this purpose, St Vincent kept the Mediterranean fleet on a permanent footing ready for battle, maintaining a very tight hold over the men he commanded, aware that the slightest hint of rebellion among the people of the lower deck, especially British mainland radicals or committed United Irishmen, could have dire consequences on his ability to maintain the blockade. Central to his thinking was that of ensuring that his officers knew their men and were vigilant in their own duties. While Bridport granted a good deal of latitude to the officers of the Channel fleet, this was not so in the fleet under St Vincent's command. Instead, Old Jarvie fostered a strictness of discipline through fear of punishment, but tempered by praise if a man was viewed as deserving of commendation. Any officer failing to meet the standards set by St Vincent was certain to receive a severe reprimand, while the slightest sign of indiscipline among the seamen serving on any ship placed under his command would always result in some form of brutal retribution.

St Vincent would often use memorandums sent to all ships' captains highlighting or naming an officer who had either performed an exemplary task or failed in some way. This was one way he kept his officers at the top of their game. Sent out in July 1797 was one such memorandum that castigated a junior officer described as showing 'vain conceit and supercilious conduct' in breaching an order that St Vincent had sent out prohibiting communication with any ship newly joining the fleet. Instead, any commander of such a ship was first to report to the commander-in-chief, with the memorandum adding that he required strict obedience to this instruction:

> *It is the Admiral's order, that when a ship-of-war is coming to join, or going to leave the fleet, no boat is sent to her without permission from the Ville de Paris [St Vincent's flagship]; and when the signal has been made for a ship going into port, all letters, &c, are to be brought, without loss of time, to the Ville de Paris, from whence they will be carefully forwarded.*

At any hint of a seaman planning a mutiny or acting in a manner that might be construed as rebellious, a court martial was immediately called with punishment, if a verdict of guilty was the outcome, always inflicted within a few hours of the court ending its session. Such speed of deliberation was not so in home waters, where everything was undertaken after lengthy consideration, due preparation and time given for a possible reprieve by the king. For St Vincent, an immediate trial followed by punishment without delay was the method he hoped to ensure that every man serving in the fleet became fully aware of the inseparability of the crime from its penalty. In home waters, those days between a sentence of execution being given and carried out were also customarily used by the condemned man to fully prepare himself for death, with the opportunity given of meeting with a clergyman over several days who would pray alongside him and take confession. That St Vincent overruled such practice unsettled the seamen of his fleet, but the commander-in-chief's intransigence and known harshness in enforcing his orders kept any man from taking action designed to reverse the timing of a hanging once ordered. It was because of his known harshness and decisiveness in such matters that Spencer, while First Lord of the Admiralty, would send ships with known troublesome crews to the fleet commanded by St Vincent.

One such ship sent by Spencer was the 90-gun second rate *London*, a ship that had played a central role in the mutiny at Spithead. Her crew, as on *Saturn* and *Marlborough*, were dissatisfied with the final determination at Spithead. On *Saturn*, the crew had sidelined their officers, with much the same happening on *London*, and for this reason she was ordered to join St Vincent so that he might ensure a return to a more orderly state of affairs. According to notes left by Benjamin Tucker, the purser on board *London* during the voyage to Lisbon where the ship was to revictual, the crew were 'in a state close bordering upon open insubordination,' with a possible plot developed by some of the crew to release a seaman who had been placed in irons and the ship then taken into a Spanish or French port. This was also the view expressed during the trial of one suspected mutineer, Richard Cole, by *London*'s captain John Purvis. While the court martial as convened off Lisbon considered there to be insufficient evidence to find him guilty of 'endeavouring to incite the ship's crew to mutiny', Captain Purvis felt there was not only a plot in hand to release the prisoner but that matters were to be taken a lot further with the ship to be taken to an enemy port.

While discontent among the crew of *London* was considerable, and ripe for the supporting of a full-scale mutiny, even the most discontented on the ship became increasingly cautious as they approached Lisbon and St Vincent's Mediterranean fleet, aware of the fearsome reputation of the commander-in-chief into whose authority they were now to pass. According to Tucker:

> *As she* [London] *approached Lisbon, the men began to bethink themselves, to whom they were going, and to show some little respect to their officers; and one or two of the Petty-officers would now and then condescend to touch their hats as the First Lieutenant passed along the decks.*

Nevertheless, according to Tucker, when *London*'s ship's barge was moored alongside St Vincent's flagship *Ville de Paris*, one of the barge crew called out to a seaman looking out of a lower deck port, 'I say, there, what have you fellows been doing out here, while we have been fighting for your beef and pork?' This a reference to the mutiny at Spithead with a suggestion that the seamen of the Mediterranean had simply offered no support and were still offering no support for those who had bravely stood out for better conditions that would benefit all men of the lower deck, irrespective of where they were serving.

In response the other very quietly said, 'If you'll take my advice, you just say nothing at all about all that here; for by God if Old Jarvie hears ye he'll have you dingle dangle at the yardarm at eight o'clock tomorrow morning.'

Despite that fearsome reputation, both English and Irish revolutionaries were propagating rebellious ideas among those who they saw as sympathetic to the cause of Ireland or supportive of French revolutionary ideals. Off Cadiz, just a few days before *London*'s arrival, a conspiracy on board *St George* had been uncovered. If carried through, this would have taken three major warships into the naval base at Cadiz to be handed over to the Spanish. It can also be assumed that upon her arrival, and with the mutiny about to be sprung, some of the discontented on *London* would have been tempted to rebel and also take that ship into Cadiz.

The planned mutiny on board *St George* had been brought to the attention of her officers on Sunday 2 July. A detachment of the marine guard were ordered on to the lower deck where they apprehended three of the organisers. To prevent any attempt by the lower deck to secure their release, all three were quickly removed from the ship, two placed in the hold of *Ville de Paris* and one sent to *Prince George*.

Initially St Vincent was allowed to think that those plotting the mutiny had restricted their activities to *St George* and no other ship. Also, the officers were given to believe that the mutiny was much more limited in its aim of preventing two seamen belonging to *St George* from being executed for sodomy, a crime, as with so many others, covered by the Articles of War, in this case Article XXIX:

> *If any person in the fleet shall commit the unnatural and detestable sin of buggery and sodomy with man or beast, he shall be punished with death by the sentence of a court martial.*

It was further mandated by St Vincent that seamen of the ship upon which the condemned men served were to act as executioners, a brutal act of retribution based on his expressed belief that it would underline to the men that they too would face execution if they breached any of the Articles of War, of which they were all too familiar. Hanging of their own, however, was something crews especially detested, and in one way heightened the possibility of mutiny, but which St Vincent effectively countered by his explicit threats of more hangings if the execution of this man did not go according to his wishes. That crews of ships in home waters were never called upon by the Admiralty to hang their own, a fact well known to the lower deck, intensified below-deck murmurings against St Vincent.

As was also St Vincent's custom, the court martial to try the *St George* mutineers had been immediately assembled, with no more than a week elapsing between the discovery of the plot and the eventual execution of the three rebel leaders. In fact, the execution that took place on Sunday 9 July had been planned for the previous day. But with the verdict not pronounced until sunset, the hanging of the condemned was put over until early the following morning with St Vincent sending a memorandum to be read by each captain to their respective crews:

> *The sentence is to be carried into execution by the crew of the* St George *alone, and no part of the boats' crews of other ships, as is*

> *usual on similar occasions, is to assist in this most painful sentence, in order to mark the high sense the Commander-in-chief entertains of the loyalty, fidelity and subordination of the rest of the fleet, which he will not fail to make known to the Lords Commissioners of the Admiralty, and request them to lay it before The King.*

The full nature of the plot that threatened the fleet off Cadiz only became clear in the hours after the court martial had reached its verdict. It was then and only then that one of the condemned chose to confess, telling all to the chaplain in attendance. In doing so, he admitted the plot to have been in contemplation for six months, indicating that those on *St George* were planning to work in concert with rebels on *Britannia, Captain, Diadem* and *Egmont*. Contact had been made by the conspirators on board *St George* with those of a similar mind on these four ships, communication between crews carried out when the vessels were revictualling off Lisbon or sent to Gibraltar for the same purpose. On such occasions, the conspirators met either face-to-face or through an agent on shore. In learning of these additional details, and never revealed during the trial of the three conspirators, St Vincent considered that on *Britannia*, 'her myrmidons would have gone the whole length' but viewed *Egmont* to be so 'highly disciplined and commanded that it would not have succeeded there.'

That the three mutineers were hanged on a Sunday caused further controversy, seen by some as a move that would profane the Sabbath. Among those who criticised him was Vice-Admiral Robert Calder, St Vincent's captain of the fleet. He requested that the executions be delayed to another day, regarding Sunday as a day given over to the Almighty. However, in making his decision, St Vincent did receive the support of Horatio Nelson, then a vice-admiral within the Mediterranean fleet and the son of a clergyman, with Nelson writing directly to Calder:

> *I am sorry that you should have to differ, but had it been Christmas Day instead of Sunday I would have executed them. We know not what might have been hatched by a Sunday's grog; now your discipline is safe. I talked to our people, and, I hope, with good effect; indeed, they seem a very quiet set.*

St Vincent did not fail to recognise that he had issued an order that could well be criticised, defending himself in a letter to the Admiralty hoping he would not be censured by the bench of bishops. In that letter he explained that there was a need to carry out the executions with great urgency:

...the criminals asked five days to prepare, in which they would have hatched five hundred treasons; besides that we are provoking the Spanish fleet to come out by every means in our power; and seven-and-twenty gun and mortar boats did actually advance, dastardly enough it must be confessed, and cannonaded the advanced squadron, now composed of ten sail of-the-line, on seeing twenty barges and pinnaces go to attend the execution of the sentence.

Clearly alarmed by this potential mutiny, St Vincent implemented a further scheme to ensure that the ships under his command were made more secure, ordering that the marines, the men who supported the officers in keeping discipline in the fleet, should be separated from the seamen of the lower deck. This was to ensure that they were not drawn into any planned mutiny and could be trusted to support their officers. It was a move that was also prompted by news from Ireland that a greater part of the militia had deserted to the rebels and that the French were boasting in their gazettes that they had emissaries in all the king's ships.

On 18 July 1797, St Vincent assembled on the *Ville de Paris* the marine captains of each ship under his command to inform them of how the policy of separating crews from the marine guard was to be put into practice, directing that on ships of three decks they would now be berthed in the after part of the middle deck. On ships of two decks, the marine guard would be quartered close to the bulkhead of the gunroom, close by the officer's cabins where they could occupy the two after-berths on each side and from where he believed they would be less vulnerable to attack. For their part, United Irishmen serving in the Mediterranean realised these orders were specifically directed against them and their hopes of taking ships into enemy ports. In an attempt to subvert this order, Irish activists set about persuading marines with whom they had contact that no separation should be made between seamen and marine. It seems also that some captains on receiving the new order showed a reluctance to introduce the new arrangement, leading St Vincent to order Lieutenant-Colonel Flight, his senior marine officer, to superintend the business and to correct any errors he might discover.

The arrival off Cadiz towards the end of May 1798 of Rear Admiral Sir Roger Curtis with the eight ships from the Channel fleet saw St Vincent again taking action against dissident crews who were defying their officers. Among the new arriving ships was *Marlborough*, the last to return to sea following the ending of the fleet mutiny at Spithead. It will be remembered that she was the ship whose commander had committed suicide at the Admiralty Office in London, proclaiming: 'There are traitors on board *Marlborough*...the country is ruined.' Under her new captain, Joseph Ellison, the warning given by her former commander came true, for while serving as part of that detached fleet under Curtis, and first serving in Irish waters to prevent the arrival of the French, a mutiny inspired by those on board supporting the cause of the United Irish had broken out, but was suppressed by the officers and marine guards. Little is known of this particular attempt at taking the ship, with Tucker referring to it as 'a very violent mutiny' that broke out in Bantry Bay. Given the significance of this particular area of water, and its use by the French as a point of invasion, the loss of a ship here to an Irish rebel-inspired mutiny could well have had significant consequences.

During her passage to Cadiz, a further mutinous act by the crew of *Marlborough* was to be witnessed when a substantial portion of her crew refused to witness the flogging of one of their number, a man who had stood up for the rights of all of the men of the ship. Peter Anderson, following the laying on the man's bare back of the first lash, loudly and defiantly accused the crew who had been called to witness this act of punishment of being 'a parcel of buggers to see a man flogged for the whole ship's company'. Following a second laying on of a lash, he then beseeched them to 'come away', with possibly thirty or more doing so.

The fact that *Marlborough* was among the new ships to be received, and aware that her crew had a troublesome history but unaware of her most recent mutiny, St Vincent ordered *Marlborough* to take her berth in the centre of the fleet but at a small distance from any other ship. This was so *Marlborough*'s crew could see that they were being threatened with the full fire power of the fleet should they continue to act in a refractory manner.

On Ellison reporting that this act of mutiny had broken out during *Marlborough's* passage to Cadiz, St Vincent immediately ordered that Anderson face trial by court martial. The outcome, which was of course in little doubt, especially given the number of officers who heard Anderson address the crew on that occasion, was him being condemned to death with the sentence to be carried out on *Marlborough* by the crew of that ship. With the hanging at the yardarm to take place on the morning after sentence had been pronounced, St Vincent confirmed that those hauling on the rope would be the 'crew of the *Marlborough* alone' and no 'crews from the other ships' to assist in any way. Somewhat alarmed, Ellison approached St Vincent on the matter, expressing his conviction that *Marlborough*'s crew would never permit the man to be hanged on board that ship.

'What do you mean to tell me, Captain Ellison, that you cannot command His Majesty's ship the *Marlborough*?' St Vincent queried before continuing. 'If that is the case, sir, I will immediately send on board an officer who can.'

'May I ask that the boats' crews from the rest of the fleet might, as always, as is customary elsewhere in the service, haul the man up?' asked Ellison, expecting that *Marlborough*'s crew would refuse to hang one of their own.

Even to such a compromise St Vincent would not give way. For him it had become an embedded principle, a means of frightening crews out of the very thought of mutiny or even of expressing discontent. If he gave way on this, he reflected, the people of the lower deck would assuredly detect a weakness that they would quickly exploit. He was having none of it.

'Captain Ellison, You are an old officer, Sir,' St Vincent continued after a short pause. 'You have served long, suffered severely in the service, and you have lost an arm in action. I should be very sorry that any advantage should be now taken of your advanced years.'

Ellison now guessed what was coming. He knew that the admiral was not about to give way.

'That man shall be hanged. At eight o'clock tomorrow morning and by his own ship's company,' St Vincent sternly pronounced. 'Not a hand from any other ship in the fleet shall touch the rope,' were his final words.

Every action necessary to ensure that nothing could go wrong was now taken, with St Vincent intent on cowering *Marlborough's* crew into total and absolute conformity. In particular, Ellison was instructed that all cannons on board his ship were to be housed and secured. Clearly, St Vincent feared that they might be used by the 'Marlboroughs' to open fire on ships loyal to the fleet and so encourage their crews to rebel.

At seven o'clock the following morning, launches armed with carronades and twelve rounds of ammunition rendezvoused close by the flagship before making passage to *Marlborough* where they would lay alongside. Should any sign of resistance occur, such as the 'Marlboroughs' opening the ship's gun ports as a sign that they might open fire, St Vincent ordered that each of the barges should immediately fire their own guns at the ship, continuing until all signs of resistance ceased. Should it become absolutely necessary, St Vincent was even prepared to see *Marlborough* completely destroyed.

Shortly before eight o'clock Anderson, who had been brought over to *Marlborough* from the flagship where the court martial had been held, was speedily placed on the cathead and haltered. On the firing of a signal gun mounted on *Ville de Paris*, the man was lifted into the air, but then suddenly dropped back. Alarm generated around the entire fleet. With every seaman forced to watch from the decks of their own ships, most believed that the execution party had indeed refused to obey – prepared to sacrifice their own lives rather than hang a fellow shipmate.

The sensation of alarm was intense.

The gun crews on the barges now within touching distance of *Marlborough* awaited the signal to fire. On those barges were men trusted and loyal, seamen gunners who St Vincent knew would carry out his instructions to the last. But what of the men in the ships drawn up to witness the hanging? Might they be less loyal to St Vincent and his harsh regime? How might they react? With sighs of relief that ran from ship to ship, audible among both officers and men, it soon became clear, and not a moment too soon. Anderson at the yardarm during the process of hanging had been dropped by accident. Unintentionally, the men on the ropes had let them slip. Knowing that if they didn't act quickly all hell would break loose, they scrambled hurriedly and with a run once again hauled the condemned man up to the yardarm where, in but a few short moments, he ceased to show any signs of life.

During the summer of 1798, in common with the Channel fleet, a mutiny in the Mediterranean fleet to support Ireland and that of republicanism was also in the advanced stage of planning but detected by the officers, leading to several of its leaders subsequently court-martialled and hanged. Among them were three Irishmen, Michael Connell and Thomas Guthrie, both rated able, and Daniel Sweeny, gunsmith, along with one of the ship's marine guards, Thomas Boyd. Considered by Vincent to be the chief organiser, however, was Thomas Bott (alias Batt), a landsman on *Princess Royal*. According to Tucker, who had now been transferred to *Ville de Paris* as St Vincent's secretary, Bott was the 'Corresponding Society's delegate on the Cadiz station'. Unfortunately for Connell, Sweeny, Boyd and Bott, and others working alongside them, they had placed faith in a Roman Catholic priest who was acting as a go-between, conveying messages between the conspirators on other ships of the fleet when they came into Lisbon's Tagus River to revictual. The conspirators believed that the priest was not only supportive of their plans but could provide advice as to when the plot should be sprung. According to Tucker's notes, the priest, who was never named, was Portuguese 'who, having been the Confessor of the lower order of the natives [in Lisbon city], had become so to most of the Roman Catholics in the fleet.' In turn, though, Isaac Coffin, the admiral superintendent of the temporary naval base that had been established on the Tagus, had induced the priest, through payment of twenty-one shillings a week, to pass on any information he gleaned from the Irish seamen while they were in the confessional box. From two of them serving on *Ville de Paris* the priest was given a letter addressed to a seaman on *Princess Royal* and which was intended for Bott. Instead, the priest passed the letter to his paymaster, with the letter indicating that the intention was to assassinate St Vincent once the rebellion had broken out on several ships. The priest also provided Coffin with a copy of the response he had given and in which he recommended that the venture be delayed. Regarding the killing of Old Jarvie, he also suggested that this should be held off but for no other reason than 'that the old gentleman was [not] yet quite prepared for so sudden an exit.'

With the names of several of the conspirators known, twenty-three or more were apprehended by the marine guard, and five of them, among them Thomas Bott, brought to trial. Following verdicts of guilty, each was hanged within hours of the court having reached its decision. A further seaman mustered to *Princess Royal*, Richard Jones, rated ordinary, was also to be hanged for his involvement in a further planned mutiny – a mutiny with the object of releasing Thomas Guthrie, he being the first of the main plotters to be placed in irons.

That more were not court-martialled resulted from insufficient evidence to ensure a successful conviction. St Vincent believed that nothing appeared more injurious to the discipline of the fleet than a failure of proof on an accusation against a man for a flagrant offence such as mutiny. Under questioning by the prosecuting officer in court it was revealed that Bott had claimed Cadiz as their future country before he went on to confess that it was the intention to hang St Vincent with command of the fleet transferred to Davidson, another delegate. Once all the officers had been turned out of their ships, except those whose duties concerned the safety of the ship and whose skills they could not replace, the fleet would sail first into the Mediterranean. Here they would meet up with the squadron under Nelson, believing that the ships under Nelson's command would join them and sail for Ireland to support the United Irish cause. Among those whose lives would be preserved would be Mr Jackson, the master of the *Ville de Paris*, as his navigational skills were required to get the rebel-held fleet to Ireland and where it was to anchor in the waters around Clear Island off the south-west coast of County Cork. However, Jackson was not a popular officer, considered too resolute in his behaviour towards the men, and it was decided he would be killed upon safely arriving off Clear Island.

Of the other eighteen who had been apprehended, but against whom it was considered there was insufficient evidence to ensure conviction, they were to be punished in a very different way, but one that did not require a trial. All of them were permanently removed from the ships upon which they had served and were then dispersed to nine ships viewed as being unaffected by thoughts of mutiny. Once mustered to their new ships, they were to be kept constantly on the poop deck at the stern where they were to eat and drink, making no form of communication with any crew member of the ships to which they had been transferred. They were granted a small act of mercy: they were not to be held in irons and allowed to move around within the confines of the poop deck. *Princess Royal*, viewed as being in a general poor state of discipline, had this problem also addressed. Her captain, John Draper, was authorised to draft the most profligate characters on his ship and to discharge them into *Romulus*, in lieu of an equal number of men given over in return.

Of this period of upheaval within the Mediterranean fleet, Jedidiah Tucker, using the notes compiled by his father Benjamin, summed up the dangers that the Irish mutinies presented for Great Britain in the war it was fighting against revolutionary France. From these notes he suggested that had not the nature of what was intended been discovered, a 'national calamity' would have ensued. The blockade of Cadiz would have ceased and the Spanish fleet would have sailed unopposed, leading to a conjunction of the fleets of France and Spain. This could easily have given the French temporary command of the Channel. Had such a combination of hostile naval forces been accomplished, with mutiny rife in the British fleet at home and abroad, England as a result would be dispirited and lose confidence. With Ireland 'only panted for revenge', who, Tucker asked, would 'venture to say the consequence?'

British warships serving in both the North Sea and the Irish Sea also witnessed the emergence of revolutionary cadres formed of United Irishmen and mainland British radicals sympathetic to the ideals of republicanism. On 25 September 1798, an attempted plot on the 50-gun fourth rate *Diomede* was uncovered. The officers were to be killed and the ship taken into an enemy port. Part of Admiral Duncan's North Sea squadron, *Diomede* was employed alongside a much enlarged fleet brought to the Texel to support a military invasion of the Batavian Republic. A newly commissioned ship, she had only been at sea for a few months, launched from the naval dockyard at Deptford in January of that same year. Consequently her captain, Charles Elphinstone, had been saddled with a hastily cobbled together crew sent to him while the ship lay moored in the River Medway off Sheerness. Large numbers came from the receiving ship *Sandwich*, the vessel that had been at the epicentre of the previous year's Nore mutiny. The nature of men now mustered to *Diomede* would have included a great many who were reluctant to serve in the navy, whether listed as volunteers or otherwise. Among those few who might have been willing to join the ship could well have been United Irishmen already intent on taking the British warship to which they were assigned into a French port. *Diomede*'s muster book indicates that out of her lower deck crew of close on 230, forty-seven (twenty per cent) were Irish by birth.

The first duty given to *Diomede* was supporting the blockade of Texel. Sailing out of the Medway at the end of June, it had become even more essential that a close watch be maintained on the roadstead here, for in August a joint Anglo-Russian invasion force would be landing on the north coast of Holland. The plan behind this invasion was the destruction of the Batavian Republic through reinstatement of the former stadtholder William V, Prince of Orange. If the Dutch fleet sheltering off Texel Island should break out, then the transport ships soon to be carrying 30,000 troops would be in great peril. Nevertheless, in the turn-and-turnabout routine adopted by Admiral Duncan in common with the same practice off Brest, Cadiz and Toulon, *Diomede* was among several ships moored off Yarmouth to revictual and for her sick to be taken ashore to a newly established naval hospital. Here, either in the town of Yarmouth or through inter-crew meetings on board the ships while moored, it was not unlikely that a conspiratorial network emerged, working alongside agents on shore. Whether a wider plan existed to include more ships in the planned mutiny other than *Diomede* can be no more than surmise, but undoubtedly a possibility.

Despite *Diomede* mustering forty-seven Irish seamen on her lower deck, the two organisers of the plot uncovered by her captain were both English by birth, George Tomms and John Wright. Sympathetic as they were to the rebellion in Ireland, a more direct connection with the Society of United Irishmen is not one that can be established. Supportable evidence does confirm their association with one particular political group, the Nottingham Corresponding Society, one of the most radical of the corresponding societies. While a decline in its membership had followed upon the passing of the Two Acts and other government repressive measures, the society was still a powerful force in Nottingham, a fact clearly demonstrated at the time of the 1802 general election when a crowd, described by one commentator as 'a republican revolutionary mob', marched to a band playing *Ah! Ça Ira*.

Unsurprisingly, neither Tomms nor Wright at their trial provided details of their connections with the society in Nottingham, although it was evidenced that Tomms promised substantial financial rewards to any who supported the planned mutiny, with this money coming from the Nottingham Corresponding Society. It was this same society that could have provided him with a link to the United Irish, for delegates from Ireland were frequently welcomed by English and Scottish radical societies, with informal alliances also established. Tomms' connection with the corresponding society in

Nottingham is further supported by him receiving letters from Nottingham sent to him by others of a radical inclination, including his brother. In one letter referring to Ireland, his brother was reported to have written of Lord Cornwallis, the lord lieutenant of Ireland and commander-in-chief of the military forces fighting the rebels, that he hoped 'he [Cornwallis] would meet with a fatal blow.' As to his own politics, it is clear that Tomms was highly supportive of France, openly declaring on one occasion, 'I will not be long out of France, for I am of them.'

For Tomms' fellow conspirator John Wright, other possibilities emerge, for not only does he appear to have had connections with the Nottingham Corresponding Society, but also with a corresponding society in Birmingham. Here too the society had a large membership, with a radical fringe that in 1795 had circulated a handbill calling the people to arms. It could be that Wright was a go-between, linking those of a more revolutionary persuasion in Birmingham with those of a like mind in Nottingham. As for Wright, by then serving in the Royal Marines as a guard on *Diomede*, this would outwardly appear a strange career move. By trade, Wright was a successful baker and maltster, with useful connections in Birmingham. One with whom he gained advantageous employment was John Ryland, a leading Birmingham wine merchant who had demonstrated sympathy with the revolution in France, attending a Bastille Day banquet in 1791. Again, no more than surmise, but Wright abandoning his trade for service in the Royal Marines may have been prompted by a desire to join the United Irish in taking a British ship into a French port.

The fact that the main organisers of the plot on *Diomede* to take her into an enemy port were both English by birth underlines a similar direction now being taken by both the United Irish and more revolutionary elements on the British mainland. Tomms even adopted the idea of taking the ship into an Irish port should one be fully secured by the rebels. However, the procedure to be adopted was different to that planned by revolutionary activists on other ships. Instead, the rebels would make their move while *Diomede* was at action stations, her guns run-out for the purpose of engaging one or more enemy warships At such time, Tomms, Wright and their fellow conspirators of the marine guard, as explained by several witnesses when the two were being court-martialled, 'would clear the quarterdeck of the quality.' Should no such opportunity arise, then it was intended that when *Diomede* was returning to port, within sight of land a trail of gunpowder should be laid for the purpose of blowing up the ship. It was then intended that the conspirators, just prior to the explosion, would commandeer one of the ship's boats and escape to the shore.

That Tomms and Wright were privates in the marine guard provides an explanation as to why they would choose clearing the quarterdeck of 'the quality', for in battle they were expected to actively handle their muskets, but aimed at the enemy rather than at their own officers. Such an act would have a clear element of surprise and confusion, something upon which Tomms was counting. At that point, one assumes, seamen of the lower deck also recruited into the plot would have hauled the ship out of battle, with the rebel marine guard threatening to shoot any man who continued to resist. If *Diomede* had been part of the Mediterranean fleet under the command of St Vincent, this alliance between seamen and marines would have been all but impossible to develop. In the Mediterranean, St Vincent had instructed his captains to separate marines from the seamen, believing that the mixing of the enforcers of discipline with those who might need to be disciplined would lead to a bonding of the two and the formation an alliance against the officers. The action taken by Tomms and Wright would seem to have proved him correct, for on *Diomede* there was no separation of marines from the seamen of the lower deck. If it had been otherwise, Tomms and Wright would not have been able to recruit into their plot a number of supporters from the lower deck, and to whom they administered oaths of loyalty.

Tomms and Wright administered oaths to an undisclosed number of seamen and marines, therefore committing them to the taking of the ship if not into a secured Irish port then into a French or Dutch port. In administering or attempting to administer that oath, Tomms and Wright had no certainty that any individual they approached would not inform the officers. This, of course, was the same for all the core leaders who attempted to establish revolutionary cadres on any ship upon which they served. For the conspiracy on *Diomede*, as on the other ships, this was to be the downfall of the organisers, it being one of the men who had actually taken the oath who was to inform Elphinstone, through approaching one of his officers, that a mutiny was in the planning. The informant named sixteen conspirators, all secured by the officers and loyal marines before being transferred to *Proserpine*, a small ship but with a crew presumed to be fully loyal. It was, of course, Elphinstone's fear that if the conspirators had been kept in *Diomede's* hold, an attempt might have been made by the rest of the crew to release them, with the even greater likelihood that the officers would be killed and the ship taken into an enemy port. The captain of *Proserpine*, James Wallis, must have had his own concerns, for his was a sixth rate frigate with a crew, when carrying a full complement, of only 200. For this reason Wallis attempted to ensure his men would remain unsympathetic to the mutineers now placed in the hold of that ship. According to one of the officers, in a letter sent back to England and published in the *Kentish Weekly Post* in October 1798:

> *As soon as they came on board, our worthy commander, Capt. Wallis drew them [the rebels brought over from* Diomede*] up on the quarter deck and turned the ship's company aft, pointed out to them, in an impressive address, the monstrous and ungrateful proceedings of the culprits before them, and his intention of keeping the culprits confined until the arrival of the* Proserpine *in England, and he hoped that they would look upon them in that detestable light they merited.*

On hearing this, the officer further recorded:

> *The ship's company gave three cheers, and during the time the prisoners were on board, not one of the crew would hold any converse, but conducted themselves in the most loyal and dutiful manner; in fact nothing could surpass their good conduct.*

Of the sixteen who had been placed in irons on *Proserpine*, only Tomms and Wright were to face a trial by court martial, due to evidence against the others considered insufficient to secure an absolute verdict of guilt.

On 30 May 1799, another attempt was made to carry into a French port several ships of the Channel fleet that were off the coast of Ireland. It was a worrying moment for the British government. Bridport's blockading fleet had failed to prevent twenty-five ships of the line under Vice-Admiral Étienne Bruix putting out from Brest, destination unknown. Later it would become clear that Bruix was bound for Egypt to extract French forces trapped there since Buonaparte's invasion the previous year. But with this unknown, Bridport assumed the French were about to launch another invasion of Ireland, leading him to take the major part of the Channel fleet into the Irish Sea. For a few days he cruised off Cape Clear before anchoring with twenty-six sail of the line in Bantry Bay expecting that he would eventually meet with Bruix's forces. One ship taken by Bridport into the Irish Sea, *Impetueux*, a 74-gun third rate, was proving especially troublesome to her recently appointed captain, Edward Pellew, forcing him to maintain order through a frequent resort to the lash. On board, and prior to her arrival in the Irish Sea, a revolutionary cadre had been formed and delegates from the cadre making contact with like-minded seamen on other ships of the Channel fleet. Seemingly, they were working to a master plan similar to that adopted by the Irish mutineers of the previous year, with delegates from *Impetueux*, during a period of revictualling at Cawsand Bay during March, making contact with delegates from other ships.

On coming to anchor in Bantry Bay, and with no news of Admiral Bruix and the location of his ships, crews were very much left to their own devices with more seamen probably drawn into the plot. On 25 May, *Impetueux*, in company with *Mars*, *Ajax* and *Russell*, was sent to take on water at Bearhaven (or Castletown–Bearhaven) on the north-west side of the bay. Here, in a small enclosed area of water sheltered by Bearhaven on one side and Bere Island on the other, the finishing touches were put to the plot. First, the crew of *Impetueux* would rise in mutiny, outwardly proclaiming discontent with their captain's frequent use of the lash and other grievances they claimed to have gone unaddressed. Pellew, meanwhile, maintained his brutal disciplinary regime. Five men were punished on the second day off Bearhaven, three receiving a dozen lashes and the other two receiving a couple of dozen lashes, while on the fourth day four more men were also lashed. With these punishments continuing to vex the majority of the crew, this may have persuaded some of the undecided to back the rebels in the taking of the ship and sailing her into an enemy port. Possibly, committed republicans on the other three ships that had accompanied *Impetueux* to Bearhaven were fully aware of what was planned. But all that is definitely known is that once *Impetueux*'s crew had mutinied, it was believed by her rebels that crews from some of the other ships in Bantry Bay would also rise and join *Impetueux* in making passage into a French port.

It was on 30 May, following the signal to unmoor and rejoin the fleet at Bantry, that the mutineers made their move, the crew having been ordered to prepare the ship for her departure from Bearhaven. Soon, as recalled by Pellew following the giving of those orders to the officer of the watch, 'a great noise' was heard with Pellew returning from his cabin to the main deck to witness the people of the ship 'about two or three hundred…pressing aft' and crying out, 'One and all. One and all. A boat – a boat.'

Asking what all this was about he received an answer from Samuel Sidney, Thomas Harrop, William Jones and several others, men who Pellew considered to be foremost in their complaints of hard usage and flogging. A letter was produced, which he was told was addressed to Bridport. It was their intention that they take it directly to the admiral, requiring a boat for this purpose. Pellew offered that either he or an officer would carry the letter, but to this he received an absolute refusal.

'No – no – no!' was the response. 'A boat of our own!' The more he attempted to pacify them, the louder were their protests. 'We will have a boat; God damn it, we'll take one,' came the response from, among others, Sidney, Harrop and Jones.

'You will, will you?' said the enraged Pellew before rushing to his cabin to retrieve his sword and to be rejoined by several of the officers who had armed themselves and were now supported by the marine guard. With these, Pellew cleared the unarmed sailors off the quarterdeck, drove them below, followed and seized nine of the ringleaders. With the crew of *Impetueux* forced into compliance, all four ships that had been taking on water off Bearhaven rejoined the main part of the fleet that following morning. On 1 June, Bridport, who had now learned the course taken by the French fleet, sent Sir Alan Gardner with sixteen sail, of which the *Impetueux* was one, as a reinforcement for St Vincent in the Mediterranean. These orders were promptly attended to by the crew of all sixteen ships, including *Impetueux*, with no other organised attempt made by any of the crews to resist the authority of their officers, either while making passage to the Mediterranean or when under St Vincent's command.

It was, however, while under the temporary command of St Vincent that eight seamen belonging to *Impetueux* were court-martialled, among them Sidney, Harrop and Jones, all on the charge that they had on Thursday 30 May assembled in a mutinous and riotous manner. It was only during the court martial hearing that the full nature of the plot became clear. One of the three, a gunner's mate, who was subsequently condemned to be hanged, provided the information in the hope that he might be reprieved. This had sometimes happened to others condemned for mutiny, especially if they had, as did this man, a previously unblemished record of service. In so doing, he confessed to the fact that if the *Impetueux* mutiny had met with success it was to have been a signal for a general revolt of the entire fleet then at anchor in Bantry Bay. The gunner's mate also unmasked another leading rebel who, though claimed as being the chief instigator of the insubordination, had contrived to keep himself in the background and so beyond the reach of evidence. This discovery, coupled with the prisoner's previous good character, encouraged Pellew to intercede with St Vincent believing the gunner's mate to be a proper subject for mercy. Upon this point, as he was with so much else, St Vincent proved to be totally inflexible. 'I am glad of it,' he said when Sir Edward spoke favourably of the prisoner's former conduct. 'Those who have hitherto suffered had been so worthless before, that their fate was of little use as an example. I shall now convince the fleet that no character will save the man who is guilty of mutiny.'

Chapter 14

Il a mort pour la liberté

Early on the morning of Tuesday 1 August 1797, all appeared quiet on board the convict transport ship *Lady Shore* as she continued her passage through the South Atlantic. It was 4 a.m. and Robert Lambert, her first mate, later recollected her position as to be roughly 450 nautical miles north-east of Cape Frio, not far from Rio de Janeiro. It was to Rio that she was bound, a friendly port in this time of war, a war in which Spain had recently allied herself with France and so was also hostile towards Great Britain. Rio, in Brazil, by contrast was a Portuguese possession, with Portugal a long-time ally of the British. Once anchored off the city of Rio, *Lady Shore* would start to revictual, taking on fresh supplies of food and drinking water. So replenished, her voyage to New South Wales would continue, this the second and longest leg of her journey.

As Lambert held steadily to the ship's wheel, he gazed into the empty void of the night with thoughts on their arrival at Rio cascading through his head. Here he was soon hoping to savour the delights of this rumbustious city, a city made rich from a vibrant trade in diamonds and gold. As daylight fell upon the ship, the sun always appearing to rise so much faster in this tropical zone, those below, the convicts, many of the crew and a fifty-strong detachment of soldiers who were also bound for Botany Bay, were supposedly asleep in their various quarters.

Unusually, the ship was carrying just two male prisoners, James Semple and Launcelot Knowles. In addition, though, and making the voyage necessary, was that of her carrying an unusually high number of female convicts, no less than sixty-six. Because of the presence of so many women and the unruly nature of the soldiers who were supposed to be guarding them, rules that never should have been broken were being broken. Fraternisation between the guards, all recent recruits into the New South Wales Corps, and the women convicts, should not have been allowed. But fraternisation was taking place, a most dangerous transgression but against which the officer in charge, Ensign William Minchin, was choosing to do nothing. Among those taking advantage of his commanding officer's laxity was Private Jean Baptiste Deseal. Having found night comfort in the arms of one female convict, the resulting passion had left him so exhausted that he had fallen into the very deepest of slumbers. That morning he was not even to be awoken by an epiphany of sound that would soon be descending upon the ship, so much clatter that would even have awoken the fictional Rip van Winkle.

Some of Deseal's fellow soldiers and a few of the crew had chosen not to take any sleep that night, nor even engage in carnal acts that might have been on offer. They had other thoughts occupying their minds. Twenty-five in number, they were about to enact a plan that would see them taking control of the ship and diverting her to the Spanish port of Montevideo. Here, having declared themselves to be enemies of Great Britain, they expected to be received with open arms. A mixed group, they included several French and Germans and a seaman from San Dominica. Significantly, also included were five Irish republicans and one English radical, all belonging to the New South Wales Corps.

Despite this diversity of nationality, all of the conspirators had one thing in common, a belief in republicanism and the revolutionary creed of *liberté, égalité, fraternité*. Maybe the five Irish guards, upon first joining the ship, would not have been fully aware of what had been achieved in France, but the injustices they believed to have been inflicted upon Ireland by the Westminster government left them wanting to know more. Delahaye, Joseph Delis, Nicolas Thierry and Le Maillot, French seamen who had been brought onto the ship to help sail her, were happy to tell them all they needed to know about the glorious revolution. In taking the ship, and it would be in the name of the French Republic, they would be doing a service both for France and Ireland. *Vive la Republique*, was their motto, their *raison d'être*, their mission in life.

Vive la Republique were the words called out as a signal that *Lady Shore* was ready to be taken and the mutiny enacted. Each of the twenty-five had a specific task, and the mutineers quickly secured the upper deck, trapping below not just seamen loyal to the ship's officers, but those of the military guard who the mutineers believed were not to be trusted. In addition, but held in a secure and separate part of the ship, were the sixty-six women convicts, or at least the ones who were not elsewhere on the ship fraternising with newly found lovers. In securing the upper deck, the mutineers not only placed armed guards over each of the hatchways but hauled into position cannons pointing down each of the hatchways as well as another two pointing aft from the forecastle deck. Primed and loaded with shards of broken glass, these they threatened to fire should there be the slightest attempt to retake the ship.

Those who might have led any resistance to the mutiny, the officers and senior members of the ship or of the New South Wales Corps, were at the time of the mutiny also asleep in their quarterdeck cabins. Here they were easily trapped. Mutineers armed with pistols covered each door and window, ensuring that no officer could escape. Only Lambert, the first mate, and John Black, the purser, put up any resistance. Rather than informing the captain and officers, Lambert, in seeing the mutineers fully armed coming on to the upper deck, chose to go to his own cabin and load a pistol. Returning to the quarterdeck, and assuring himself that mutiny was intended he again returned to his cabin from where he fired his pistol, hitting one of the leading mutineers, Christopher Delahaye, fully in the breast. At first it appeared that Delahaye was only slightly wounded, for although he fell to the ground, he was soon back on his feet, firing his pistol at Lambert before once again falling from loss of blood. The plight of Lambert was no better than that of Delahaye, for in being brought under fire, he also fell to the ground where he was run through with a bayonet before managing to run into John Black's cabin. By this time, Black had been awoken from his sleep by not just the sound of gunfire but cries of murder. Almost as soon as he was out of his bed, the badly wounded Lambert crashed through his cabin door. Black later wrote, 'I fired one of my pistols, the ball of which took one of the mutineer's hats off his head, without doing any other execution.'

James Wilcocks, the captain and owner of *Lady Shore*, also being awoken by the commotion on the quarterdeck, ran out of the roundhouse where he was quartered at night to be confronted by two of the armed mutineers who demanded that in the name of the French Republic he give up the ship. This he refused, but in attempting to regain his own cabin to arm himself, he was brutally attacked and bayonetted just below the heart. According to Black, Wilcocks fell to the ground but managed to pull himself to his feet, making a spring towards the after hatchway. On doing so he 'received another stab at the neck with a knife and fell down the hatchway, a musket was fired after him in his descent, but without taking effect.'

The man who should now have taken charge was William Minchin, the commanding officer of the detachment of soldiers, who might, if he had been a better commander, have regained control of the ship. However, Minchin had already shown himself unable to control the men he commanded, orders he issued were often ignored and Minchin failed to take any action to punish them. In Portsmouth, before the ship sailed, Ensign Minchin had gone ashore leaving his sergeant, Hughes, in charge of the detachment. Hughes, despite this order, also went ashore and was still absent when Minchin returned. As if this in itself was not conduct to be harshly punished, the re-appearance of Hughes on a boat rowed from the shore saw the sergeant once again defying his commanding officer. Ordered to immediately come on board, Hughes replied that he would not do so until the goods he had acquired in town were out of the boat. According to an account later supplied by Semple, one of the two male convicts:

> ...*the officer [Minchin] repeated his commands, and Hughes replied in a language which I will not repeat; strange to tell, the officer calmly walked into his cabin, without taking the least notice of the insult.*

Part of this has to be put down to Minchin's lack of command experience. An ensign, the very lowest of officer ranks, he had served for only a few months, seeing little of how other officers successfully commanded their men. His, without doubt, was a most unsuitable appointment, placed in charge of a detachment of soldiers who would have proved difficult for even the most experienced of commanders, much less one as untried as Minchin. Those placed under Minchin were themselves little more than convicts, recruited from among the worst elements of society. Of those on board, some were straight out of prison, offered early release if they volunteered to join the New South Wales Corps. Six of them had been taken from London's Savoy military prison and ordered to serve in that regiment for life. Others were simply deserters and troublemakers from other regiments or men caught by an army press gang and forced into military service against their will.

    Captain Wilcocks, having fallen down the hatchway, managed to drag himself into Minchin's cabin, expecting the ensign to have armed himself and ready to take action against the mutineers. Of this he was to be sadly disabused. Minchin and his wife, who was travelling with him, were both hiding under the bunk bed. Bleeding profusely, Wilcocks fell onto the bed and in a faint voice informed Minchin that the ship had been seized and that the mutineers 'have murdered me'. Unable to do little else, he called on Minchin 'to give up the ship'.

    Prior to this moment, both Lambert and Black had looked to join Wilcocks in order to continue the fight against the mutineers, attempting to enter the captain's cabin by way of the saloon. This lay under the poop deck and interconnected with Black's cabin. In passing into the saloon, the two men were able to see into the captain's cabin, witnessing Wilcock's last moments as he was again stabbed before receiving a fatal pistol shot to the head. It was while in the saloon, and not daring to move as otherwise the mutineers would have spotted them, that Black could also see into his own cabin where a mutineer was stabbing his bed with a bayonet, apparently believing that the purser might be hiding under the sheets. In his later account, Black described the overwhelming fear that enveloped him:

IL A MORT POUR LA LIBERTÉ

Certain of Lambert's death, and fully convinced Captain Willcocks had not escaped – uncertain of the fate of those below, and covered with poor Lambert's blood – if I attempted to move from the place where I stood, as nothing but a canvas screen separated me from three or four of them, with their pieces cocked, and ready to fire at anything they saw. It is easier for you to conceive, than me to describe my sensations during this interval. I remained in this situation some time, [even hearing] one of them lamenting my death.

The other witness who was to leave an account of what he observed, Major James George Semple, was very much a square peg in a round hole. Yes, he was being transported as a convict, and yes he was a man with high military rank. He had fought for Britain in the American Revolutionary War and later, so he claimed, as a soldier of fortune in various European armies. That he had been recently sentenced to a term of seven years in Botany Bay had followed upon his conviction at the Old Bailey for defrauding a number of tradesmen. Highly literate, and one who was forever courting public attention, his account of events on *Lady Shore* was later published as part of his autobiography. While Semple was a known liar and a well-practised confidence trickster, his account of the mutiny appears accurate, although he may have exaggerated his own role in opposing the mutineers. Only one of two males, and also as a result of his social standing, Semple had been accorded certain favours by Wilcocks, allowed to be housed in the forepart of the ship where he even socialised with the officers. In having been granted this favour, it was to give him that morning a front row seat that allowed him to witness the unfolding events being played out. Also given similar treatment to Semple was the second male prisoner, Knowles, formerly the Duke of Portland's porter. He too had been found guilty of fraud and ordered to be transported for seven years.

According to Semple's account, he heard Wilcocks calling for his assistance as the captain lay dying on his bed, Wilcocks aware that despite his conviction as a fraudster, Semple had considerable military experience. Semple confirms in his account that the captain was very much in favour of giving up the ship, for in being so close to death he had nothing to hope for other than 'to expire in peace'. As for Minchin, of whom Semple had long held a low opinion, Semple noted that he also showed no desire to fight the mutineers, imploring Semple to talk to the mutineers and assure them that no further resistance would be made:

To the Captain I answered, that whatever might, in his own opinion, rend to his advantage or convenience, I should most readily do, but to Ensign Minchin, I felt myself as a soldier, obliged to speak in

> *another tone. Him I told, that HE, and HE ONLY, was the proper person to speak to the mutineers...and that it was his duty TO SUBDUE THEM OR DIE!*

Semple also claims to have produced a plan that might well have resulted in the eventual defeat of the mutineers and one that could have avoided undue loss of further lives:

> *I called to his recollection...that, as well as the ammunition, we were masters of the provisions; that we had only to defend the hatchways, and keep the mutineers where they were; and that, having neither bread nor water in their reach, want of refreshment and rest would soon reduce them to sue for mercy on their knees: I even proposed to him [Minchin] to choak the rudder, and cut away the masts between decks, in which case the wreck would have fallen on their heads, and they had not one implement of any kind to clear it with...*

But with such measures Minchin did not agree, repeating his own desire to give up the ship:

> *I went therefore to the hatchway, where the sentinels presented their pieces to my head; but three Frenchmen, a German, and several Irish at that moment appearing, I communicated my business. They remained upon deck, and myself below; and while we were in that situation, they assured me that they wished not to hurt anyone; but that they wanted their liberty and would have it or die: they added, that if the Captain and Mr. Minchin would come to the hatchway, and give their word of honour that no resistance should at any time be made, all should be at peace, and we should be well treated.*

While it was agreed that the captain was in no position to come to the hatchway, the mutineers accepted that the assurance need only be given by Minchin. The ensign was finally persuaded to come to the hatchway to make the promise as demanded, calling out to the mutineers that the ship had indeed been surrendered to them:

> *Upon this the mutineers gave three cheers, fired two of the great guns, and a volley of small arms, and laid on the hatches, fore and aft.*

Neither Delahaye nor Wilcocks were to survive their wounds, both dying soon after and buried at sea on Monday 2 August. Delahaye, as a leader of the mutineers, was accorded a special ceremony with the mutineers firing a volley of small arms and fixing to his body the inscription *Il est morte pour la liberté* – He died for freedom. For Wilcocks, the mutineers agreed to permit any honour requested, but it was thought proper to do no more than raise to half-mast 'the English colours'. Not wishing to be taken into Montevideo where Semple and the other loyalists would be treated as prisoners-of-war, Semple requested that they be given the ship's long boat so that they could make for the coast of Brazil. Here they would not be imprisoned, but more likely quickly repatriated back to England.

It was on 15 August, when about 340 miles from Brazil, in the latitude of Cape Sta-Maria, that twenty-nine of those who the mutineers considered least valuable to their cause, including Semple, Black and a number of women convicts and their several children, were ushered into the boat and cast adrift. The precise number of children is unknown, for this was never recorded, although the youngest was an infant of less than five weeks. Despite appalling weather, and the distance that had to be sailed, the boat reached the port of San-Pedros where they were hospitably received.

As for *Lady Shore*, she successfully reached Montevideo, dropping anchor on 27 August 1797 with Delis introducing himself as the captain. The mutineers did not, perhaps, receive the welcome they were hoping for. The Spanish were unhappy at receiving a ship taken by mutiny. For his part, and now clearly standing out as the overall leader, Delis argued that *Lady Shore* had been taken as a prize for and on behalf of the French Republic. As an ally of France he insisted that they should be accepted as true friends in the ongoing war against Britain. In two minds as to how they should treat these new arrivals, a compromise was reached. The mutineers, while looked upon with little respect, were nevertheless given a small income to maintain themselves but informed that they must remain in Montevideo. Eventually, and with considerable reluctance, the authorities did finally accept *Lady Shore* as a prize, purchasing her for the sum of 53,207 pesos, which was distributed among those officially credited as playing an active part in the taking of the ship.

The outbreak of mutiny on *Lady Shore* had been little short of inevitable. Apart from her officers, each and every person on board had a serious grievance that could only be eased by taking the ship into an enemy port. Those who had the greatest of grievances were the convicts. Unusually, of course, and apart from Semple and Knowles, they were all women and, as such, played no active part in taking the ship. This does not mean that in fraternising with their military guards and seamen they did not bring some influence to bear, possibly encouraging their new found sexual partners to rebel and take the ship anywhere other than the penal colony in New South Wales.

Those placed over the convicts, the detachment of soldiers from the New South Wales Corps, also had a long list of grievances. None were willing volunteers, knowing that on being sent to New South Wales they would never return to England, for a posting there was for life. They were the dregs of society and, following their assembly at barracks located in Chatham, their discontentment had soon become plain for all to see, constantly proving themselves rowdy and insolent. To get them to Deptford where they were to board *Lady Shore*, they had to be marched under close escort, but even so, eight managed to escape, disappearing into the Kent countryside, never to re-emerge.

Yet for a mutiny to be successful on a convict transport ship, something more was needed than a set of discontented individuals. Over the many decades in which convict ships departed England for New South Wales, it is known that there were several attempted mutinies, but only the one on *Lady Shore* proved successful. On the other transport ships there were many who were all too willing to inform while outwardly appearing to support whatever was being planned. In doing so, they counted on being generously rewarded, likely to receive favourable treatment by the officers in command and also at the penal colony when they landed. According to a paper written by Maxwell-Stewart, convicts were routinely punished for mutinous actions during the voyage itself, and any plots being hatched by small groups of conspirators were transmitted to the officers when the wider circle of convicts learnt of what was afoot. For those leading and organising the mutiny on *Lady Shore*, the potential for being informed upon still existed, but was mitigated by the existence on board the ship of a number of men committed to a wider revolutionary cause, forming among themselves a cadre that would hold strong against an informer, with many on the ship being unaware that such a plot was to be actioned.

Admittedly, before the ship sailed there had been talk of mutiny with the high-status convict Major James Semple reporting that he had been told there would be an attempt to take the ship. He was even asked if he would lead it. But this was a separate group of discontented individuals, men who simply desired to avoid a future life in a penal colony and who, in turn, sought any leader who could make this possible. Those who organised the successful mutiny had no need to seek out someone to lead them for they had the confidence to organise themselves, creating a well laid out plan that would only be hatched when the ship was well away from England and with no possibility of meeting a British warship that would bring about the recapturing of *Lady Shore*. It was for this reason that the mutiny was sprung while off the coast of South America, so placing the ship within close reach of various ports of the Spanish empire that they knew would allow them refuge, albeit reluctantly in the case of Montevideo. Finally, and securing the ultimate success of the mutiny, was that among the mutineers were men with seafaring skills, men who had sailed the seven seas and even knew the waters in this part of the Atlantic.

That important leadership quality came from several former prisoners-of-war who had joined the ship when they had been drafted into the New South Wales Corps. Delahaye was one named as a leader, possibly the main organiser, but certainly among the most active, with three others, Joseph Delis, Nicolas Thierry and Le Maillot, also taking noticeably leading roles, the last name acting as the ship's *Secretaire à board de la prise*. In addition, they had the support of Conrad Locher, an officer in a Swiss regiment that was fighting alongside the French, who had been captured at sea when the ship upon which he was a passenger had been taken by a British frigate. At the time Locher was bound for the important French possession of Isle de France (modern-day Mauritius) in the Indian Ocean. As an officer with command experience, it seems likely that he would have played a significant role in helping organise the mutiny, his command experience likely to have proved invaluable.

Delis and Thierry, as well as leading the mutineers, were seamen, formally crew members of *La Bonne Citoyenne*, a captured French privateer, and as such they helped ensure that once the ship was taken, it would survive the vicissitudes of the sea before entering a port of safety. Thierry had been *La Bonne Citoyenne*'s coastal pilot and Delis the chief helmsman. Cristobal Martinez, a Puerto Rican seaman, was also important to the success of the mutineers, for he had essential knowledge of the South Atlantic and the location of various ports that might accommodate *Lady Shore* once taken.

Not to be forgotten, and very much a part of the core group, were the five Irish guards on the ship together with one single Englishman. In common with a number of others now serving aboard *Lady Shore*, these six had been offered the choice of serving in the New South Wales Corps or serving out a long sentence in the Savoy Prison. But what is of particular significance, is that the majority of those within the corps had not involved themselves in the mutiny, while those who did were for the most part Irish. So why should this be? Why should Irish members of the New South Wales Corps be the most prone to join a mutiny?

At this point they almost certainly cannot be considered part of the United Irish plot to take and hand over to the French a number of British warships. Nevertheless, as Irish Catholics, each would have been subject to the overall pressure suffered by all Catholics in Ireland. Those men on board were not skilled artisans, otherwise they would not have volunteered for military service in the first place. Their various crimes that had first brought some of them into the Savoy Military Prison further demonstrates their unsuitableness for military service. In Ireland they and their families would have greatly suffered through both poverty and being on the front line of a violent society in which Catholics suffered the most. Treated as an underclass, the Catholics in Ireland were among the poorest of any community in the whole of Europe. With only small parcels of land upon which large families attempted to survive, they had been given little choice but to find employment within the British Army. But before doing so, each would have become familiar with the Catholic secret societies working throughout rural Ireland that were dispensing retribution upon Protestant landlords and employers – the White Boys, Right Boys and Defenders. In turn, countered by Protestant gangs, violence was endemic across Ireland, with such violence seen as customary and legitimate. For the Catholics, however, the French Revolution had taken on particular significance. Replication of such a revolution in Ireland was considered a means of overcoming their various problems. With the Defenders in particular having adopted a more radical agenda, and one influenced by events in France, support for the ideals of the revolution even if not well understood would have created a desire to work alongside those who were determined to oppose the English establishment. It was such feelings that would have brought the Irish into the mutiny on board *Lady Shore*, as it did also on board the ships of the Channel fleet during the following year.

Those on board *Lady Shore* who were later to plan and organise the mutiny may well have been encouraged by events that they came to directly witness. In April 1797, immediately prior to the vessel's departure from England, she had sailed to Portsmouth to take on additional stores with all on board seeing for themselves the amazing sight of the entire Channel fleet of the Royal Navy in mutiny. Contact between the seamen and soldiers of *Lady Shore* and those in mutiny would have been impossible to prevent. Indeed, we already know that Minchin was unable to control his men. At least some of the New South Wales Corps went ashore without gaining his permission. Here also were activists of the Society of United Irishmen, and while they had little or no influence on the course of the fleet mutiny at Spithead, they would certainly have been radicalising Irish crews into thoughts of future mutinies, mutinies that could be staged for the specific benefit of Ireland. Soon *Lady Shore* sailed, probably ordered to take a sudden departure to get those on board away from the disturbances in Portsmouth and her own crew taking similar action. But in doing so she sailed on to Torbay, where almost certainly further news percolated through of a similar mutiny having broken out in the Sound. With such memories in mind, the Irish contingent on board *Lady Shore* sailed into the Atlantic to form a comradely alliance with those who had once fought for the Republic of France. Between them they formed a secret inner committee that planned and directed the mutiny, a mutiny so precisely planned that taking the ship was as smooth an operation as could possibly have been conceived.

Despite the obvious potential for mutiny, *Lady Shore* was the only convict ship to witness a successful mutiny. In part, this was because pressure was placed on the Transport Board to reconsider its recruitment of prison ship guards from the ranks of deserters and others formally held in a military prison. On news being received in England of the mutiny, the owners of both *Minerva* and *Friendship*, the next two convict ships to be transported to Australia, refused to allow guards drawn from military prisons, agreeing with the Transport Board that they employ 'their own men, in addition to the ship's officers and crew, specifically to act as guards'. Subsequently, a return was made to the use of a more professional military to provide detachments of guards for ships transporting convicts. But by then a more careful vetting of officers and men had been introduced.

One other further convict transport ship came close to being taken in a successful mutiny that occurred on 29 July 1800. This was *Ann*, which departed Cork on 26 June 1800 conveying a total of 171 convicts, made up of 147 men and twenty-four women, to Port Jackson. Most of the male convicts were Irish, the majority, some 127, rebels who had been arrested and convicted for their part in the uprising of 1798. Those rebels, of course, had a level of unity not possessed by the more typical convicts who had little in common with each other, other than taking actions that were entirely self-serving. For the Irish rebels it was their beliefs and the oaths taken that would keep them true to the cause of Ireland that drove them forward and created on any convict ship upon which they were being transported a unique unity of purpose.

The object of the *Ann* mutineers was, most certainly, to gain their freedom, but more specifically to regain the shores of Ireland so that they might help rekindle the fight against the English hegemonic elite to which they were opposed. For this reason, there was no waiting until the ship was off the coast of South America, where the ship once taken would be unlikely to be intercepted by a patrolling British warship. In such more distant waters, as with the mutineers on board *Lady Shore*, they could have taken the ship into the guaranteed safety of a Spanish port. While this might have given them freedom, it would not have guaranteed an easy return to Ireland. For this reason, the mutiny was sprung just a few days after leaving Cork and while *Ann* was to the west of Greenock in latitude 6.32 north, and longitude 21.34 east. At the time, the lower deck, where the convicts were held, was being fumigated with gunpowder and vinegar, a standard practice when there was a risk of typhus, commonly referred to as gaol fever and spread by human body lice. In overcrowded and unhygienic conditions, such as gaols and convict ships, the disease could spread rapidly. Fumigation killed off the lice, although it was not realised at the time that the disease was caused by lice, only that fumigation helped curtail any outbreak. Through the heating of the gunpowder and vinegar, a vaporous smoke was created that allowed the mutineers to act without being initially seen. In a letter later published in a number of newspapers, including *Porcupine* and *London Chronicle*, Stewart, the captain of the ship, outlined what happened:

> *The instant the smoke began, I was seized by the throat by a convict, vociferating death or liberty. The gunner and mate were seized at the same time by others; and the party of them upon deck, about thirty, wrenched a cutlass from one of the sentinels, and some iron bars from the cab house.*

However, without the support from any of the military guard, the mutiny was quickly quelled. Stewart continued:

> *I extricated myself from the man who first seized me, and was rescued from the crowd by two convicts and got upon deck. The mate and gunner being still in their custody, and the mutiny still continuing, recourse was had to firearms, when one man attempting to take a pistol from a seaman was shot dead, and two more were wounded.*

Marcus Sheehy was viewed as the ringleader and upon him apparently confessing his guilt he was, upon the agreement of all the officers of the ship, immediately shot, in the presence of the convicts. Christopher Grogan, a ringleader in the fighting that took place on deck, was in turn sentenced to 250 lashes. According to Stewart, this was sufficient to end 'this disagreeable affair' with *Ann* arriving at Buenos Ayres on 22 August. from where he wrote his account.

Chapter 15

Bloody Mutiny

The seizing of a British warship by her crew and the taking of that ship into an enemy port was no fanciful idea. During the French Revolutionary War, the crew of British warships *Marie Antoinette*, *Hermione*, *Danae* and *Albanaise* did just that. None, though, were major warships. All were smaller vessels on detached duties away from the main fleet, with *Marie Antoinette*, a 10-gun schooner captured from the French in 1793, *Hermione*, a 32-gun fifth rate frigate, *Albanaise*, a brig previously captured from the French, and *Danae*, a corvette that had also been captured from the French. It should also be said that the factor directly inciting each of those mutinies was the ill-treatment of the men by the officers who commanded them. This ensured that there was a common cause uniting the entirety of the people of the lower decks of each of these ships. Ireland was not the reason for which they mutinied, although it is noticeable that in all four cases there is considerable evidence that among those who mutinied were a disproportionate number of Irish seamen in both the organising and actioning of those mutinies. The point here is that ships most vulnerable to a successful mutiny were smaller ships, ones where a discontented element of the crew might more easily dominate, and through being out of sight of the main fleet, not likely to be impeded when sailing on a course that would take the vessel into an enemy port.

Of those four mutinies, the taking of *Hermione* into the Spanish port of La Guaira in modern-day Venezuela is the most well-known. The ship's captain, Hugh Pigot, was a cruel and sadistic tyrant whose behaviour as a disciplinarian was unlike any other officer in the British Royal Navy. It was a series of events taking place on the evening of Wednesday 20 September 1797 that acted as the catalyst for the mutiny, but already there existed among the majority of the crew a seething underlying hatred towards Pigot. Stationed in the Mona Passage, the strait separating the islands of Hispaniola and Puerto Rico, the topsails were being reefed for the night, a regular task that involved reducing the area of sail exposed to the wind by tying them up at particular points. Undertaken by the ship's topmen, a dozen or so of whom passed along a yard and hauled up the sail, using the reefing sewn into the sail to secure it. At the best of times this was dangerous work that could only be performed by the most skilled members of the crew, the topmen of the fore, main and mizzen masts, while precariously perched on the ship's upper spars 50 feet above the ship's swaying deck. Deciding that this work was not being performed with sufficient haste, or to his immediate liking, Pigot clutched his speaking trumpet and called to the men on the mizzen mast, 'I'll flog the last man down.' It was a chilling threat made by a captain already known by his men to be over-keen on flogging, with not a man doubting that it was a threat he was fully prepared to carry out.

In this day and age, Pigot would have been diagnosed as suffering from oppositional defiant disorder (ODD), a condition that includes a persistent pattern of anger, irritability, vindictiveness and a refusal to accept the norms of society. As captain of *Hermione*, Pigot had absolute authority over all who served under him, both officers and men, with nobody in a position to assuage his anger, however unreasonable might be his actions. This the mizzen topmen knew, and in fear of the threat to each of them now given, they began to rush their work, with three men tragically losing their footing and tumbling to the deck below, their deaths an inevitable outcome. It was, however, Pigot's next order that was to seal his fate, and which brought on the mutiny.

'Throw the lubbers overboard,' he demanded of the men nearest to him.

Such disdain for the now three dead topmen, their lives lost because of Pigot's callous threat to flog the last man down, was seen as insufferable and a singularly brutal instruction. For the men of the lower deck, it fuelled their mounting resentment against him, turning it into a burning rage that engulfed each man in an unstoppable desire for revenge. Immediately there were murmurs of protest from the men of the topmast, but Pigot was having none of it. To quell their protests he ordered several of them to be flogged for insubordination. This he said was to be carried out the following day.

Overnight the topmen and others, the most respected members of the crew, met and decided that Pigot's reign of brutality had to be brought to an end. They could take no more and they knew the rest of the crew were with them. It was agreed that they would now act against him, but not until the following night when all would be ready to pursue a hastily assembled plan.

The following morning, at eleven o'clock, a possible fourteen topmen were flogged in turn, each receiving a dozen lashes. The rest of the day outwardly appeared much as normal, but come the evening all hell broke loose, with the ship engulfed in bloody mutiny. Pigot, two of his officers and a midshipman were violently set upon by men wielding cutlasses and axes. While still alive, they were thrown overboard. Pigot may well have been the one who gave the orders for so many excessive punishments, but it had been the officers who had ensured that his orders were carried out to the letter. As for the clerk, he had protested little against the punishments and would have given evidence against any man who might later fall into the hands of the Admiralty.

Having taken the ship, an inner core of eighteen seamen proceeded to meet in the captain's cabin, taking decisions for future actions. Among them were three seamen of Irish birth, of which one in particular was to come to the fore, 35-year-old Laurence Cronin, the surgeon's mate. A native of Belfast, the Irish city with the strongest links to the Society of United Irishmen, Cronin had not been an initial organiser but appears to have had a considerable impact on subsequent events, especially with regard to the death of several officers. A born orator, Cronin clearly made his mark on the day following the taking of the ship. Calling upon 'the people [of the ship] to be assembled around the skylights overlooking the lower deck gun room' he read out a paper he had written previously, which outlined the conduct of the captain and officers. Indicating himself to have been a republican ever since the start of the war, he proclaimed the mutiny to be a good thing, but that they must go further, 'that all the officers must be put to death as it was of no use to put [just] one to death.' To those assembled around him, he made it clear that not one single mutineer would be safe from being hunted down by the Admiralty if a single officer was left alive, for any such officer would be able to identify them and ensure that many of them would be hanged.

By all accounts it was an electrifying speech, for while the original organisers considered that there had already been enough killings, Cronin's enthusiasm caught the mood of the majority. According to the ship's master, Edward Southcott, one of the few of the petty officers to survive, 'The scene now became dreadful, and the greatest confusion prevailed.' Fuelled as they were by excessive consumption of spirits taken from the stores, the majority assembled began to bellow against the remaining officers, 'Hand 'em up! Pass the buggers up! Kill them all! 'Once again blood flowed freely, the remaining officers alongside a second midshipman as well as the captain's clerk viciously attacked and flung into the sea whether dead or alive.

Despite the renewed onset of bloodshed, not all of the petty officers were killed, with some later testifying against one of the mutineers who fell into the hands of the Admiralty, and so justifying Cronin's argument. Yet how far could they go? Kill all of the officers, petty officers, as well as any man who demurred from the killings or had not supported the mutiny from the outset? To this, Cronin produced a solution, one almost certainly based on the associations he appears to have had with various radical bodies, maybe as a Defender or United Irishman. This was to force every man who survived the days of slaughter to take a sacred oath that was designed to protect one and all. Taken in the name of God, it was a declaration by each, once he had departed the ship, 'not to know one another, in any part of the globe, man or boy, if they should meet, nor call each other by their former names.' This last was a reference to a further idea put forward by Cronin, that each man should also take on a new identity, a disguise that would help keep them safe from the inevitable and unceasing anger of the Admiralty. Finally, the oath was concluded by each man stating, 'This is my oath and obligation, so help me God.'

While such oaths were taken seriously by ships' crews and were used time after time to bind rebel groups and mutineers, there was really little possibility that all, especially those forced to take the oath, would adhere to the terms it attempted to impose. Over the following decade, and the result of a determined effort on the part of the Admiralty to punish as many of the mutineers as possible in a desire for retribution, a total of thirty-three *Hermione* mutineers were eventually apprehended and brought to trial. Most were taken at sea, found serving on captured enemy privateers or warships or upon merchant ships stopped and searched by Royal Navy warships whose officers had been given names and descriptions of those who had been most active in the mutiny. If the oath had been fully binding, the evidence against all thirty-three would have been minimal and unless all thoughts of a just trial were abandoned, most would have escaped the penalty laid down for mutiny: execution by hanging. Of that thirty-three, twenty-four were hanged and one transported to Botany Bay. It was 'Hermiones' who had taken the oath, some of them forced to do so even though they opposed the mutiny, among them a midshipman and surviving petty officers, who would think nothing of breaking the oath, and giving evidence against those who had played an active role. In addition, some of those who played a more minor role in the mutiny but would still face the death penalty if put on trial, having fallen into the hands of the Admiralty chose to testify against others who had played a more active role. In the event, only a small number of those known to have led the mutiny were brought to trial, disappearing from the gaze of the world. Among them was Laurence Cronin who, according to one author, stayed in La Guaira, running a business.

In determining to sail the ship into the Spanish port of La Guaira, 500 miles to the west of the Mona Passage, a high degree of navigational skill was required. This may partly explain why Southcott's life was spared, for while only a petty officer, ranking below that of a lieutenant, he was the ship's navigational officer, regularly taking the ship's position and setting the sails for the required course and sea conditions. Without Southcott the ship would have been without a member of the crew sufficiently adept in safely guiding the ship towards La Guaira. William

Turner, formerly the master's mate and appointed by the mutineers as the new ship's captain, might have learnt a few things from Southcott, but within two days of the ship having been taken he admitted to being unsure of their correct position. At this point Southcott was taken on deck and forced to use his quadrant to calculate the position of the ship that allowed Richard Redman, a leading mutineer who had served as coxswain, to lay off a new course.

As for the reception given to *Hermione* by the Spanish authorities upon her arrival at La Guaira, this was somewhat mixed. No prize money was distributed to the mutineers, although they were given subsistence money and accommodation before many of them dispersed, most aiming to enter the United Sates. A total of fifty were, however, retained by the Spanish, required to continue serving on *Hermione* once she was taken into Spanish service. While the Spanish were happy to gain a frigate, their navy generally short of warships in the Caribbean, and consequently pleased that the British Navy was now depleted by one frigate, they did not care for the way it had been achieved. For should the mutineers have been better rewarded, including the distribution of prize money, this not only went against their tradition of service and authority but could well encourage their own seamen to act in a similar fashion. Unlike the government of revolutionary France, with which Spain was admittedly in alliance, Spain was a monarchy and one that would naturally fear revolution and the possibility of also becoming a republic. Thus, a ship brought into one of her ports by those rejecting the authority of another monarchical state had to be held with utmost suspicion. Yes, the Spanish authorities in Montevideo had paid out prize money, but a clear difference was that among those who took *Lady Shore* were a number of men who had actually served France in uniform, so justifying the action of the ship being taken as a wartime prize, not by her own crew in mutiny.

Possibly acting as an inspiration to those organising the mutiny on *Hermione* was the mutiny on *Marie Antoinette* that had preceded the *Hermione* mutiny by just ten weeks, having occurred on 7 July 1797. More significantly, the *Marie Antoinette* mutiny had also taken place in the Caribbean, with news of this known to the crew of *Hermione* immediately prior to her leaving Cape Nicholas Mole (Haiti) for the Mona Passage. In many ways, the two mutinies were very similar. The crew of *Marie Antoinette* murdered her commander, Lieutenant John McInerheny, and several officers, throwing them overboard while also restraining the remaining officers and loyal crew. The schooner was then carried into a French port, Gonaïves, in Saint-Domingue. Here the mutineers were financially rewarded with the loyalist members of the crew, who had been taken as prisoners, sent by the French to the British-held port of Cape Nicholas Mole. Little is known of this mutiny, although it was acknowledged that McInerheny was another brutal officer, similar to Pigot, treating his men harshly and with disdain, so giving those on board *Marie Antoinette* little choice other than to take the ship and run her into a French port.

It was in March 1800 that the crew of one British warship, *Danae*, played out the dreams of the United Irishmen in the sense of this vessel being taken into Brest and handed over to the French. While some of those responsible were politically motivated, strongly sympathetic to the republican cause, the taking of the ship was not part of a wider republican plot. Most of those active in the mutiny were simply discontented individuals, unhappy with being pressed into naval service and seeing the taking of the ship as the only means by which they could regain their freedom and a return to the life they really wished to live. By all accounts, William Jackson, a determined radical, was the leader of the mutineers. He had once served on *Pompée*, already mentioned as one of the most radical ships of the fleet, which mutinied at Spithead, with the *Naval Chronicle* in 1800 suggesting that Jackson had served as Parker's secretary at the Nore. This, however, is an unlikely possibility as Jackson is shown to have been at Spithead mustered on *Pompée* at this time. Another key member of the *Danae* mutiny was Ignatius Fieney, who was undoubtedly a United Irishman. Rated an able seaman, Fieney was Irish, a former priest and, according to evidence presented by *Danae*'s first lieutenant in a court martial of one of the mutineers who was subsequently arrested in London, 'a lieutenant in the rebel army'. Of the forty-one mutineers whose names were subsequently recorded at Brest, a total of twenty claimed to be Irish, with twelve claiming to be American. Only five admitted to be English. J.D. Spinney, in checking those names against a *Danae* muster list, found that at least twelve of the alleged Irish and four of the alleged Americans were born in England.

It would seem that the mutiny was supported by forty of the crew with the ship appearing to be crewed by a large number of discontented seamen. Nevertheless, the ship's commander, Captain Lord Proby, the eldest son of the Earl of Carysfort, was no tyrant. Many of the crew remained loyal to him. However, the mutineers were well-organised. The conspirators met in the maintops, well out of the hearing of loyal crew members and officers. Oaths were also admitted in secret, with officers later admitting that they had not the slightest knowledge of any conspiracy in the making. On 15 March 1801, the day of the mutiny, *Danae* was off Ushant on the north side of the island, well away from any other British warship and within easy reach of the Goulet that the mutineers realised would take her safely into the roadstead. It was for this reason the mutineers struck when they did, requiring only a couple of minutes to take the ship. Darkness having fallen, most of the officers had turned in for the night, as had most of the crew. *Danae* herself was flush-decked, which made the taking of the ship so much easier as all off duty loyal crew and officers would be below deck. All that was required was for the mutineers to overpower the ship's master who was the acting officer of the first watch, alongside two midshipmen who were also on duty. With the mutineers who had crept on deck soon numbering in excess of twenty, most brandishing cutlasses, this was a simple task. The master and the two midshipmen were bundled below and all of the hatches sealed. While the noise of those early scuffles did alert other officers of what was taking place, none managed to gain entry to the deck. They were all pushed back by the mutineers. While a few sustained injury, none was killed. The mutineers had agreed among themselves to take no lives. Soon the call went out, 'The ship is ours now, and we are masters.'

Danae had lain overnight off the Breton coast near Point St Mathieu. Contact was made with the French early the following morning, with two pilots sent on board to bring the ship safely through the Goulet and into the Rade. Whether as a true sympathiser of the republican ideal or simply to curry favour with the French, one further *Danae* mutineer, William Moorland, the gunroom cook, declared upon the first arrival of French troops onto the frigate, '*Vive la Republique Francaise.*' Others were later to be seen wearing in their hats tricolour cockades as a symbol of their support for the republic and all for what it stood. While those of *Danae* who had remained loyal to the officers, together with the officers, were soon to be returned to England under a prisoner exchange agreement, the mutineers, of course, chose to remain in France. Here they were generally well received, provided with subsistence money, and upon the sale of *Danae* at Brest, a share of the money received by the French government for her sale into private hands. Indeed, each of the mutineers as acknowledged by the French, would eventually receive a little over 1,156 French Francs (approximately £2,000 in today's money). On his return to England, and as presented to his court martial looking into the loss of *Danae*, Proby downplayed any advantage gained by the mutineers in taking the ship, fearing that the slightest hint of financial reward for taking a vessel into an enemy port might induce others to do likewise. However, one thing Proby did let slip was that he became aware that the French were hoping to acquire further British warships in the same way. Seemingly it had been mentioned to him that although the agents of the French government expressed their 'abhorrence of the treason', he still had to admit that the mutineers 'were given some encouragement', further adding that they were in hope 'of getting possession of our entire fleet in the same way'. For this reason Proby wanted to make it known that the mutineers faced a few difficulties. According to him the French authorities refused to enter them on board any of their warships, believing those who could betray their own country were not to be trusted. Proby also indicated that the mutineers had difficulty in finding accommodation upon first arriving in France, as houseowners did not wish to receive them.

Eight months later, on 23 November 1800, *Albanaise* sailed into the Spanish naval port of Malaga, taken there by several of her crew following the overpowering of her officers. Previously a French naval brig, *Albanaise* had been captured in the Mediterranean by the Royal Navy and taken into service as a bomb ketch. Under Lieutenant Francis Newcombe, who had been given the rank of master and commander and who proved himself a resourceful officer, *Albanaise* successfully captured several enemy ships, among them a small Spanish vessel on the very evening of the mutiny. At that time *Albanaise* was in the Alboran Sea, at the western end of the Mediterranean, escorting a convoy of seven merchantmen carrying cattle and barley from the North African port of Arzeu to Gibraltar. While *Albanaise*'s allowed complement was 100, she was perilously short of seamen, for as each prize had been taken, the number of men remaining on board had been gradually reduced through the releasing of seamen to sail each of the prizes into a British naval port. For that latest capture, a further four men under the master's mate, John Terrel, were now shed, instructed to sail the prize quickly into Gibraltar, with the convoy continuing but at a much slower pace. As well as being short of her full complement, a large portion of her crew were men who had been recruited in various Mediterranean ports. British seamen were in short supply due to the massive expansion of the Royal Navy in this long and continuing drawn-out war with revolutionary France. Indeed, most ships of the British Navy, but especially those serving in more distant waters such as the Mediterranean, Caribbean and Indian Ocean, had become increasingly reliant on recruiting natives of nearby foreign lands. On board *Albanaise* were a number of Portuguese and Spanish, and it was this group of seamen alongside at least two Irish crew members, Patrick Kennedy and Hugh Keenan, who were to turn against the ship and mutiny. While it is impossible to explore the motives of the Irish who mutinied, other than a possible sympathy for the United Irishmen, it might be assumed that the Portuguese and Spanish mutineers resented the lack of freedom and general harshness of the conditions under which they were required to serve. Maybe they were further motivated by the sight of the shoreline of southern Spain well within sight as *Albanaise* continued her journey towards Gibraltar, fostering among those who eventually mutinied a desire for a return to their own homeland rather than an undetermined length of time at sea. Certainly there is no evidence of the *Albanaise* mutineers expressing revolutionary sentiments.

BLOODY MUTINY

It was on the night of 22 November that the mutineers struck. As with *Danae*, *Albanaise* was flush-decked, with the captain and officers as well as the crew having their sleeping quarters below and access to the deck obtained through a hatchway. Thus it was possible, once the mutineers had assembled on deck, to easily trap officers and crew members below by sealing the hatches and placing a guard over them. As for the officer of the watch, the one officer who would, at night, remain on deck overseeing the steering of the ship, he was a young midshipman who was easily overcome. Only Newcombe, the captain, put up any real resistance. With much of the ship already under their control, three mutineers entered the cabin where Newcombe was asleep. In the darkness, and suddenly aware that all was not well, he was able to reach for his loaded pistol, fire it and kill Hugh Keenan, one of the mutineers. In turn, however, he was soon overcome by the others who had entered his cabin, each man armed.

Newcombe was later to learn that the mutiny had been in the planning for several days. He also came to believe, following discussions with some of the crew while held in a Spanish prison, that it was Terrel, the master's mate and one of the Portuguese seamen who was to have led the mutiny. Terrel being ordered to Gibraltar with the last taken prize meant he was not present on the ship at the time of the mutiny. Jacob Godfrey, a further Portuguese seaman, stepped into his role. Godfrey was also one of those who had entered Newcombe's cabin, warning the captain following the death of Keenan, 'If you cannot behave like a gentleman and lay still, we'll have life for life.' To complete the account, Godfrey was later to fall into the hands of the Admiralty and court-martialled in January 1802 when he was found guilty of 'having aided and assisted a mutiny on board that ship, and running away with her in November 1800'. He was duly hanged. Terrel was also arrested, having not attempted to run from his service in the navy, but the evidence against him was questionable. While allowed to continue serving, the accusation was constantly held over him with a second court martial held in June 1802 that finally absolved him on an inconclusive verdict of 'charge not proven'. Three more of the *Albanaise* mutineers were also tried in 1802. Of these, one was acquitted, another sentenced to 300 lashes, and the third, Patrick Kennedy, sentenced to be hanged. Kennedy, who was Irish by birth, was another who had entered Newcombe's cabin on the night of the mutiny, holding a pistol to the captain's head and threatening him with instant death if he made any resistance. Adjudged one of the ringleaders, Kennedy was hanged at Plymouth on 16 October aboard *Hussar* in full view of all ships moored in the harbour.

From an examination of these four mutinies where British warships were, during the French Revolutionary War, actually taken into enemy ports, it is possible to analyse why the Irish mutinies of 1798 were destined to fail. Beyond that it is also possible to consider what might have happened should the mutinies have actually been unleashed and the likely course of events that would have followed. A major reason for the failure of the mutinies of 1798 was a lack of secrecy. Knowledge of the planned mutinies was, in most of the ships involved, known throughout the ship and so, despite an unwillingness to inform on their shipmates, the enormity of what was being planned was ultimately communicated by at least one crew member to those in authority. On *Danae* and *Hermione*, recruiting by the primary activists of a large section of the crew and the subsequent actioning of the mutiny was conducted within the space of a few hours rather than over a period of several weeks. Secrecy of the plot from loyalist members of the crew and officers was achieved through the core activists meeting not on the deck of the ship but in the working top on the foremast, where they could not be overheard and their presence unlikely to raise suspicion. While on board *Danae* and *Hermione*, a division between loyalist and rebels was apparent. This was not as great as on the ships of the Channel, North Sea and Mediterranean fleets. The 'Hermiones' had all suffered at the hands of 'one of the most cruel and oppressive captains belonging to the British Navy', and through being subjected to the whims of this tyrant were almost fully united in a determination to end his tyrannous reign of power. For *Danae*, while a considerable loyalist crew were opposed to an Irish component of the crew taking the ship into Brest, they had no awareness, until the rebel crew made their first move, that a mutiny had been planned. Upon the signal being given, most of the loyalist members of the crew, because of the action taking place at night, were in their hammocks, easily trapped in the lower deck, with the rebels taking command of the upper deck.

PART 7

The Admiralty Takes its Revenge

Every man serving on board a British warship in the eighteenth century would have been mindful, whether a volunteer or pressed, that the penalty for mutiny was death. At least once a month, the captain of every naval ship in service was required to read to his assembled crew the Articles of War, the codified rules and orders of service which, in having to be obeyed, governed life on board a British warship. Given that some ships remained in commission with the same crew for three, four or even five years, a typical serving man of the lower deck may well have heard the Articles read to him by the captain in an unwavering monotonous tone some dozens of times. Many seamen were doubtless able to commit to memory the wording of one particular all-encompassing sentence:

> *Any person in or belonging to the fleet shall make, or endeavour to make, any mutinous assembly on any pretence whatsoever every person attending herein, and being convicted thereof by the sentence of the court martial, shall suffer death.*

Nothing could be plainer, nothing could be simpler. Any seaman associated in any way with a mutiny on a British warship could, if brought to trial and found guilty, face execution. But the Admiralty did not consider these simple words to be a sufficient deterrent. When a man was hanged for mutiny, his final death throes had to be witnessed. And not just by those who had served alongside him but by seaman of the entire fleet, or as many as were serving on the warships which, in the course of their duty and at the time of the execution, lay in close proximity.

In the few cases where a rebel crew successfully took the ship upon which they served into an enemy port, the Admiralty was especially anxious to demonstrate that they too would not be forgotten and that death also awaited them should they fall into the clutches of the navy. The depths to which the Admiralty was prepared to go was well demonstrated in 1790 when the frigate *Pandora* was ordered to Tahiti to search out and bring back to Britain the *Bounty* mutineers. In this she was only partially successful. Several mutineers, including Fletcher Christian, remained undiscovered through having fled to the Pitcairn Islands. The mutineers who successfully took *Danae* and *Albanaise,* together with those who took the transport ship *Lady Shore*, could never have felt entirely safe from a revengeful Admiralty. Some in particular, those who subsequently chose to serve on board a French warship or privateer or who chose to return to the British Isles, were especially at risk. As will be shown, several did fall into the hands of the Admiralty, recognised when the enemy ship upon which they served was captured by a British warship or seen by one of their former officers when simply walking the streets of London. In other words, their deed, an act so feared by the Admiralty, was one that the Admiralty could never afford to forget.

Chapter 16

Hanging, Transportation and the Lash

Following a five-day-long hearing held on *Cambridge*, the Plymouth Harbour flagship, Bartholomew Duff was executed. One of the key leaders in the failed attempt by the United Irishmen to take ships of the Channel fleet to the French, Duff, alongside Lawrence Buckley, Michael Butler, John Desmond, John Mahon, and John Cotton, also belonging to *Caesar*, were simultaneously hanged on that ship, three at each of the foreyard-arms. All six had stoically accepted the passing of their sentences, expecting nothing less from an enemy with whom they considered themselves to be at war, and whom they bitterly detested. Accordingly, from the time of the sentence being passed until the stretching of their necks on the long drop, none offered the slightest sign of contrition. In Ireland, among the rebel community, nothing less was expected of them, for to them they were heroes, martyrs to the cause. For readers of various newspapers across England, of which few had sympathy for the Irish cause, there was a simple lack of empathy, an inability to understand why seamen of the Royal Navy, whatever their heritage or the conditions under which they served, should show such disloyalty during a time of war.

The six sentenced to be executed had not been the only members of *Caesar*'s lower deck to be tried by court martial. Others, through being partially found guilty, were ordered to receive 200 lashes 'on their bare backs', to be carried out two days prior to the hanging of the six key *Caesar* rebels. Both the floggings and the hangings were spectacles intended for all to witness, acts of brutality staged for the purpose of intimidating any other seaman who might be tempted to plan or join a mutiny.

On Tuesday 28 August, the day the floggings were to be administered, the men to be punished were taken from *Caesar*, to where they had been returned following the trial, and each put into a separate launch that would be towed to each warship moored in Plymouth Sound. Eventually a long flotilla of small craft would form, each ship of the fleet having to send a boat manned and armed to attend and assist. Once all was ready, and the entire flotilla lined up, Sir George Home, *Caesar*'s captain, read aloud the sentence of the court martial before ordering the master-at-arms to oversee the portion of the punishment to be inflicted upon the mutineers while they were alongside his ship. On board each boat, those ordered to carry out the floggings took up position and would use the cat o' nine tails with unusual fearsomeness, the master-at-arms having warned his men that there was to be no mercy shown to the miscreants who had threatened to take that very ship into an enemy port. Upon each man receiving the due number of lashes assigned to that ship, his back was inspected by a surgeon's mate who made a judgement as to whether the prisoner was able to bear further punishment. Once this was done, a blanket was thrown over the shoulder of each man, and with the punishment completed the flotilla headed to the next vessel. Proceeding the flotilla at a faster pace was a light gig, the dispatch-boat, a lieutenant on board to inform the captain of the next ship to be approached that the men to be flogged were about to arrive alongside.

Now making headway towards *Cambridge*, the first of the boats carrying a mutineer had at the bow a fifer who had struck up the *Rogue's March* accompanied by a muffled beat played out on a drum. On reaching *Cambridge*, the men on the towing boats lay on their oars as each in turn was hooked on to the ship, the sentence of the court again read aloud. Those selected by the boatswain's mate to carry out the next portion of floggings jumped into the launches, each having ready to hand a fresh and unused cat o'nine tails. They too were energetic in their task, for as each lash pounded down on the backs of the men being flogged, little visible flesh would soon remain. From the nape of the neck to below the shoulder-blade a deep purple mass was all that was to be seen, more blood slowly oozing as each stroke was laid on. The screams and groans that each tormented man initially tried to suppress were now unrestrained. Such cries went unheeded. It was a procedure that might have continued for several hours, but those under punishment could only take so much before mortality threatened. Death was not the object, the sentence given was flogging not death and the surgeon accompanying the flotilla was there to see that all, while under great pain, remained alive. Finally, the surgeon accompanying the flotilla declared that he could not allow punishment to continue and it would need to be suspended until each man was once again fit enough for the lashings to be finished at some future date.

On that same day, during the afternoon, the six mutineers held on *Cambridge* and condemned to be hanged were also taken to *Caesar* where they remained under the watchful eye of the ship's marine guard. As with the flogging of the *Caesar* mutineers, the execution was designed to instil fear into the minds of those who served on the lower deck, a further warning of the perils that faced a mutineer serving on board a British warship. For this purpose, the crews on board every ship in harbour or victualling in Cawsand Bay were, as with the floggings, forced to witness the final grotesque moments of these very public multiple hangings.

While the first act in the performance of the execution had already been played out, the court martial and the passing of a sentence of death, approval of the death had to be given by the king. Rarely was this anything more than a formality, and once his approval had been given, the Admiralty in London had it officially transmitted to Admiral Sir Richard King, commander-in-chief, Plymouth, so that he could make the necessary preparations.

On board *Caesar*, Home, on receiving notification that the executions were to go ahead, ordered the ship to be made ready, a scaffold had to be erected and placed over the cathead – the two beams that supported the ship's anchors when they were raised or let go. Duff and his fellow conspirators, while held below in the hold and under the guard of several marines, would clearly have heard the sound of hammering and what it represented. How much sleep they got over the following two nights is debatable. On that fateful Thursday, 30 August, the day of execution, the six were roused from their hammocks at 6 a.m. To help them sleep, each man may have been offered an extra tot of rum to calm them, but if so it went unrecorded. Maybe also some of them managed a bite of bread given for breakfast, possibly accompanied by a few extra sips of rum. Soon after, *Cambridge* fired a single gun and ran-up a yellow flag, the signal of death, answered by *Caesar* also running up a yellow flag. This was to alert the fleet as a whole to the forthcoming spectacle and that it was now time for each ship to send a boat manned with armed marines to assist in the execution. It was also a signal to each captain to assemble their crews on deck and read to them the Articles of War and to acquaint them with the crime for which the men of *Caesar* were about to be executed.

Some 100 boats eventually clustered around *Caesar*, a few to help and assist, but most to add to the drama, for those on board in closely witnessing the hangings were expected to relay to their fellow shipmates all that they were to see. At 11 a.m., Duff and his fellow conspirators were brought on deck, their arms tightly bound to their sides. Likely they were unnerved by the immediate sight of a double row of armed marines, all standing to attention along the entire length of deck and through which each had now to pass. Arriving at the platforms secured over the catheads, the port admiral's warrant of execution as addressed to Captain Home was read by the clerk of the ship, who fully recited the king's approbation of the proceedings. Possibly the prisoners were allowed a few last words. In so doing, they would have been words adhering them to Ireland and a call for its independence. For this reason, it went unreported.

With each of the condemned declaring themselves ready, the master-at-arms gave instructions for a halter to be placed around their necks and their legs bound. The halter was spliced to the reeve rope, and a cap, whether they wished it or not, placed over their heads. With each man secured and in position, the order was given to proceed. A length of rope running up to the spar was attached to the halter, running back down to where it was to be hauled by a dozen or so men once the signal was given.

That signal was the firing of two cannons immediately under the two catheads. This was the last scene of the final act and choreographed to absolute perfection, allowing no man to forget what he was to witness. Through these guns being fired simultaneously, a huge plume of smoke arose from the forecastle, obscuring for a moment the six convicted mutineers. Then, above the smoke dramatically appeared and in rapid succession each of the hanged men, maybe some still alive and others with broken necks, but each body, lifeless or in final convulsion, shaking from side to side, as it came to a halt high above the deck. Visible to both the oarsmen of the boats gathered nearby and to each of the crews ordered by their captains to observe this final moment of the condemned mutineers, it was meant to be shocking, and that it surely was. Finally, the bodies having hung for an hour were cut down and conveyed to the Royal Hospital for interment.

And now the epilogue.

The message to be broadcast by the drama of those hangings was not just for the men mustered on the ships at Plymouth, nor for the Channel fleet in general. It was a message for the entire navy. To this end, captains of all ships were called upon by the Admiralty to read to their men the sentence and fate of those six mutineers, that of swinging at the end of a rope.

One ship's captain who duly carried out this instruction was Sir Thomas Livingstone on board *Expedition*, a 44-gun frigate lying off Blackstakes in the River Medway. His was a ship with a sizeable Irish contingent, and they seemed suitably cowed, their response being an assertion of loyalty to their captain. Yet, in reality, all might not be as it outwardly appeared. In truth, it is impossible to assess their actual commitment to the navy, but to do otherwise than protest loyalty was certainly a wise move. Indeed, there may even have been an element of compulsion, given that the main organiser of a letter sent to the captain was Patrick Bruman, the master at arms, and the petty officer responsible for discipline. It was a letter signed by the ship's thirty-one Irish seamen together with several inferior officers and Bruman himself. It was dated 31 August:

> *We, the Irish part of the company belonging to his Majesty's ship under your command, feel ourselves called upon to declare, that*

> *we look with the utmost abhorrence and detestation on the crimes for which the said six men suffered: and that we will do our best endeavours to detect and bring to punishment any man or set of men, who may attempt to suborn us, or any individual of us from that affection and attachment we bear our King and Country; and we further declare, that we will defend them as we always have done, with the utmost of our ability against both our foreign and domestic foes. We have only, Sir, to say, that if our enemies have formed a hope that the Irish seamen will ever betray their King and Country, they will find their mistake whenever we are brought into action with them — We wish, Sir, that you would forward this declaration to the Admiralty, in order that it may he made public, and we subscribe ourselves with dutiful respect.*

Punishments similar to those inflicted upon the *Caesar* mutineers was to become a familiar sight witnessed by the mass of British seamen during the year 1798, of which the mutinies inspired by the United Irishmen were to result in over thirty being hanged from the yardarm, all in full view of numerous assembled ships. In July, Stevens and Mullins of *Adamant*, together with Timmings and Cormick of *Haughty*, were hanged in Portsmouth harbour. On 27 September, eleven mutineers of *Defiance* were also hanged at Portsmouth and on 27 October, eight of *Glory* were hanged at Plymouth, while others found guilty of mutiny from those two ships were lashed round the fleet during this same period. During the second week of November, George Tomms was hanged from the yardarm of *Diomede*, the ship upon which he had once served, while his co-conspirator, John Wright, received the first part of 500 lashes given alongside ships in port. During the summer, eleven men were hanged in the Mediterranean under the orders of St Vincent. Surprisingly, despite a considerable amount of evidence brought against those planning to mutiny on *Captain*, a total of twelve, none was condemned to be executed. Apart from one, against whom the charge was not proven, all the others were to be lashed around the fleet, some to receive 100 lashes, others 200, a few 300, while McGee, Grumley and Duggan, the identified leaders, 400 lashes. Why this should be lies beyond discovery, although by December, when the twelve faced court martial, it may have been felt that the point had been made and further executions surplus to requirement. Although it also needs to be said that a man receiving 400 lashes was unlikely to live, dying in considerable pain.

While the six mutineers of *Caesar* had all been executed alongside each other at exactly 11.30 a.m. on the bow of *Caesar*, different arrangements were made for the larger number of *Glory* and *Defiance* mutineers, also ensuring that the executions could be clearly seen by crews from a large number of ships. From *Defiance*, while all eleven were executed on the same day, the hangings were conducted on five ships: *St George, Repulse, Le Tigre, Le Puissant* and *Resolution*. Each was utilised for this purpose with scaffolding erected on each of their bows. William Lindsey was hanged on *St George*; Nicholas Ryan and Cornelius Callaghan on *Repulse*; Thomas Laffin and Michael Kelly on *Le Tigre*; Richard Kennedy and Edward Swinney on *Le Puissant*; and John Brady, David Reed, Thomas Derbyshire and Edward McLaughlan on *Resolution*. Stationed in either Portsmouth Harbour or within the Spithead anchorage, the executions all took place in the morning between 9 a.m. and 11.30 a.m.. It was reported in several newspapers that 'the whole of them, to the last, protested their innocence, and met death with the most manly fortitude and becoming resignation.' Of the eight seamen on *Glory* sentenced to death, two ships were commandeered, the frigate *Thisbe* anchored at the mouth of the Hamoaze and *Captain* in Cawsand Bay, with four seamen executed on each ship:

> *At eleven o'clock this morning [27 October 1798], four Seamen, lately belonging to the* Glory, *of 98 guns, were executed on board the* Thisbe *Frigate, in Hamoaze, for attempting to excite a mutiny, and afterwards to murder the Officers belonging to that Ship; and at half past twelve o'clock four other seamen, lately belonging to the said Ship, were executed on board the* Captain, *of 74 guns, in Cawsand Bay, being implicated in the same horrible crime.*

Among those who witnessed the execution on *Captain* were the twelve of her crew awaiting trial, a point noted by several newspapers:

> *There are now on board the* Captain, *a number of her crew, in irons, for mutinous intentions, whilst on her last cruise, who, it is said, are to be removed to Portsmouth, preparatory to their being tried. These men, no doubt, were spectators of the melancholy fate of the deluded wretches turned off this day on board their ship; and if their minds are not too hardened, it may prepare them for the approaching prospect of a punishment that may await them, if convicted of the crime they now stand accused of.*

Although it was not always clear, for it was rarely formally reported, it seems that each man as he stood before the yardarm awaiting a tightening of the noose that would end his short time on earth, was given the opportunity of saying a few final words. Some, as with the *Defiance* mutineers, apparently protested their innocence. Others were stoic and resolutely confronted their fate, and one or two expressly forgave all who had had a part in bringing them to trial and passing a death sentence. Possibly Timmings or maybe Cormick were the exception, in that one of them, in stating that he was at peace with the world, did turn his venom on the man upon whose evidence he had been convicted, and upon whom he spoke with the strongest displeasure, hoping that upon him his former shipmates would take their revenge.

Following these executions, it was required that the body of each of the hanged should remain strung up for all to see for an hour before being cut down. Many officers, however, believed that some of those hanged for mutiny, because of the very seriousness of this action, with its potential to considerably weaken the navy, should remain much longer in chains after execution. This was the expressed view given at the court martial of John Evans, a corporal of marines, and James Dixon, both of *Saturn*, in 1797. However, on being referred to twelve judges for their opinion, they failed to sanction the judgement of the court, deeming it as derogatory to the authority of a naval court. In the meantime, Evans and Dixon had to wait five months before they were eventually executed.

Given the seriousness of mutiny as a charge, the string of courts martial did sometimes show a degree of compassion, especially for some of the accused from *Defiance*. While nineteen of the twenty-five were originally adjudged to 'suffer death by being hanged by the neck', of that number, eight were 'humbly' recommended for mercy, but on condition they be transported 'or such other conditional pardon as His Majesty shall be graciously pleased to grant.' Finally, five of the accused against whom it was considered that the charges had been only partially proved were to be flogged, two to receive 200 lashes and twelve months' solitary confinement and three to 100 lashes and six months' solitary confinement, with a fifth not to be flogged but to serve twelve months' solitary confinement. Just one of the twenty-five, John Donnelly, was acquitted.

The effect of these public executions or floggings around the fleet upon the thousands of seamen who were forced to witness them can only be surmised. Undoubtedly it did have the effect of discouraging shipboard mutinies from those least committed to a particular cause. Samuel Leech, a seaman in the British Navy who later wrote of his experiences, may well have witnessed the hanging of the six *Caesar* mutineers when writing of why mutinies were not a more frequent occurrence on board British warships:

'Why did not your crew rise in resistance to such cruelty?' is a question which has often been proposed to me, when relating these

facts to my American friends. To talk of mutiny on shore is an easy matter, but to excite it on shipboard is to rush on to certain death. Let it be known that a man has dared to breathe the idea, and he is sure to swing at the yardarm.

Here, in the following passage, Leech is almost certainly referring to the hanging of the *Caesar* mutineers:

Some of our men once saw six mutineers hanging at the yardarm at once in a ship that exhibited the incipient beginnings of mutiny. Let mutiny be successful, the government will employ its whole force, if needful, in hunting down the mutineers; their blood to the last drop, is the terrible retribution it demands for the offence. That demand is bound to be met, as was the case with the crew of the Hermione *frigate, and the crew of the ill-fated* Bounty, *whose history is imprinted on the memory of the whole civilised world. With such tragedies flitting before our eyes, who need ask why we did not resist?*

One officer ordered to take charge of the launch carrying a seaman punished to be flogged around the fleet later wrote of his feelings. Describing himself as an 'Old Officer of the navy' and written sometime around 1832, it seems likely he is referring to an episode that occurred during the lengthy period of war with France:

It was at a few minutes before eight o'clock in the morning, when the First Lieutenant of the ship ordered me to take charge of the launch, and see the punishment carried into effect. Had he given me orders to mount the sides of an enemy's frigate, at the head of a launch's crew, it would not have distressed me half so much, as I might have considered that my good luck might bring me a Lieutenant's commission; but here was a service devoid of honour and full of painful consequences, from which, however, there was no chance of escape.

I must needs obey; and the heaviest, bitterest hour of my life was when I stepped into the boat to superintend the infliction of 500 lashes on the back of poor Evan Evans, a half-idiot Welshman. The men on board were ordered up to the rigging, so that every person on board might see the whole operation. The Captain, taking off his hat, which was followed by all on board and in the boats, which were lying on their oars within earshot, then proceeded to read the sentence of the court martial. This effected, the Boatswain of the ship himself stepped into the launch; the blanket was removed from the culprit's shoulders, and he, the Boatswain, inflicted the first twelve lashes. The poor idiot screamed, and groaned, and struggled; but all this, like the struggles of the dying sheep under the knife of the butcher, passed unheeded. The Boatswain returned on board, and two Boatswain's mates came down and completed the number of fifty lashes.

This same scene was repeated first alongside the admiral's ship and then alongside two other warships in the harbour, with the writer emphasising his own feeling of disgust, condemning himself 'for ever becoming one of the many unfeeling wretches who were so seriously occupied in torturing this poor wretch.' And wondering also if others felt as disgusted as he did. Two hundred lashes had now been inflicted with a cat o' nine tails, the equivalent of 1,800 strokes:

At this period I gave the Doctor a hint, by asking the Master-at-Arm in a loud tone, how many lashes the prisoner had received. "Two hundred lashes, exactly, Sir," was the reply. I knew this very well, but, it answered the purpose; for I saw the doctor look at me, and then ordered him to be taken down.

Five weeks later the punishment was continued, Evans received a further 183 lashes before the surgeon finally deemed him incapable of taking any more, and the Admiralty later remitted the final 117 lashes. Nevertheless, the ordeal had proved just too much. Evans died a few months later, with the writer concluding that 'this was just what I expected: for it was clear that the first flogging had given the death-blow to the unfortunate Welshman.'

Among those of Irish Catholic descent, or others who agreed with radical political programmes, they would seethe with anger and frustration when forced to witness the tortured bodies and final death throes of Irish radicals and nationalists. For the bulk of English seamen, there may well have been a high level of approval, especially when it was known that oaths being taken by Irish mutineers included such wording as 'kill or destroy the Protestants'. This led to a distaste on the part of some crews when seamen on board a ship that had witnessed an attempted Irish mutiny were dispersed and placed on board other ships. Following the attempted mutiny on *Adamant*, many of the crew were sent on board other vessels, including ten sent to *Surprise*, the ship used during the following year for a cutting-out expedition that successfully saw the retaking of *Hermione*. On boarding *Surprise*, the seamen from *Adamant* were immediately ostracised, informed that 'they were mutinous rascals, and that they would neither admit them into their messes, or have the slightest communication with them whatever.' The ship's commander, Captain Hamilton, immediately turned the hands up, and, after highly commending their spirit of loyalty and attachment to their country, told them that they ought not let their zeal lead them into becoming unjust:

> *...that it was true that the* Adamant's *crew had behaved in a mutinous and very scandalous manner; but as the ringleaders had already met the punishment they so richly deserved, and as there was no positive proof or, indeed, any immediate reason to suppose that the men he had just received from that ship had been the least active in the mutiny, it would be highly unjust to consider them being of that number, at most they could be only regarded as suspicious characters, and might be watched accordingly. In the meantime, he strongly recommended to them to live amicably together; as for his own part, he had not the slightest doubt of their good conduct in future.*

Apparently this speech had the desired effect and, according to the various newspapers that reported it, 'all in a moment returned to harmony with the hope expressed that this will serve as a lesson to all ships that may fall into similar situation.'

Where mutinies had been successful, the Admiralty took what revenge it could. But when a ship was taken into an enemy port the task was more difficult, with many of the mutineers simply disappearing, never to be heard of again. Some stayed close to the enemy port in which refuge had been first sought, while a few, including some from *Hermione*, *Lady Shore* and possibly *Marie Antoinette*, sought and found refuge in the USA. Those at most risk were former mutineers who returned to sea – after all this, for the majority of those who mutinied, service at sea was their one and only trade. Of the *Lady Shore* mutineers, of which there were at least twenty-five, the Admiralty was able to take revenge on two, one of whom was Patrick Kelly who was Irish by birth and a private in the New South Wales Corps. At that time he was under punishment for desertion and had been offered release from prison if he agreed to take a posting to Botany Bay. Following the mutiny, and once he had received his share of the prize money,

HANGING, TRANSPORTATION AND THE LASH

he took passage in a French schooner bound for Isle de France. Unfortunately for him, this vessel was captured by a British warship and Kelly was taken to Jamaica. Here, in this lively sea port full of naval seamen, he was recognised and, following a brief trial, found guilty of complicity in mutiny and executed at Gallows Point, near Kingston.

A second *Lady Shore* mutineer, Jean Prevot, was executed in London at Execution Dock, which overlooked the Thames at Wapping, on 27 December 1799. He had been taken while aboard the French privateer *La Républicaine*, captured in the West Indies by the Royal Navy frigate *Tamar*. Not being a mutineer on a British warship, his send-off was different to that seen in the naval ports. The barge on which he was taken to Execution Dock was attended not by naval officers but by men of the City of London, including the water bailiff, who carried the silver oar, the sheriff, and the city marshals. Prevot had been found guilty of murdering James Wilcocks, the captain, through plunging a knife into his neck. Newspapers seemed particularly intrigued by Prevot's youthful looks and general demur and duly reported in *Saunders's News-Letter*:

> *Yesterday, about one o'clock, Jean Prevot was removed from Newgate prison to his sentence for the murder of Captain Wilcox [sic] of the Lady Shore transport to Execution Dock, attended by the Sheriff and city officers, where he was launched into eternity about three o'clock in the afternoon, amidst a vast concourse of people on the occasion. This unhappy culprit appeared not to be more than 17 years of age, and at the time he was removed from the condemned cell, was not the least affected with his situation. On entering the cart a settled smile appeared on his countenance, which continued, with momentary intervals, till he arrived at the place of execution.*

Chapter 17

Trial by Courts Martial

It was on Thursday 27 September 1798 that the eleven mutineers of *Defiance* were hanged in view of naval ships both anchored in Spithead and moored in the harbour. Among those launched into eternity was Thomas Derbyshire, a man who might so easily have avoided this fate if the courts martial system by which he was condemned had rules and processes that did not work so blatantly against the men of the lower deck as opposed to those of the quarterdeck. Effectively, he was condemned not by his own words, nor any of the witnesses brought by his captain, Theophilus Jones, who was the prosecuting officer. He was condemned by Luke Behanah, the single witness that Derbyshire himself had called for the purpose of proving his loyalty to both king and country.

The court martial was in its fourth day and for Derbyshire the trial was going reasonably well. He was one of the twenty-five seamen of *Defiance*'s lower deck charged with a multiplicity of mutinous acts that included organising a mutiny and uttering seditious words. Up until that day and the calling of a witness by Derbyshire for his own defence, all that had been said against him was that he had been frequently seen conversing with some of those who were standing trial alongside him. Admittedly, some witnesses called by Captain Jones claimed that he had taken the oath binding the mutineers to the taking of the ship, but Derbyshire claimed this not to be true. Instead, he suggested that the witnesses making this claim had been mistaken, confusing Derbyshire with another seaman, the oath being sworn in poor light. Daniel Lynch, a seaman of the lower deck, had made this claim on the first day.

As Lynch stood before the court, Jones asked him, 'Did all the prisoners take the oath in your presence?'

'No, not all of them,' came the reply. 'I saw Brady, Lindsey, Hopkins, Mahane, Dunn, Cannon, Reed, Derbyshire, Ryan, Callaghan, Kennedy take the oath.' Continuing to expand, Lynch added, 'Laffin had the book in his hand but whether he kissed it or not I cannot tell. I saw Devoy, McGuire, Hoare and McLauchlin also take the oath.'

It was a long list of names, and one that could easily be challenged on grounds of confusion and misremembering. Derbyshire, with Lynch still in the courtroom and sworn to tell the truth, was soon after given his chance to question that statement.

'Do you recollect who gave me the book to swear at the time you say the people were swearing?'

'Yes, it was David Reed,' responded Lynch.

'Was it day or night I took the oath?'

'It was betwixt the two lights.'

Again, a skilled legal practitioner would have made more of this, because in the half-light it was more than possible that Lynch had been mistaken. A further point that could have been made was that Lynch, in making a whole series of accusations against those now facing court-martial, was settling a vendetta. He too had been one of those apprehended by Jones on 24 August and placed in the coal hole, but had no liking for his fellow Irish compatriots. Not only had he clashed with Derbyshire on previous occasions, but he blamed him and several of the others on trial for his incarceration in the coal hole. To anyone who would listen, and before his release from the coal hole, he made it clear that he would get his revenge.

However Derbyshire, through having no courtroom experience, made little use of this earlier enmity and the possibility that Lynch was deliberately hostile and overkeen to gain favouritism with Jones. However, one prosecution witness called by Jones did present Derbyshire with the equivalent of a 'Get Out of Jail Free' card. On the morning of the third day Jones called another of his carefully selected witnesses for the prosecution, John Hall, English by birth and a man who had shown no previous sympathy with the mutineers. But in common with most of those of the lower deck, he was aware of what was being contemplated by a section of the crew, mostly Irish but some Jacobin sympathisers from mainland Britain. Turning his attention to Hall, Jones commanded him to relate to the court any expressions he had heard Richard Kennedy make use of while serving on *Defiance*.

'It was God bless and prosper the United Irish.'

'Where was Kennedy at that time?' asked one of the senior captains called to help determine a verdict on each man being court-martialled.

'Between the first and second gun on the starboard side of the galley between the hours of four and seven o'clock.'

'Did you discover any persons near him at the time he used the expression?'

'Yes, there was Thomas Derbyshire, Thomas Jourdaine and Edward McLaughlin. There were more, but I cannot recall them.'

After ascertaining that Kennedy had not reported this to any officer, giving fear that he would be set upon by members of the smoking club as his reason, Hall was asked one further question.

'Did the persons you have named as present when those expressions you have stated were made use or make use of any expressions of approbation or disapprobation?'

'Thomas Derbyshire said that that was too bad by God almighty.' This was the 'Get Out of Jail Free' moment. A witness called for the prosecution had certainly condemned Kennedy, another of the leading mutineers, but Hall had indicated that Derbyshire was much more mild-mannered, did not approve of the violent language sometimes being directed towards the English, and might be taken as one who was not supportive of taking *Defiance* into a French port.

This is how naval courts martial of the eighteenth century worked in practice. They had an outward appearance of fairness but were heavily weighted against any lower deck seaman who appeared before such a court. While a prosecuting officer such as Jones had an abundance of education and the support of fellow officers who made up the rest of the court, a seaman was very much on his own, dependent on his own native wit and determination. Jones could even call on professional legal advice, something denied to the ordinary seaman. Court proceedings were managed by a legal officer employed by the Admiralty who mixed in the same circles as the officers, but not men of the lower deck. This was the judge advocate general, there to present his opinions on the matter of civilian law and navy rules while helping push forward procedures to help the trial run smoothly. It was the judge advocate who took the minutes, read out the warrant that authorised the court to assemble, read the charges against those to be tried, and administered the oaths taken by each witness when called to give evidence.

In the case of Portsmouth, overseeing the court martial of those accused on *Defiance*, the judge advocate general was Moses Greetham (jr), a practising solicitor with prestigious offices in the centre of Portsmouth. He had originally been appointed deputy judge advocate for the navy in 1784 when only 22 years of age, but later promoted to judge advocate. At Portsmouth he officiated at some of the highest profile trials in naval legal history, notably those of Captain Bligh and the *Bounty* mutineers in 1792. At Plymouth where the *Caesar* mutineers were tried, the judge advocate was Sir Charles Morgan, a man equally experienced in matters of law having been called to the bar in 1750, four years later appointed a king's councillor, and also succeeding his father as deputy judge advocate before becoming judge advocate in 1770. Not all those appointed judge advocate had this same high level of experience, especially when courts martial were held on foreign stations. One known in particular to the author, a distant relative through his mother's side of the family, was John Philip Castang, who was Horatio Nelson's secretary and appointed by Nelson as judge advocate during one trial held in December 1796 at Corsica on a deserter. While a highly capable secretary, Castang had no legal experience whatsoever. Volunteering for the navy in 1793 (but more likely pressed), he was rated able, suggesting an earlier seagoing career. A merchant by trade, his mother owned a tobacconist shop in London's Tottenham Court Road. He was later to set himself up as a shopkeeper after his subsequent service in the navy as a purser.

As for the court itself, those who might otherwise be referred to as the judge and jury, this was entirely drawn from serving naval officers, men a world apart from the lower deck and whose sympathies would rest entirely with the prosecuting officer who had initiated the charges and with whose plight they would be in sympathy. At any naval court martial, those with the rank of captain of ships held in that port at the time a court martial was called were expected to attend and make judgement on the accused. Few excuses were accepted for a failure by a captain to attend, although on the calling of the *Defiance* court martial, two captains were given leave, one on the grounds of ill-health and the other because of already having received Admiralty leave from his ship. The captain who claimed illness, Sir Thomas Williams, commander of *Endymion*, before his absence was accepted had to have his ill-health confirmed on oath by his ship's surgeon's mate. As for the captains who were present to make judgement on those accused of mutiny on board *Defiance*, there were eight in total, each taking position behind a long table, three seated to the left of Captain John Holloway, second in command of naval ships at Spithead and Portsmouth and who sat as president of the court, and four to his right. At the far end of the table, taking copious notes and ready to offer legal advice, was Greetham. In front of the table was positioned a chair for witnesses when called to testify, with a further set of chairs to one side occupied by the accused. This arrangement in practice would be the same for a court martial held on all the seamen accused of mutiny during 1798.

Initially, the court-martialling of the accused on *Defiance* might have seen a greater number brought to trial than the twenty-five who were finally named. On 24 August, with Captain Jones having learnt that mutiny was being planned, he had called upon the ship's marine guard to apprehend over 100 seamen and one marine of the lower deck. These men he had placed in the ship's coal hole and after hold, but he was then forced to release many of them either because of having insufficient evidence or because some were willing to provide evidence against those with whom they had formerly conspired. Of that latter group, at least ten went some way further, agreeing also to give evidence in court against one or all of the twenty-five eventually charged. It is easy to see why they did so. Undoubtedly, the majority of them knew that they were equally culpable, and if they did not co-operate with Jones, they would be facing a similar charge of mutiny, knowing that the most likely penalty was hanging from the yardarm or flogging round the fleet. A further incentive given to them, and one eagerly accepted by most, was that of a discharge from the navy, ensuring that they never need return to *Defiance* and possible retribution by others of the crew who had once been members of the smoking club.

A question to which there is no definitive answer is how Jones went about selecting men to be tried and why some but not others were offered the possibility of exoneration if they gave evidence against their fellow conspirators. Some of those who did provide evidence had to admit that they had been members of the *Defiance* smoking club when mutiny was discussed or when toasts disloyal to the Crown and British Navy were drunk. Being present on such occasions was in itself a crime, unless immediately reported to an officer. When those witnesses were asked by the court why they had not reported what they now claimed to know and now willingly told the court, they usually claimed it was through fear of retribution from the main core of conspirators. One witness, George Turner, a corporal in the marine guard, told the court, 'I was afraid of them.' Apparently he went on to add, referring to Edward McLaughlin, one of the Irish conspirators who was later hanged, 'I was afraid because he was drinking last Christmas with another man and he knocked up a row in the berth before he went away.' Of two other conspirators Turner added, 'William Lindsey tried to kick me up as I came from under the half deck. I was afraid of James Lawless [who] used to get drunk and abuse me.' While Lindsey was one of the eleven to be hanged, Lawless was to be flogged around the fleet with 200 lashes. Another witness, John Hall, gave as his reason for not reporting seditious remarks he had heard, was a fear that members of the smoking club would 'afterwards hurt me'.

Going back to the question of what factors determined Jones to offer an amnesty to some but not others, much appears to have hinged on their ethnicity and religion. Jones himself was Irish but born into an elite Protestant family, the second son of Theophilus Jones, a member of the Irish House of Commons. Such a background created within him a significant prejudice against Catholics of his own country and, as a result, believing the plot on *Defiance* to have been generated wholly by Irish Catholics without any significant support by those of English, Scottish or Welsh descent. Why else would he fail to prosecute a number of seamen born outside of Ireland who were equally as culpable as those brought to trial? Among those he did not choose to prosecute was Englishman Jack Crow, the ship's armourer, a man often associated with the smoking club and who agreed to supply the conspirators with weapons. Similarly, John Longmore, Thomas Goldsmith, Thomas Downey and John Drinkwater, all English by birth, were referred to in the trial as frequently seen among the conspirators when planning the mutiny and within hearing distance of numerous disloyal toasts. Some of these men were undoubtedly Jacobins, who would as much welcome a French invasion of Ireland as did those Irish seamen whom he did prosecute. In truth, all those prosecuted by Jones, bar one, were Irish, while of those who can be identified as members of the smoking club, but not brought to trial, seven were English and one was Scottish. Of the remaining two, both admittedly were Irish, but one of them, Daniel Lynch, was a Protestant.

It was the early afternoon on the fourth day of the trial that Greetham was instructed to call into the courtroom Luke Behanah, a 49-year-old Londoner rated on the ship as a landsman. He was the witness previously named by Derbyshire, the witness who would effectively damn him in the eyes of the court. Quickly ushered into the room, Behanah found himself in a totally alien environment. Standing stock still, he was being carefully eyed by the eight senior naval officers of the court, together with the captain of *Defiance*, all members of a social class and with a lifestyle a million miles from his own.

'Luke Behanah?' Greetham promptly queried for the benefit of the court. 'You are now required to answer questions put to you. You will answer truthfully, and according to the oath you must now swear. Repeat after me.'

Having established that Behanah understood what was now required of him, Greetham proceeded to slowly read out, frequently pausing, the oath required of every witness brought before a naval court martial and as laid down in the official instructions of the Royal Navy.

'I Luke Behanah, do most solemnly swear,' Greetham begun.

'I Luke Behanah, do most solemnly swear,' repeated the nervous seaman.

And so it continued, With regular pauses:

> *I Luke Behanah, do most solemnly swear, that the evidence I shall give before the court, respecting the present trial, I will, whether demanded of me by question or not, and whether favourable or unfavourable to the prisoner, declare the truth, the whole truth and nothing but the truth; so help me God.*

Behanah and Derbyshire were mess mates, constantly eating and working together, with a trust borne over the three years that they had both served on *Defiance*. Why else would Derbyshire have called Behanah as his only witness? Surely Behanah could be trusted to say good words of his fellow mess mate. And doubtless that was what he intended, possibly regretting his effort at providing additional information beyond the question he was asked. Derbyshire rose from his chair, where he had been seated alongside the other defendants. As he put his first question, the others looked on disconsolately, some knowing that in the previous three days of the trial their fate, be it hanging or flogging, was sealed beyond question.

'Did you ever hear me,' asked Derbyshire, directing his gaze towards Behanah, 'make use of any bad expressions to the detriment of either king or government?'

'Never,' responded Behanah. And this was where Derbyshire expected his mess mate to stop. Maybe even add a few remarks that would strengthen this decisive answer, adding 'since all the time I've known him'. But the over-truthful Behanah continued.

'But once at dinner time, as I was leaving the gun room, I came to the mess to dinner.' Maybe at this point Derbyshire's heart began to sink. What was his only witness about to say? Certainly something that Derbyshire was not expecting, nor wished for. If they had had time to properly prepare, a meeting prior to the court martial perhaps he might either have warned Behanah of the consequences of what he was about to say, or not called him at all.

'They were contending,' continued Behanah in a relentless drone that was beginning to unnerve Derbyshire, 'about the disturbances in Ireland, how the English had used them in putting men and women to death.'

There was nothing Derbyshire could do to stop him. He simply did not have the legal training to interject with a further question hinting at Derbyshire saying nothing that would incriminate him.

'They asked me what I thought,' continued Behanah, a man who had sufficient nous to not implicate himself. His answer was that he threw the question back at them.

'What else can be expected? The Irish are killing the country.' And now came the bombshell. 'Derbyshire made answer and swore with an oath, if we came into action at any time he would give no assistance.' In other words, if *Defiance* was confronted by a French warship, Derbyshire would refuse to do his duty that required of him to work one of the guns.

This completely damned Derbyshire. To refuse to assist his shipmates when in action against an enemy warship was a simple hanging offence in its own right. To try and recover the situation, Derbyshire fired out another hastily thought-out question.

'Was I drunk or sober when I said this?' hoping that Behanah would say the former, so suggesting that Derbyshire would never say such a thing when in his right mind.

'Sober to all appearance,' came the answer, a final nail in Derbyshire's self-inflicted sentence of death.

Derbyshire, in being accused of swearing an oath that if *Defiance* came into action at any time he would not give assistance, was in breach of several of the Articles of War that had authority from various Acts of Parliament. These Articles, which could also be amended from time to time 'at the pleasure of the king', were displayed on every ship of the Royal Navy in a most public place and, as mentioned above, were required to be read to the entire ship's company at least once every month. In these Articles, almost every possible offence that could be committed in the navy was laid down alongside the punishment for committing the offence. For Derbyshire, according to Behanah's testimony, he was in potential breach of Article XII:

> *Every person in the fleet, who through cowardice, negligence, or disaffection, shall in time of action withdraw or keep back, or not come into the fight or engagement, or shall not do his utmost to take or destroy every ship which it shall be his duty to engage, and to assist and relieve all and every of His Majesty's ships, or those of his allies, which it shall be his duty to assist and relieve, every such person so offending and being convicted thereof by the sentence of a court martial shall suffer death.*

However, while this undoubtedly damned Derbyshire, the original charges of mutiny and making contact with an enemy or rebel were the ones of which he and the others were charged, all punishable by death and covered by several additional Articles, specifically Articles III, XV and XIX. Of these, Article III laid down:

> *If any officer, mariner or soldier, or other person of the fleet, shall give, hold, or entertain intelligence to or with any enemy or rebel, without leave from the King's Majesty, or the lord high admiral, or the commissioners for executing the office of lord high admiral, commander-in-chief or his commanding officer, every such person, so offending, and being thereof convicted by sentence of a court martial, shall be punished with death.*

Article XV:

> *Every Person in or belonging to the fleet, who shall desert to the enemy, pirate, or rebel, or run away with any of His Majesty's*

ships or vessels of war, or any ordnance, ammunition, stores, or provisions belonging thereto, to the weakening of the service, or yield up the same cowardly or treacherously to the enemy, pirate or rebel, being convicted of any such offence by the sentence of the court martial, shall suffer death.

Article XIX:

If any person in or belonging to the fleet shall make, or endeavour to make, any mutinous assembly on any pretence whatsoever every person attending herein, and being convicted thereof by the sentence of the court martial, shall suffer death: and if any person in or belonging to the fleet shall utter any words of sedition or mutiny he shall suffer death, or such other punishment as a court martial shall deem him to deserve: and if any officer, mariner or soldier, in or belonging to the fleet, shall behave himself with contempt to his superior officer, such superior officer, being in the execution of his office, he shall be punished according to the nature of the offence by the judgment of a court martial.

Courts martial, when appointed, were extremely disruptive of naval affairs, especially in wartime, it being a requirement that captains of ships in the port where the court was held were required to attend. Consequently, this prevented a large number of ships sailing, having to await the conclusion of the court martial and the return of each captain to his ship. The court martial appointed to try the *Defiance* mutineers sat from 8 to 14 of September (Sunday the 9th excepted), preventing eight ships returning to sea as well as *Defiance*, as Theophilus Jones, her captain, had also to be present at the trial.

To initiate a court martial, the first step was that the complaint being made against an individual or individuals had to be made in writing and, if in home waters, addressed to the senior naval officer of the port to which the ship had returned. In bringing a charge against those accused of mutiny on *Defiance*, Jones addressed his letter to Peter Parker, commander-in-chief of his majesty's ships at Portsmouth and Spithead. This letter had to include the names of those to be charged, the place, time and in what manner the act was committed. If the request for a court martial was approved, the commander-in-chief had to then pass these details to the judge advocate, who would examine each of the witnesses under oath, preparing copies of all statements made for the trial. In his letter dated 2 September, Jones named those he wished to bring to trial, more than thirty in number, stating it was 'for having previous to the ships putting out from Cawsand Bay in the month of July last held a mutinous assembly or meeting on the starboard side of the galley of the said ship at which…an oath was taken,' with Jones then providing the wording of that oath.

At the trial itself, and following the taking of evidence from witnesses, Moses Greetham reduced the number against whom he considered there was sufficient evidence to twenty-five, arraigning against them a number of specific charges. These charges were read to the court shortly after it came into session, those named being John Brady, William Lindsey, John Hopkins, James Mason, Christopher Mahane, Terence Dunn, Thomas Jourdaine, James Cannon, David Reed, Thomas Derbyshire, Nicholas Ryan, Cornelius Callaghan, Owen McCartey, Richard Kennedy, Thomas Laffin, Patrick Devoy, John Donnelly, Peter McGuire, John Hoare, Edward Swinney, Patrick Hynes, Michael Foy, Michael Kelly, and Edward McLaughlan, all seaman, together with James Lawless, a private in the ship's marine guard.

Having read the names of those being court-martialled, Greetham enumerated the charges now brought against them:

> …*For making and endeavouring to make such mutinous assemblies as aforesaid on board His Majesty's said ship* Defiance, *for uttering words of sedition and mutiny and for concealing mutinous practices and designs and traitorous and mutinous words spoken to the prejudice of His Majesty's government and words, practices and designs tending to the hindrance of His Majesty's service and for being present at a mutiny and seditious meetings or conspiracy without using their utmost endeavours to repress or reveal the same.*

At this point all of the witnesses, to be called by Jones and any by the defendants, would be present in the courtroom, but on the charges having been read would be ushered out into a waiting area to be called in as and when they were required to give evidence. As in the case of Behanah, before giving their evidence, each would need to swear the oath as read to them by Greetham. For examining witnesses at a naval court martial, the procedure was laid down in *Naval Regulations and Instructions* under Article VIII:

> *In the examination of witnesses the following method is to be observed: first, to call such as are in support of the charge, who are*

to be questioned by the accuser, if any, the court, or judge advocate, and afterwards by the party upon trial. Such as are produced to invalidate a charge are next to be examined, and the party accused is to begin with his interrogatories, if he shall think fit. If a question proposed is objected to, the opinion of the court is to be admitted or dropped as the majority shall agree.

As confirmed by Article VIII, any individual so named was then permitted to ask questions of the witness. But few had the skill to make full use of this right, some merely asking if they were sure they were correct in the accusation being made.

The first witness to be called was Laurence Carroll, Jones' chief witness who established the case against all the prisoners with but just one exception, that of John Donnelly. Indeed, it is difficult to see why Donnelly, other than being Irish and against whom Jones had a prejudice, was included among the prisoners in the first place, given that none of the thirty-one witnesses called by Jones implicated him in any way, other than his being seen in the company of some of the mutineers. This the court also recognised, passing on Donnelly a verdict of not proven, so releasing him at the end of the trial to rejoin his ship. As required, before giving his evidence, Carroll duly took the oath, with Jones asking him first if he knew the names of the prisoners who had been called out.

'Yes,' Jones responded before pointing to each in turn and naming them.

'Do you know that the prisoners were present at a meeting held at the starboard side of the galley in the month of July last before the ship sailed from Cawsand Bay with Sir Alan Gardner?'

'I do but I cannot swear positively to John Donnelly being there and I am not sure that Cornelius Callaghan and even McCartey was there.'

'Do you know,' came the follow-up question from Jones, 'that an oath was taken by the remainder of the prisoners except John Donnelly, Cornelius Callaghan and Owen McCartey?'

'I did.'

Carroll, under continuing questioning from Jones, did later also provide evidence against Callaghan, but not against McCartey. When asked by Jones to relate any seditious or mutinous expressions he had heard made by any of the prisoners, he referred to the letter he had written to his brother, Laurence, in which he had wished that the rebels had been defeated.

'Cornelius Callaghan told me,' Carrol explained. 'I ought to be knocked down for I was no Irishman for writing such a letter.'

A few minutes later he added, 'Callaghan often drank the health of the United Irish and hoped that they had Spike Island at the entrance to Cork Harbour.'

Under questioning, Carroll outlined the wording of the oath, an oath that he himself had taken, saying that it had been administered to him by Lindsey. Yet in saying this, Carroll had implicated himself in the mutiny and, as such, was guilty of a serious felony and liable to the death sentence. Of course an agreement had been struck between Carroll and Jones that allowed Carroll's role in the planned mutiny to be swept aside. This, of course, on condition that he provide evidence against the other prisoners. As to why he had taken the oath, Carroll had a ready explanation, stating to the court, 'When I made a scruple to take the oath, McLaughlin and Reed said that my life would be taken if I did not and everyone that did not. They brought me into it.'

While other witnesses were also to confirm that McCartey, Callaghan and Donnelly may not have taken the oath, McCartey and Callaghan, unlike Donnelly, were to be found guilty, Callaghan sentenced to be hanged and McCartey to 100 lashes and six months' solitary confinement. According to one of Jones' witnesses, and whom the court chose to believe, McCartey had often stated that he would rather that the United Irish would get the better of the king's army. Of Callaghan, another witness reported him as giving the toast, 'Success to the United Irishmen and may they gain their ends.'

Doubtless Jones was most determined to ensure that there was sufficient evidence against the core Irish leadership of those who had planned to take the ship. Among these appear to have been Lindsey, Brady and Reed, with Jones using a number of the witnesses to demonstrate their guilt. Carroll had confirmed them as mutineers, referring to Reed as one who had threatened him if he did not take the oath. Daniel Lynch told of Reed expressing a wish that the French might land in Ireland. It was Lynch, who had been present at the oath taking, who also confirmed that it was Lindsey who had both recruited many into the mutiny scheme and had sworn them in with the oath, including Lynch himself. To Lynch, who it will be remembered was an Irish Protestant, Lindsey had offered this as encouragement.

'Daniel Lynch,' Lindsey reportedly said. 'There are many Jacobean Protestants in the ship to get free of their slavery and confinement.'

'If I was there, in Ireland,' he told Lynch on one occasion, and referring to the rebel army, 'I would be worth one hundred of their officers. I could teach them how to make signals and the telegraph,' Lindsey continued, still referring to the rebel army. 'They would know from one hill to another over all Ireland the same as our admiral knows his fleet or squadron.'

As evidence of Lindsey and Brady being leaders, Lynch told how they were the ones who organised the meetings, appointing lookouts to ensure they were not surprised by an unwanted intruder. Lynch himself acted as lookout when the oath was being sworn over a Catholic prayer book.

'He [Lindsey] and Brady put me at the station to look out and warn them if anybody came they would conceal the book.'

According to Lynch, Brady and Lindsey were as one in supporting the United Irishmen in their fight for an independent Ireland. They both agreed that if the French did land it would save many Irish lives from further English atrocities. This, in turn, was supported by numerous other witnesses called by Jones, with two of those witnesses reporting that Brady had at one time avowed that he would be quite happy to rise from his hammock one midnight to cut the throat of a Presbyterian.

William Thomson, Jones' third witness, confirmed that it was Lindsey who had administered the oath to him, also relating the wording of the oath. On being asked by Jones if he had had any particular conversations with Lindsey, Thomson responded in the affirmative. 'Lindsey said that he wished that all the United Irish might survive and win the day.'

Over the five days, the evidence supplied by Jones' thirty-five witnesses against the prisoners steadily mounted, although one witness selected by Jones must have had second thoughts, not wishing to inform on his fellow shipmates in such a public forum. This was James Mason, who was probably a black seaman, for of one thing he did report was that of being frequently woken at night and called 'a black bugger' by Laffin and Dunn, prisoners who would later receive the death penalty but with the latter recommended to the mercy of the king. Other than that he would testify of hearing or seeing no more against any of the named prisoners, something that Jones was not expecting. To such questions as 'have you had any oath proposed to you within the last six months' and 'did you see all the prisoners assemble together' or 'have you not observed that Lindsey was notoriously busy amongst them', his stock answer was the single word 'no'. Jones, having previously met Mason, was expecting a series of answers that would continue to weigh against the prisoners, and he became increasingly annoyed, with the court eventually ordering that he be confined on the grounds of his 'reluctance in answering the questions' and afterwards cautioned by the court 'to be more careful in his conduct for the future'.

The reluctance of a witnesses to give evidence against a fellow seaman in court, and despite an agreement that they would provide such evidence, was a scene played out in several of the trials. In failing to produce anything other than a series of monosyllabic answers when called by Captain Elphinstone of *Diomede* to testify against George Tomms and John Wright, Marine Sergeant Daniel Alexander was punished by the court with three months in the Marshalsea Prison. His crime, that of 'prevaricating'. Similarly, seaman Jonas Brown of *Amelia* was given, during the trial of Robert Larken and Dennis Broughall, a three-month sentence of solitary confinement in the Marshalsea Prison for also having prevaricated.

Finally, on the fifth day of the *Defiance* trial, 13 September, with all the witnesses having been called, both those brought forward by Jones as well as the prisoners, the court was cleared to allow the captains present to reach a verdict upon each of the individuals who had stood before them. The procedure for determining a decision was laid down in a set of instructions for service at sea, with the judge advocate general normally required to draw up a set of agreed questions to help determine 'the innocence or guilt of the person upon trial'. To help ensure that the more senior officers did not unduly influence the junior officers of the court, when taking opinion on any matter as regards these questions, 'the youngest officer shall vote first, proceeding in order up to the president.' In finding any of the accused to be in breach of any of the Articles of War established by law, the court then had to consider the punishment to be given, again with each captain present voting in accordance with their age, the youngest first. How any disagreement was fully resolved, other than by further discussion and voting, is unclear, and it is likely that the views of the more senior would prevail over those of the more junior captains.

Derbyshire, the man who probably could have avoided the fate of execution if the court martial system had not been so heavily weighted against him, had at least been given a small amount of time to prepare his defence, although in calling Behanah he achieved nothing more than a sentence of execution. Thomas Boyd, the marine guard found guilty of attempting to help Thomas Guthrie, a seaman accused of mutiny on *Princess Royal*, to escape incarceration on the ship, was given even less opportunity to prepare his defence. St Vincent, his commander-in-chief, as noted, was one who insisted that a man accused of a crime worthy of a court martial should be tried with urgency. Fairness did not seem to enter into St Vincent's thinking, with the gap between the discovery of a supposed mutinous act and the resulting trial compressed into a minimal amount of time. In the case of Marine Boyd, no more than four days elapsed between his being placed in irons and his execution on 7 July. The trial, held on 6 July on board *Prince* while off Cadiz, lasted no more than a few hours, with the court arriving at its decision before the end of the day, adjudging Boyd 'to suffer death by being hung by the neck until he is dead by the yardarm.'

As commander-in-chief on a foreign station, St Vincent was allowed to assume powers not available to those commanding the home fleets, so permitting him to determine both the date of holding a court martial and the sanctioning of a date for the carrying out of sentences. He, of course, always chose the following day for an execution, with Boyd hanged from the yardarm of *Princess Royal* on 7 July. Most problematic for Boyd, irrespective of his guilt or otherwise, was that of him learning of the charges against him on the afternoon of the 5th, giving him only eighteen hours (assuming he took no sleep) to prepare his defence. As with Derbyshire, he was not permitted to meet with any witness he might choose to call, trusting that any witness produced would respond favourably to a series of unrehearsed questions that would be put to him while under oath. In his own hastily written words, produced for the benefit of the court, Boyd made it clear that he had been given very little time to prepare his defence:

> *I most humbly beg to state that when the judge advocate gave me a copy of the charges yesterday [5 July] and for which I am now brought before you for trial, he, I am certain, saw my astonishment, as well as might my captain, the prosecutor.*

As with Derbyshire, Boyd's questioning of both his and the prosecution witnesses, through his own basic lack of any legal skills, was lame to say the least, often going no further than asking them to confirm that he was a seaman of good character and that none directly overheard him plotting to release Guthrie. Evidence against him was, at the most, circumstantial and underpinned by hearsay, with the case against him lacking any real foundation. St Vincent, even if he had gone to the effort of reading the minutes of the court martial, had little interest in overruling the product of such an unfair trial, for his interest was that of instilling fear into the hearts of the lower deck, and for this Boyd was no more than a sacrificial lamb.

Returning to the trial of the twenty-five accused of mutiny on *Defiance*, nineteen were sentenced to be hanged, of which eight were recommended 'to His Majesty's Mercy on condition of transportation, or such other conditional pardons as His Majesty shall be graciously pleased to grant.' Against four other prisoners, where it was considered that their transgressions were only part proved, two were to receive 200 lashes and twelve months' confinement in either the Marshalsea Prison or a prison hulk, and two were sentenced to 100 lashes and six months' solitary confinement. The lashing, in all four cases, was to be on their bare backs 'with a cat o' nine tails on board of or alongside such of His Majesty's ships and vessels for the time being at Portsmouth.' One of the accused, again because of the charge not being fully proved, was to be confined for twelve months and was not to be lashed, while Donnelly, the charges against him having not been proven, was acquitted.

Once Greetham, as judge advocate, had drawn up in writing these sentences, they were approved and signed by each member of the court before the accused were re-admitted to hear the sentences given. Finally, it was the duty of the judge advocate to send the original sentences and the minutes of the court martial to the secretary of the Admiralty for the information of the Board of Admiralty and retention.

Jean Prevot, one of the two *Lady Shore* mutineers who had fallen into the hands of the Admiralty following the capture of *La Républicaine*, on which he had been using the assumed name of Jean Sanlard, was hanged in public at London's Execution Dock. Through him being a French citizen and not mustered to a British warship, he underwent a civil trial held in the Admiralty Division of the Old Bailey. Widely reported in newspapers, as indeed had the mutiny itself, it is the newspapers that provide the only available detail of the course of the trial and what the defendant and witnesses said when giving evidence. The chief witness brought forward to testify against Prevot was Minchin, the ensign who was in overall command of the military detachment assigned to *Lady Shore*, who told the court that he had been awoken at around quarter past four on the morning of the mutiny by 'a great noise and disturbance a-head'. This induced him to proceed to the hatchway, which he found to be battened down with the captain lying beneath, 'weltering' in his own blood.

'What is the matter?' Minchin asked the captain. To this he received no answer, claiming that he carried the captain to his own bed, where he saw his wounds dressed by the surgeon.

Minchin, of course, was concealing the fact that he was, at the time of the captain having been stabbed, hiding with his wife under his bed, and that Wilcocks had made his own way into Minchin's cabin. Semple would later tell of this in his published account, but this would not be available for general reading for several years. Black, in his account, which had already been published, confirms that Minchin and the captain were both present in Minchin's cabin at this time, so it is possible that the rest of Minchin's evidence is correct, although of this there can be no certainty as Minchin had already lied to the court.

'The captain,' Minchin then stated to the court, 'said, that when he heard the noise a-head, he ran out, and coming to the ladder next the hatchway, he felt a wound from a bayonet in the breast. Proceeding a little farther, he [Captain Wilcocks] was met by French Jack.'

Here Minchin was using the name by which Prevot had been generally known while aboard *Lady Shore*, going on to say that it was 'French Jack, who stabbed Wilcocks with a bayonet in the neck.'

Doubtless the jury and other members of the court were shocked by this revelation, with Minchin adding that as soon as it was daylight he went out and saw Prevot standing sentinel on the hatchway.

'He was standing at the hatchway with a brace of pistols at his sides, a cutlass in his hand, and on his head the hat which Captain Wilcocks usually wore when on board.'

Over the next fifteen days, before Minchin and others were set adrift in the ship's longboat, Minchin informed the court that Prevot often stood sentinel at the hatchway and was always active in the mutiny. To this he added that in his hearing, and while speaking to one of the Irish mutineers, Prevot had frequently boasted that this was not the first mutiny in which he had been concerned nor that Captain Wilcocks was the first man whom he had assassinated. Apparently this declaration was made in the English language.

Several other witnesses were called, all of whom had shared the indignity of being cast adrift in the ship's longboat and had now, along with Minchin, returned to England in 1799 following negotiations by the British government with the Spanish government in Madrid. None were present in the cabin when Wilcocks supposedly indicated Prevot as the man who inflicted the last wound upon him, but several agreed that they had heard Prevot boasting of being involved in an earlier mutiny and Wilcocks not being the first man he had killed. Robert Welsh, a private in the New South Wales Corps, testified to 'frequently' seeing the captain in the cabin following the attack upon him, with Wilcocks telling him that it was Prevot who had stabbed him in the neck. Welsh further said that he had, and again using the word 'frequently', seen Prevot on deck armed in company with the other mutineers. At other times he had seen Prevot acting as a sentinel over a cannon loaded with glass and ready to be fired should any of the loyalists attempt to retake the ship.

Another of the witnesses, Frances Hughes, the wife of Sergeant Hughes and who was accompanying him to Botany Bay, told of how she had heard Prevot boasting to some of his fellow mutineers that 'he had finished the bastard', referring to Captain Wilcocks. While this may have been her wording, another newspaper, the *St James Chronicle*, reported her as having given Prevot's words as 'Damn him. I finished him. I stabbed him in the neck – he was not the first I served in my time.'

Prevot was not really in a position to call any witnesses for his own defence, as those who might have offered any counter statements would have been men who the Admiralty would be looking to prosecute. In general, it would appear, Prevot showed little interest in defending himself, only claiming that he had been forced to take part in the mutiny and had not murdered Wilcocks. Had Semple been called as a witness, he would at least have undermined some of the evidence given by Minchin as to Prevot's guilt. But with several witnesses having claimed to have heard Prevot boasting of his attack upon Wilcocks it is unlikely that he would have received anything other than a death sentence. As to Prevot's reaction to his fate, it was reported that he 'seemed wholly to disregard the sentence, and laughed in the face of the court as soon it was pronounced.'

Conclusion

What Might Have Been – A Personal View

The taking of British warships into enemy ports by discontented or politically motivated crews, while rare, was during the French Revolutionary War an occurrence much feared by the Admiralty. Apart from those ships discussed in this book, and putting aside for one moment the attempted Irish mutinies of 1798, there is much evidence that on other British warships similar actions were discussed by portions of their crews. *Pompée*, one of the most active ships during the mutiny at Spithead, saw a petition drawn up calling for the removal of Prime Minister William Pitt and an end to the war with France. This, in itself, was an extremely radical move that, if successful, would have changed the very nature of the governmental process in Britain. In taking this action, some of the lower deck also went a good deal further, threatening to sail the ship while off Ushant into Brest. Prior to the North Sea fleet mutinying and joining the rebel fleet at the Nore, an earlier mutiny had been foiled on board *Inspector*, a 16-gun sloop. It was a plot uncovered on 24 May while the ship was in the port of Hull. According to Charles Lock, her captain, the object was to sail the ship to France, but the mutiny only to be enacted when *Inspector* had sailed and had 'got below the *Nonsuch*', a former 64-gun ship that was serving as a floating battery at the port's entrance. Lock also accused one of the mutineers, Thomas Potts, of saying that they would, 'take the ship off to France and that the officers may then stand clear, for that he would stick a knife in any bugger that did not stick by them, was he certain of going to the yardarm next minute.'

According to Lock, 'Many other mutinous words were spoken by Potts to the ship's company recommending them to leave off work and to cut a man down whom I [Captain Lock] was going to punish.'

In 1797, *Inflexible*, widely regarded as the most radical and committed vessel of the ships in mutiny at the Nore, fired her guns on other ships when their crews appeared to be wavering in their support for the mutiny. At the time *Inflexible* also had on board delegates who were threatening to take the ship to France or find refuge in Ireland. Leading Nore mutineer William Gregory declared, 'Is there not many among you here as fit to be our sovereign as George Rex? He has power and we have the force of gunpowder.'

Lieutenant Forbes of *Sandwich*, the parliament ship at the Nore, indicated that red cockades were worn by the most prominent mutineers, signifying that 'between forty and fifty of the ship's company [*Sandwich*] might have worn them at different times.' The taking of ships to some neutral port was supposed to have been considered by Richard Parker and other delegates towards the end of the mutiny. To prevent the taking of ships from the Nore into an enemy port by some of the most militant crews, the Admiralty instructed Trinity House to remove the navigational buoys that lined the Thames, so leading to the possibility of a ship sailing for France instead running on to one of the many sandbanks that littered the estuary.

That *Pompée, Inspector*, nor any of the ships in mutiny at the Nore did not attempt to break for France was primarily because those who favoured such a radical action were very definitely, at this point in time, a very small minority. By contrast, *Hermione, Danae* and the other British warships taken into enemy ports had, whether resulting from the mutineers being of a radical persuasion or otherwise, a sufficient number of men favouring this very idea, able to overpower those crew members who remained loyal. These were also ships operating independently of the main fleet, ensuring that interception by larger and more powerful units of the British Navy was unlikely, an important factor in the successful taking and sailing of each ship into a French or Spanish port.

In reality, though, just how close did any of the ships of the planned Irish mutinies of 1798 come to be taken to France and what were the problems that would be confronted once any ship had been taken? While the actual number court-martialled and punished in some way was a relatively small proportion of each ship, a much larger number were initially taken and placed in irons with a likely larger number of sympathisers on each ship going undetected. As to whether this would have produced a number sufficient to take a ship and hold on to that ship until it reached a French port is a question impossible to answer. However, helping boost those numbers was that traction for a ship-board mutiny or rebellion came not from just those who thirsted for the freedom of Ireland or radical political change in mainland Britain but from among those with other resentments, such as enforced impressment or lack of shore leave. It is possible, therefore, that the numbers necessary to take one of those ships upon which a revolutionary cadre had been formed might well have existed. If so, and with all other factors favourable to such an outcome, the objective might just have been achievable.

Of course Irish Catholics of the lower deck, immersed as they were in all-pervading anti-English sentiments, were the element on a British warship most favourable to the taking of that ship into an enemy port. While this unity of culture was a point of strength, it was also a major point of weakness, inhibiting the accord that needed to be developed between all who were discontented. On board *Caesar*, it was the disunity of sectarianism that primarily led to the planned mutiny failing on the very eve of it being actioned. On some ships, however, both Irish republicans and discontented English did work alongside each other. In part, this was an outcome of the radical societies in mainland Britain and links created with the Society of United Irishmen. Through a process of constant messaging, these societies, in combination, helped create an underlay of revolutionary thought that was often powerful enough to overcome entrenched sectarianism of the individual. While none of those radical societies in England or Scotland, unlike the United Irish, had reached a point where they could be seen as a vanguard party able to assume a leadership role in fermenting revolution, they were nevertheless highly active and well organised. Prior to the naval mutinies of 1797 the London Corresponding Society not only had branches in all the key naval towns, which of course included London, but had sent to Chatham and Portsmouth two of its leading members, John Binns and John Gale Jones, who addressed numerous meetings in and around these two key areas for the recruitment and retention of seamen.

How then might the mutinies on the various ships that had formed revolutionary cadres, particularly those of the Channel fleet, if actioned by a sufficient number have been played out? Beginning here with the officers, would the majority have been slaughtered as occurred on *Hermione*? Certainly there was a call for this to happen. Yet this has to be weighed against time available. If ships had been captured close to the French shoreline, time might not have been available, or once having taken the ship the desire to kill might have been seen as an unnecessary act for the purpose in hand. Once brought into a French port, all officers would have been treated as prisoners-of-war, even offered freedom to live outside of a prison if they gave their surety that they would not attempt to escape. As for the loyalist seamen of the lower deck, they would have been sent to a prison camp from where there was the possibility of an early return to England under a prisoner exchange agreement.

An essential task following the taking of any ship would have been its successful navigation into a French port, most obviously Brest. If taken through the Goulet and into the Rade de Brest, any vessel would have been secure from attack by other elements of the British fleet. On board *Defiance*, and according to William Lindsey, the mutiny leader, 'any man in the ship could carry her [*Defiance*] into Brest [as] it was a broad deep water,' appointing John Hopkins, one of the Irish rebels, to steer the ship into Brest. This, however, was an incorrect assumption. The Goulet through which *Defiance* would need to pass was a treacherous stretch of water. Attempting to pass through on anything other than a flowing tide or positioning the ship too close to the centre of the Goulet passage would both prove hazardous, with the ship likely to run aground and end up a complete wreck. Other naval ports on the Atlantic coast, including La Rochelle and Orient, were equally as difficult to navigate, so confronting rebel crews with similar access problems. Regan on *Glory*, of course, gave this more considered thought, selecting an unnamed but competent member of the ship's crew as master for taking the ship into an enemy port. That *Hermione* was successful in sailing a distance across the Caribbean of 500 miles to enter the port of La Guaira was a result of the ship's master proving, under extreme duress, sufficiently co-operative to take sightings of the sun and establish the ship's exact position. For ships of the Channel fleet, if taken by their crews, the most obvious solution would be that taken by the crew of *Danae*, of alerting the authorities ashore as to the mutineers wishing to enter the Rade for the purpose of surrendering the ship and there await the arrival of a pilot. However, that in itself would take time, with the possibility that her desertion, having been reported to the main fleet, could result in a determined attack by ships still loyal and untroubled by the threat of mutiny.

Making contact with the French would have been relatively easy, if only by flying a white flag or a French *Tricolore* over the Union flag and which would have been quickly spotted by lookouts stationed at one of the many forts and batteries lining the coast. As to the reception the mutineers might have received, this would have been considerably better than the *Hermione* mutineers did at La Guaira, where the Spanish viewed the taking of a ship by mutiny quite abhorrent. France, however, would have been very different. Proby, following the loss of *Danae*, quickly informed his superiors upon his return to England that the French were in hope 'of getting possession of our entire fleet in the same way'. Indeed, in 1798, with the French in the process of preparing ships at Brest for an invasion of Ireland, they would have doubtless been fulsome in welcoming the mutineers, with their arrival in Brest eased by the presence of Wolfe Tone. Holding the rank of *chef-de-brigade*, Tone was fully engaged on work associated with the sailing of the third expedition to Ireland and which departed Brest on 16 September under the naval command of Vice-Admiral Jean-Baptiste-François Bompart (1757-1842). Should any ship succumbing to mutiny have entered Brest, or any other French port prior to the sailing of the expedition, it would have greatly strengthened French resolve and the re-use of those ships in the expedition against Ireland would have given the expedition that did sail a greater possibility of success.

The French, of course, would have willingly paid reward money to those bringing in such prized ships as a first, second or third rate of the Channel fleet, aware that such payments would act as a spur to other warship crews who were on the verge of joining a mutiny. Given, also, that these ships would have been brought into a French naval port specifically for the cause of Irish freedom, it seems not unlikely that the French would have wanted to make greater use of those seamen on board who wished to continue serving at sea. Admittedly none was capable of commanding a ship of war, but many were highly skilled seamen, and some would have had a considerable knowledge of the waters around Ireland. Even more important, these men would have brought considerable intelligence regarding the size of the blockading force that lay off Ushant when it was most likely to be at sea, and the use made of Cawsand Bay and Spithead as revictualling anchorages. Here, both Charles O'Neal and John Brady would have been extremely useful having mixed with the officers of the *Glory* and *Defiance* quarterdecks in their roles as ships' barbers.

While one ship being detached from the Channel fleet might not have had an especially terrible impact upon the course of events in the English Channel, the loss of five, six, seven or eight ships would have been nothing less than a disaster. At the very least, the British Navy would have lost some 4,000-6,000 skilled seamen at a time when recruiting seamen into the navy was, to say the least, somewhat challenging. In addition, the Channel fleet could really only oppose the French Navy if it was of a size equal to the number of ships available to the French. With the French able to assemble twenty or more warships, with an additional number from the British Navy, this would have made the French Navy in the Atlantic almost unassailable. To this number can also be added the ships of the Batavian Navy, still a sizeable force even after the Battle of Camperdown. However, not all of any newly acquired British ships might have been available for an invasion of Ireland as the French also had difficulty in recruiting seamen. But certainly, some would have been available. If nothing else it might be assumed that most of the Irish seamen, maybe as many as 800, would have joined the ranks of the French Navy in a determined effort to free Ireland from British rule.

Here, though, I do need to make it clear that it was most unlikely, even if each of the plots had not been discovered, for the plan to take a fleet of British ships into enemy ports to meet with success. At the outside, a particularly determined large number of Irish crew and radical revolutionaries from mainland Britain might just have taken one or two ships into enemy ports. But it is unlikely that these would have been the larger ships such as *Caesar, Captain, Defiance, Diomede, Glory* or *Neptune*. Much more vulnerable were the smaller vessels

WHAT MIGHT HAVE BEEN – A PERSONAL VIEW

serving in detachment from the main fleet and with smaller crews. Nevertheless, to the United Irishmen, in formulating a plan to encourage Irish republicans to enter the Royal Navy alongside Irishmen already serving on the lower decks of British warships, it was a plan designed to hit at the very heart of the English-based establishment and the means by which it held power. If the Royal Navy could not effectively patrol the seas around the British coastline, or if the French Navy was placed in a stronger position, then the sea lanes to Ireland lay wide open. Here, to once again quote Wolfe Tone, 'It is in Ireland, and only in Ireland that she [England] is weak.' Upon the landing of a large force of French troops, a much larger number than were landed at Bantry Bay or planned to be landed off Tory Island, Ireland would have fallen. Tone had said a French Army of 20,000 was desirable, adding that he would even accompany 'a corporal's guard'. Such would have been a staggering blow to England, making invasion of the mainland so much easier, leading in turn to the eventual fall of England.

Bibliography

Primary Sources

British Library Newspaper Library
Caledonian Mercury
Chester Chronicle
Derby Mercury
Exeter and Plymouth Gazette
Hampshire Chronicle
Ipswich Gazette
Ipswich Journal
Kentish Weekly Post or Canterbury Journal
London *Gazette*
London *Times*
Madras Courier
Manchester Mercury
Morning Chronicle
Morning Post
Oxford Journal
Reading Mercury
St James Chronicle
Salisbury and Winchester Journal
Saunders's News-Letter
Staffordshire Advertiser

The National Archives, Kew (TNA)

ADM1/102	Letters from Flag Officers, Channel Fleet: 1795
ADM1/107	Letters from Flag Officers, Channel Fleet: 1797
ADM1/524	Letters from Commanders-in-Chief, North Sea: 1797

BIBLIOGRAPHY

ADM1/727	Letters from Commanders-in-Chief, Nore, 1797
ADM1/1518	Letters from Captains: Robert Barlow
ADM1/3685	Letters from the Solicitor of the Admiralty and other Crown legal officers, 1797
ADM1/5337	Courts Martial Papers, *Defiance* mutiny of November 1795
ADM1/5339	Courts Martial Papers, April-June 1797
ADM1/5343	Courts Martial Papers, January-March 1798: Ferrier of *Defiance*; Broughall and Larken of *Amelia*; *Adamant* Mutineers
ADM1/5345	Courts Martial Papers, Timmings and Cormick of *Haughty;* Richard Jones of *Princess Royal*
ADM1/5346	Courts Martial Papers, August-September 1798: *Defiance*
ADM1/5347	Courts Martial Papers, Tomms and Wright of *Diomede;* Charles O'Neal of *Queen Charlotte;* the several accused of mutiny on *Glory,* Richard Cole of *London,* Peter Anderson of *Marlborough*
ADM1/5486	Courts Martial Papers: Nore Mutiny, 1797
ADM1/6034	Naval intelligence papers, 1798-1801
ADM36/11909	Muster Book: *Defiance,* 1795
ADM36/11931	Muster Book: *Saturn, 1798*
ADM36/12492	Muster Book: *Amelia, 1798*
ADM36/12495	Muster Book: *Glory, 1798*
ADM36/12567	Muster Book: *Neptune,* August-September 1798
ADM36/12751	Muster Book: *Caesar, 1798*
ADM36/14439	Muster Book: *Defiance,* 1798
ADM36/15214	Muster Book: *Diomede,* 1798
ADM51/1206	Captain's Log, *Defiance,* April 1797
ADM51/1241	Captain's Log, *Impetueux,* May-June 1798
ADM51/1272	Captain's log *Amelia,* 28 August 1797–31 August 1798
ADM52/2695	Master's log *Amelia,* 28 August 1797–27 August 1798
HO42/212	Letters and Papers. Correspondence relating to Post Office, Customs, Excise
PC2/197	Records of the Privy Council, 1815
PRO30/8/331	Letters of Lord Westmoreland, as Lord Lieutenant, 1790-96

National Archives Scotland (NAS)

GD 26/15/55	Resolutions and Constitution of the Society of United Scotsmen, a society for promoting an equal representation of all the people in Parliament, 1797

Parliamentary Papers (PP)

Royal Commission on Irish Education, First Report of the Commissioners, 1825

Printed Books and Papers

Bartlett, Thomas, 2011, *Ireland: A History* (Cambridge: CUP)
Bartlett, Thomas, 1985, Select Documents XXXVIII: 'Defenders and Defenderism in 1795' in *Irish Historical Studies*, Vol. 24, No. 95 (May, 1985), 373-394
Black, John, 1798, *An Authentic Narrative of the Mutiny on Board the Ship* Lady Shore (Ipswich)
Byrn, J., 2009, *Naval Courts Martial, 1793-1815* (Navy Records Society)
Carleton, William, 1834, *Traits and Stories of the Irish Peasantry* (Dublin: W.F. Wakeman)
Cashel, Alice M., 1925, 'Education in Ireland in the 18th Century' in *The Irish Monthly*, Oct., 1925, Vol. 53, No. 628, 513-518
Corbett, Julian S., 1913, *The Spencer Papers*, Vol. II (London: Navy Records Society)
Forester, C.S. [ed], 1994, *The Adventures of John Wetherell* (London: Michael Joseph)
Frykman, Niklas, 2020, *The Bloody Flag: Mutiny in the Age of Atlantic Revolution* (Oakland: University of California Press)
Hardie, Elsbeth, 2019, *The Passage of the Damned: What happened to the men and women of the* Lady Shore *mutiny* (North Melbourne: Australian Scholarly Publishing)
Hawkins, Anne & Watt, Helen, 2007, 'Now is our time, the ship is our own, huzza for the red flag: Mutiny on the Inspector, 1797', in *The Mariner's Mirror*, 93:2, 156-179
Jones, John Gale, 1797 (republished 1997), *A Political Tour Through Rochester, Chatham, Maidstone, Gravesend etc* (Rochester: Baggins Book Bazaar)
Kennedy, W. Benjamin, 1974, 'Catholics in Ireland and the French Revolution' in *Records of the American Catholic Historical Society of Philadelphia*, September, December, 1974, Vol. 85, No. 33 and 4
Konstam, Angus, 2020, *Mutiny on the Spanish Main: HMS* Hermione *and the Royal Navy's Revenge* (Oxford: Osprey Publishing)
Laughton, J.K., 1906, *Letters and Papers of Charles, Lord Barham, 1758-1813*, Vol. I (London: Navy Records Society)

BIBLIOGRAPHY

Lavery, Brian, 2020, *Nelson's Navy: The Ships, Men and Organisation, 1793-1815* (Oxford: Osprey Publishing)

Leech, Samuel, 1844, *Thirty Years From Home or a Voice from the Main Deck* (Boston: Tappan & Dennet)

Lyons, Tony, 2016, 'Inciting the lawless and profligate adventure' – The Hedge Schools of Ireland in *History Ireland*, Vol. 24, No. 6, 28-31

MacDougall, Philip, 2013, *London and the Georgian Navy* (Stroud: The History Press)

MacDougall, Philip, 2020, 'L'estuaire de la Tamise et les eaux côtières du Kent' in Histoire Économie et Société 39anné(1): 59-77

MacDermot, Frank, 1939, *Tone and His Times* (London: Macmillan)

Madden, R.R., 1842, *The United Irishmen, Their Lives and Times* (London). Also available at: https://archive.org/details/unitedirishmenth11madd

Mahan, Alfred, 1902, *Types of Naval Officers Drawn From the History of the British Navy* (London: Sampson Low)

Mason, William Shaw, 1819, *A Survey of Tullaroan* (Dublin: Faulkner Press)

Maxwell-Stewart, Hamish (2013) 'Those Lads Contrived a Plan' Attempts at Mutiny on Australia-Bound Convict Vessels in Anderson, Claire [Ed], Frykman, Niklas [Ed], Lex Heerma van Voss [Ed], Marcus Rediker [Ed], 2013, *Mutiny and Maritime Radicalism in the Age of Revolution: A Global Survey* (Cambridge: Cambridge University Press)

McArthur, John, 1805, *Principles and Practice of Naval and Military Courts Martial* (London). Also available at: https://archive.org/details/principlesandpr00margoog

McDowell, R.B., 1943, *Irish Public Opinion, 1750-1800* (Westport: Greenwood Press)

McDermott, Frank, 1968, *Theobald Wolfe Tone and His Times* (Dublin: Anvil Books)

McFarland, E.W., 1994, *Ireland and Scotland in the Age of Revolution* (Edinburgh: University Press)

Mewett, Ryan E., 2017, *Commissioned Officers' Place in Late Georgian Society* (unpublished MA thesis: Faculty of Humanities and Social Sciences, University of Portsmouth)

Morris, Roger (ed), 2001, *The Channel Fleet and the Blockade of Brest, 1793-1801* (London: Navy Records Society)

Morris, Roger (2011), 'Crew Management and Mutiny' in MacDougall, P. and Coats, A.V. [ed], 2011, *The Naval Mutinies of 1797: Unity and Perseverance* (Woodbridge: Boydell Press), 106-119

Nicol, John, 1822, *The Life and Adventures of John Nicol, Mariner* (Edinburgh: W. Blackwood)

Osler, Edward, 1854, *The Life of Admiral Viscount Exmouth* (London). Also available at: https://archive.org/details/lifeofadmiralvis00oslerich

Pfaff and Hechter, 2020, *The Genesis of Rebellion: Governance, Grievance, and Mutiny in the Age of Sail* (Cambridge University Press)

Pope, Dudley, 1963, *The Black Ship* (London: Weidenfeld and Nicholson)

Pope, Dudley, 1987, *The Devil Himself* (London: Martin Secker & Warburg)

Roger, Nicholas, 1986, *The Wooden World: Anatomy of the Georgian Navy* (London: Collins)

Roger, Nicholas, 2021, 'The Politics of Mutiny: The *Pompée* at Spithead and beyond, 1797' in *The International Journal of Maritime History* Vol. 33(3) 464–488

Saxby, R.C., 1960, 'The Escape of Admiral Bruix from Brest' in *The Mariner's Mirror*, 46:2, 113-119

Semple, James, 1799, Excerpt from *Memoirs of the Northern Imposter, or Prince of Swindlers: Being a Faithful Narrative of the Adventures and Deceptions of James George Semple, Commonly Called Major Semple, Alias Harrold, Maxwell, Grant, &C. &C* (London)

Slope, Nick, 2011 'Discipline, Desertion and Death: HMS *Trench*, 1796-1803' in MacDougall, P. and Coats, A.V. [ed], 2011, *The Naval Mutinies of 1797: Unity and Perseverance* (Woodbridge: Boydell Press), pp. 226-42

Spinney J.D., 1956 'The Danae Mutiny', *The Mariner's Mirror*, 42:1, 38-53

Strauss, E., 2022, *Irish Nationalism and British Democracy* (London: Routledge)

Thompson, E.P., 1968, *The Making of the English Working Class* (Harmondsworth: Penguin)

Tone, Theobald Wolfe, 1791, *An Argument on Behalf of the Catholics of Ireland* (Dublin). Also available at: https://archive.org/details/argumentonbehalf00tone

Tone, William Theobald Wolfe, 1826, *Life of Theobald Wolfe Tone* (Washington: Gales & Seaton). Also available at: https://archive.org/details/lifetheobaldwol01tonegoog

Tucker, Jedediah Stephens, 1844, *Memoirs of Admiral the Right Hon[orabl]e the Earl of St. Vincent* (London: R. Bentley). Also available at: https://archive.org/details/memoirsadmiralr01tuckgoog

Webb, Alfred (1878) *A Compendium of Irish Biography* (Dublin: Gill & Son). Also available at : https://archive.org/details/compendiumofiris00webb

Weber, Paul, 1997, *On the Road to Rebellion: United Irishmen and Hamburg, 1796-1803* (Dublin: Four Courts Press)

BIBLIOGRAPHY

Electronic

Davis, Michael T., 2008, London Corresponding Society available at https://doi.org/10.1093/ref:odnb/42297 [accessed February 2023]

Lee-Jane Giles, 2016, Research tells tale of 1797 Plymouth Channel squadron mutiny at https://www.plymouth.ac.uk/news/research-tells-tale-of-1797-plymouth-channel-squadron-mutiny [accessed March 2023]

First Report of the Royal Commission on Irish Education (1819) available at https://archive.org/details/op1244151-1001 [accessed June 2022]

'Political and Administrative History: Political History to 1832', in A History of the County of Warwick: Volume 7, the City of Birmingham, ed. Stephens, W.B. (London, 1964), pp. 270-297. British History Online http://www.british-history.ac.uk/vch/warks/vol7/pp270-297 [accessed April 2023]

Discussion of Sources

Prologue: *Vive la République!*

While as indicated the events described in and around the Rade de Brest on the seventh of *Fructidor* in Year VI (24 August 1798) of the calendar of the revolution are fictional, the account is based on real events played out by other British naval warships such as *Danae* and *Albanaise* that were taken into enemy ports (see Chapter 15). The presence of Wolfe Tone and the names of some of those complicit in the taking of *Defiance*, a ship which, during that year, very definitely had on board a revolutionary cadre, is based on fact, facts extracted from the court martial papers and the muster book that lists all members of *Defiance's* crew. However, as for 24 August being the one in which *Defiance* came into the Rade, this in truth was the day that the planned mutiny on *Defiance* was uncovered with over 100 seamen and one marine of her crew arrested as complicit.

Chapter 1: The Ships

Reliance for this chapter has been placed primarily on various contemporary official documents located at the National Archives (Kew) and which include letters to the Admiralty from flag officers of the Channel fleet for both 1795 (the first *Defiance* mutiny) and 1797 (the fleet mutinies) together with letters from Admiral Duncan, the commander-in-chief (North Sea), the captain's log of *Defiance* (April 1797), papers relating to *Inflexible* and her role as a leading ship at the Nore in 1797, and court martial papers, April-June 1797 (*Defiance* mutineers). Letters sent by seamen or their friends and families that were intercepted by the government are also to be found at the National Archives, held under correspondence relating to the Post Office (see primary sources as given above). Contemporary newspapers also provided essential background detail, including the *Chester Chronicle* (5 May 1797), *Ipswich Journal* (22 April 1797), *Kentish Weekly Post or Canterbury Journal* (21 April 1797) and *Portsmouth Gazette* (26 June 1797).

DISCUSSION OF SOURCES

Chapter 2: The People of the Ships

For more detail on impressment and the social hierarchy on board a naval warship of the late eighteenth century, particular use was made of Mewett (2017) and Rogers (2010), while I have also explored the same subject in one of my earlier books, MacDougall (2013). The quote by James Oglethorpe was taken from his own pamphlet 'The Sailor's Advocate', as reproduced in Bromley (1974 pp.71-84) but originally published in 1728. For the discussion on the value of quota men I referred to Dugan (1966, p.62), Lavery (2020, p.128), Lewis (1960, pp.116-27), Kindleberger (1992, p.18) and Slope (2011, p.257). On the nature of officers and different attitudes between the Channel and Mediterranean fleets, both Mahan (1901) and James (1950) proved invaluable while the specific reference to the frigate *Thames* and Admiral Cockburn was drawn from Morris (2011, pp.108-9 and 116-7). The quote taken from Niklas Frykman can be found on page 60 of his book *The Bloody Red Flag* while the correspondence between Kempenfelt and Middleton was taken from Laughton (1906, pp.299 and 306). For the activities of Theophilus Jones, captain of *Defiance*, use was made of both the *Defiance's* captain's log book and papers from the court-martialling of twenty-five of the crew that he prosecuted for mutiny in 1798.

Chapter 3: Harsh Laws and Discrimination

An important element in the call to arms spurring many Irish Catholics into rebelling against the English hegemonic control of Ireland, and certainly a factor encouraging the planning of mutinies on board British warships, were the hedge schools, and for these schools I drew detail from Lyons (2016, p.28), Carleton (1834, pp.234-6), Mason (1819, p.148), Dowling (1968, p.48) and Cashel (1923, p.513). The First Report of the Royal Commission on Irish Education is available online (archive.org) to which I especially referred to pages 755-6. Much has been written on the penal laws of Ireland and their impact upon Catholic society, and I can do no more than recommend Bartlett (2011) as further reading on this subject.

Chapter 4: The Society of United Irishmen

In assembling the views of the various strata of late eighteenth century Irish society, of particular value were McDowell (1943), Strauss (1951) and Kennedy (1974, p.222). Background and quotes accorded to Wolfe Tone were drawn from

Curtin (1985, pp.463-6) and Tone's own writings as given in Bartlett (1985, p.375) and McDowell (1943, p.215). On increasing radicalism as identified by the Earl of Westmorland I quoted from a letter sent to Pitt dated 4 January 1793 (Pitt Papers). On Defenderism I referred to Bartlett (1985), and for Tone's time in America and France I leaned upon McDermott (1968) and Tone (1826).

Chapter 5: 'Mankind are naturally friends to each other'

John Gale Jones' own account of his presence in Chatham, attending meetings of local corresponding societies and boarding a prison hulk to speak to French prisoners, was republished in 1997 with background detail in the introduction that I wrote. His greeting to these prisoners, *'je suis Anglois, mais je suis un Citoyen. J'aime votre Patrie, and je souhaite qu'elle seroit libre'* translates as 'I am English, but I am a citizen. I love your country, and I wish it to be free.' Government-acquired information on the activities of the corresponding societies and other radical groups during the period of the English Reign of Terror are to be found at the National Archives (Kew), to which I drew upon HO42/41 (ff. 98, 298-11, 213-16, 298) and also made use of the Constitution of the Society of United Scotsmen held at the National Archives Scotland (GD26/15/55). Quotes from Thompson and Roger appear in Thompson (1968 p.162) and Roger (2001 p.475). McCarthy's overstay in London is recorded in further documents held at Kew, ADM1/3685 (17 June 1797) and ADM1/727 (25 July 1797) while references relating to radical and revolutionary activities within the fleet at the time of the Nore mutiny and referred to here are to be found in ADM1/5340 (12 July 1797), ADM1/3685 (minutes of the court martial of James Lewin) and ADM1/5486 (minutes of the court martial of Thomas Jephson). Also proving of value for the writing of this chapter: McFarland (1994) and Graham (2000).

Chapter 6: The Blockade of Brest

The discussion on the value of Ushant as the fleet rendezvous when blockading Brest is informed by Morris (2001, pp.2-21), with Morris also discussing the difficulty of large ships sailing to Ushant from Spithead and the more advantageous geographical location of the Sound. The quoted document from Berkeley dated 16 April 1799 is from Morris (2001, pp.356-7), as is the quoted letter from Keats to Warren (Morris, 2001, p.151).

DISCUSSION OF SOURCES

Chapter 7: Bantry Bay

For the actions of the Channel fleet during the vital period covered in this chapter, reliance was placed on the correspondence of Lord Bridport and Naval Intelligence papers, both held at the National Archives (see bibliography above). Also consulted: Morris (2001) and Elliott (1982).

Chapter 8: *Amelia* and *Haughty*

A number of newspapers carried details of both the mutiny at the Cape and the execution of James Dixon (seaman) and John Evans (marine corporal) of *Saturn*. In particular for these two events I drew upon the *Hampshire Chronicle* (30 December 1797) and the *Kentish Weekly Post* (19 December 1797). In describing the mutiny on board *Amelia*, I made particular use of documents held at the National Archives (Kew), including her captain's log, master's log and muster book alongside the minutes taken of Broughall and Larken's court martial (ADM1/5434, 8-9 March 1798). The words and expressions of Larken and Broughall as quoted are the sentiments they expressed, a point also made by those giving evidence and so not necessarily the exact words. The description of the execution of Broughall and Larken was taken from the *Hampshire Chronicle* (24 March 1798). For the planned mutiny by Timmings and Cormick on board *Haughty*, the minutes of their court-martialling (ADM1/5345) and letters from Captain Smith (ADM1/1518/50 f.111-2) proved invaluable, as did a newspaper account appearing in the *Kentish Gazette* (17 July 1798). Timmings and Cormick were both hanged at Spithead in full view of the fleet on Thursday 12 July 1798.

Chapter 9: All Not Well Within the Fleet

Events described as taking place on *Marlborough* are documented in letters to Bridport from his captains and also in various newspaper reports including the *Hampshire Chronicle* (8 July 1797). Newspapers also frequently reported the apprehension of British seamen found on captured French warships and privateers. The five Nore seamen delegates in Hamburg were also reported in newspapers, including the *Ipswich Gazette* (10 March 1798). Bourdon's report to the Directory is to be found in the French archives, but here requoted from Frykman (2020, p.178). Details of the known plots and preparations for the planned mutinies on the several ships of the Channel fleet are once again taken from the court martial papers held at the National Archives (Kew) and listed in the bibliography above under 'Primary Sources'.

Chapter 10: *Captain*

All actions described, including conversations and places where meetings took place and other statements made, are based entirely on the minutes taken during the course of the court-martialling of twelve seamen of *Captain*. Some additional detail was provided by *Captain's* ship muster book. References for these are listed in the bibliography above under 'Primary Sources'.

Chapter 11: Organisation and Leadership

Material relating to the mutineers on board the various ships referred to is drawn from the minutes made of various court martials and ship muster books as listed in the bibliography above under 'Primary Sources'.

Chapter 12: *Caesar, Defiance, Glory* and *Neptune*

For the writing of this chapter, reliance again was placed on the minutes of the courts martial of those accused of mutiny on board *Caesar, Defiance, Glory* and *Neptune* but supplemented by ships' muster books and contemporary newspaper reports. Details of these sources are provided in the bibliography above.

Chapter 13: Cadiz! Our Country

In providing an account of the threatened mutinies on ships under the command of St Vincent, one source proved invaluable: the notes written by Benjamin Tucker who joined the Mediterranean Fleet as a purser on board *London*, but later appointed by St Vincent as his secretary. These notes were subsequently edited and published by his son Jedidiah Tucker. See bibliography, with this chapter informed by pages 312-341. In particular, Tucker provides much

DISCUSSION OF SOURCES

detail on the arrival of both *London* and *Marlborough* off Cadiz, with details provided by Tucker supported by the minutes of Peter Anderson's court martial (ADM1/5344, 28 May 1798) and the court martial of Richard Cole (ADM1/5347, 18-19 October 1798). Tucker's reference to 'a very violent mutiny' breaking out in Bantry Bay can be found in Tucker (1844, p.304). *Regulations and Instructions Relating to His Majesty's Service at Sea*, otherwise known as the Articles of War, are reproduced in Byrn (2009, pp.23-4). The court considered there was insufficient evidence to convict Richard Cole of 'endeavouring to incite the ship's crew to mutiny', but it is clear that *London's* captain, John Purvis, felt that there was a plot in hand to release the prisoner and that matters were to be taken a lot further (see ADM1/5347). Following *Ville de Paris* returning from Cadiz to Portsmouth, four Irish marine privates were also court-martialled for uttering treasonous remarks and were sentenced each to 500 lashes around the fleet, Dugan (1966, p.429). Details of charges against Michael Connell, Thomas Guthrie, Daniel Sweeny, Thomas Boyd and Thomas Bott (alias Batt) are filed under ADM1/5434. Boyd, the marine, was charged with attempting to murder his marine lieutenant, for the purpose of releasing Guthrie who had already been placed in irons for attempting to organise a mutiny. The primary evidence given against Boyd was him having several conversations with Bott.

For *Diomede*, apart from contemporary newspaper reports, considerable reliance was placed on the minutes of Tomms and Wright's court martial and the ship's muster book. Thompson (1968) and Stephens (1964) provide detail on the strength of the Nottingham Corresponding Society.

Tucker (1844) and Captain's Log, *Impetueux*, May-June 1798 are the sources used for the *Impetueux* mutiny. Bearhaven rather than Berehaven (*Baile Chaisleáin Bhéarra*) results from spelling as used in those documents.

Chapter 14: *Il a mort pour la liberté*

Two first-hand accounts, both used in the writing of this chapter, provide insight into the mutiny and how it was organised: Black (1798) and Semple (1799). That female convicts had found for themselves lovers from among the seamen or soldiers was confirmed by Jean Baptiste Deseal, and reported in several newspapers including the *Ipswich Gazette* (7 December 1799), when he was brought back to England in 1799, Deseal admitting that on the night of the mutiny he had been sleeping with one of the convict women. The New South

Wales Corps was a prison guard regiment formed to serve in New South Wales, and often recruited from the worst elements of society.

Chapter 15: Bloody Mutiny

The *Hermione* mutiny is well documented by James (1822), Pope (1963) and Konstam (2020). The courts-martial papers of the several *Hermione* mutineers are located at the National Archives, especially for the years 1798 to 1801. For the mutiny on *Marie Antoinette*, reliance was placed on several newspaper accounts including the *Oxford Journal* (11 November 1797). The *Danae* mutiny is best covered in Spinney (1956) and Pope (1987), while the reference to Fieney is to be found in the court-martial minutes ADM1/5356 (10 June 1801). Finally, for *Albanaise* I was reliant upon ADM1/5360 (Jacob Godfrey, court martial), ADM1/5361 and ADM1/5362 (5 October 1802), court-martial of P. Kennedy, the *Naval Chronicle*, Vol. 8, p.347 and The London *Times* (19 Oct 1802).

Chapter 16: Hanging, Transportation and the Lash

The final fate of many of the mutineers was primarily drawn from newspaper reports usually provided by local correspondents who may well have witnessed the hangings from a distance. In particular, I drew upon the *Hampshire Chronicle* (10 September 1798), *Staffordshire Advertiser* (21 July 1798), *Chester Chronicle* (5 October 1798 and 1 November 1798), *Oxford Journal* (3 November 1798), *Chester Chronicle* (20 July 1798) and *Madras Courier* (4 July 1798). The speech made by Captain Hamilton of *Surprise* was reported in several newspapers, including the *Manchester Mercury* (31 July 1798), the *Ipswich Journal* (28 July 1798) and the *Oxford Journal* (28 July 1798). Leech provides his account in Leech (1843, p.89). For the execution of Prevot see the *Salisbury and Winchester Journal* (2 August 1802) and *Saunders's News-Letter* (28 December 1799).

Chapter 17: Trial by Courts Martial

The primary sources for this chapter are the hand-written minutes of the *Defiance* court martial produced by Greetham and held at the National Archives

DISCUSSION OF SOURCES

(ADM1/5346) and, to a lesser extent, minutes taken of several of the other courts-martials involving attempts to take ships into enemy ports. Regarding procedures followed at a naval court martial, this is detailed in *Regulations and Instructions Relating to His Majesty's Service at Sea* and reproduced in full by Byrn (2009 p.23). All references to Thomas Boyd's trial are drawn from the minutes of his court martial (TNA ADM1/5343, 6 March 1798). For the trial of Prevot, reliance was placed on *Saunders's News-Letter* (27 December 1799), *St James Chronicle* (21 December 1799) and *Chester Chronicle* (27 December 1799).

Conclusion: What Might Have Been – A Personal View

Only a very limited amount of new material was used for the writing of this conclusion, with details relating to the mutiny on *Inspector* taken from Hawkins & Watt (2007), while the brief mention of the Nore mutiny relied upon the Nore courts-martial papers as referred to in the bibliography above.

General Index

A

Acts of Parliament, 53, 119, 167
   Quota, 21
   Seditious Meetings, 49
   Treasonable Practices, 49
Admiralty, Board of, xii, xiii, 4,–5, 13, 17, 19, 23, 34, 64, 68–9, 71, 73, 84–7, 94, 139–40, 145, 152, 175, 179
American Revolutionary War, 23, 129
Articles of War, 147, 151, 167, 173, 195
Associated Friends of the Constitution, 52

B

Bantry Bay, 46, 63–8, 123–4, 183, 195
Bastille Day, 42, 120
Batavian Republic, 64, 118–19
Bearhaven, 123–4, 195
Binns, John, 50–1, 53, 180
Bligh, Captain William, 15–16, 162
Botany Bay, 125, 129, 140, 158, 176
Bounty payments, 21, 26, 95
Bourdon, Léonard (French Agent), 84–5, 193
Brest, 46, 63–8, 71, 122
   blockade of, 4, 59–62, 86–8, 100
   description of, 57–8
   navigation into, 89, 94, 97, 102, 181
   reception of mutineers, xvi–xxi, 142–3, 146
Bridport, 1st Viscount Alexander Hood, xx, 3, 6, 62, 64–5, 193
   actions, Spithead mutiny, 6, 65–6
   asks for a return of Irish on ships, 23
   disposes ships against French invasion, 66, 68, 100–101, 122
   receives letter from *Impetueux*'s crew, 123–4
   relaxed attitude to discipline, 25, 108
Buonaparte, Napoleon (future Emperor of France), 95
   Egyptian expedition, 67, 122

C

Cadiz, xiv, 94, 110–1, 112–14, 116–18, 173, 195
Calder, Vice-Admiral Rober, 112
Cape Clear, 67–8, 122
Castang, John Philip, 163
Castlebar, 78, 163
Cawsand Bay, 85, 100, 103
   rebel meetings, 92, 95, 97, 169–70, 182
   revictualling station, 68, 73, 85, 90, 94, 123
   yardarm hanging, 76, 154
Channel Fleet, *passim*

GENERAL INDEX

Chatham, 3, 95, 132
   Visit of John Gale Jones, 50–1, 180, 192
Cockburn, Admiral George, 26, 191
Collingwood, Vice-Admiral Cuthbert, 21
Collooney, 47–8
Colpoys, Vice-Admiral Sir John, 63–4
Curtis, Rear-Admiral Sir Roger, 29, 67, 113–14

D
Defenders, 41–5, 134, 139, 192
Dublin Castle, 35, 40, 43, 47
Duncan, Admiral Adam, 11, 15, 30, 65, 118–19, 190

E
Eaton, Capt. John, 82–3
Ellison, Capt. Joseph, 83, 113–15

F
Flogging, 30, 47, 92, 166
   Caesar floggings, 149–51
   Description of, 157
   Hermione floggings, 138
   Impetueux floggings, 123–4
   Marlborough floggings, 114
   tool of social control, 27, 164

G
Galloway, Alexander, 51
Gallows Point, Kingston, Jamaica, 159
Glasgow Society for Burgh Reform, 52
Goulet de Brest, xix, xx, 71, 100, 142, 180
   Danae, entry through, 143
   defences, 72
   hazards of navigating, 62, 181

Graham, Aaron, 51
Grain, Isle of, 9

H
Hangings, xii, 5, 69–70, 85, 88, 147, 155, 196
   Albanaise, 145
   Amelia, 73–5
   Articles of War punishment, 111
   Caesar, 149–51, 156
   Defiance (1796), 15, 153–4, 160, 164, 166, 171, 174
   Glory, 153–4
   Haughty, 80, 153, 193
   Hermione, 140
   Impetueux, 124
   Lady Shore, 175
   Nore mutineers, 13–14
   St Vincent's frequent use of, 109–112, 114–16, 173
   Saturn, 155
   Tone, Wolfe, 48
Hamburg, 66, 84–5, 193
Hardy, Capt. Thomas, 26
Home Office, 11, 47, 49
Howe, Admiral Richard, 1st Earl Howe, 4, 7, 10

I
Impressment, 18–19, 72–4, 88, 128
Ireland,
   Cromwellian massacres, 36
   hedge schools, 35–8, 191
   Norman Conquest, 35–6, 38
   Presbyterianism, xviii, 35
   Protestants and Protestantism, xix, 36–7, 39, 41–4, 47, 97, 101–102, 134

Roman Catholic, 42–5, 96, 116,
133–4, 157
  Clergy, 42
  discrimination against, xviii,
35–6, 38–40, 164
  landowners, 42
  societies, 39
    See also Defenders
Williamite Wars, 36–7

J
Jackson, Revd. William (French agent), 45
Jervis, John, 1st Earl of St Vincent, 26, 89, 108, 173–4, 194
  attempted assassination of, 116–17
  criticism of Channel Fleet, 29
  disciplinary methods, 24, 108–17, 124, 153
  reputation, 25
  separates marines from seamen, 121
Jones, Capt. Theophilus, 54–5, 97, 99, 102, 161–5, 171–3
Jones, John Gale, 50
Judge Advocate General, xiv, 162–3, 168, 170, 173–5

K
Kempenfelt, Rear-Admiral, 27–8, 191
Kilcummin, xi, 11, 47, 68
Killala, 48

L
Leith Road, 15–16, 96
Lisbon, 110, 112, 116
London Corresponding Society, 50, 180

M
Marshalsea Prison, 41, 76, 172–4
Master-at-Arms, xiii, 9, 149–50, 152, 157,
Mediterranean Fleet, xiii, 1, 61, 88–9, 146, 194
  discipline in, 7, 24–7, 108, 110, 112, 121, 191
  planned mutinies in, 94, 112, 116–18
Middleton, Charles 1st Lord Barham, 28, 191
Minchin, Ensign William, 125, 127–30, 134
  testimony against Jean Prevot, 175–7
Mona Passage, 137
Montevideo, 107, 126, 131, 133, 141

N
New south Wales, xii, 107, 125
New South Wales Corps, 125–8, 132–4, 158, 176, 195–6
Nore Mutiny, 9–15, 30, 65, 69–71, 82–4, 98, 118, 191–3, 197
  London Corresponding Society and, 50–1
  radicals/revolutionaries and, 21, 51–2, 178–9
  Richard Parker's secretary at, 142
Northern Star, 43
North Sea Fleet, viii, 27, 34, 178

O
Orde, Rear–Admiral Sir John, 7
Ouessant, *see* Ushant

P
Paine, Thomas, 21
Penal laws, 38–44, 191

Pigot, Capt. Hugh, 137–42
Pitt, William, 6, 11, 21, 45, 65, 178, 192
Plymouth, 7, 9, 29, 73, 83, 88–9, 145, 151–2, 162
    dockyard, 6–7, 60–1, 72, 74
    flagship, 149
    North Corner Street, 88– 90, 92
    Sound, 4, 7, 10–11, 16, 59, 82
Pointe de Mathieu, xix, xx
Portsmouth, 4–10, 25, 28–9, 127, 134, 162–3, 168, 174, 195
    Binn, Johns, at, 50–1, 53, 180
    dockyard, 60, 94
    Harbour, 6, 153–4
    receiving ship, 95
    Spithead mutineers at, 51–3
    United Irish Club, 20
    United Irish delegate at, 84
Press gangs, 18–19, 72–4, 88, 128
Prevot Prison, Dublin, 48

Q
Quota Acts, 21

R
Rochefort, 67–8

S
St Vincent, *see* Jervis, John, 1st Earl of St Vincent
Savoy Military Prison, 128, 133–4
Semple, James, 125, 128–32, 175, 177, 195
Ships
    Convict Transport
        Ann, 136
        Friendship, 135
        Lady Shore, 107, 125–36
        Minerva, 135

Naval, British
    Adamant, 4, 15, 79–80, 88, 157–8
    Ajax, 123
    Albanaise, 137, 144–5, 190, 196
    Amelia, 4, 71, 74–7, 82, 84–5, 87, 172, 193
    Atlas, 7, 8–9
    Bounty, 16, 148, 162
    Britannia, 13, 112
    Caesar, xiv, 4, 7, 85, 88, 90–1, 94–5, 97–8, 100–106, 149–51, 153, 155, 162, 180, 182, 194
    Calypso, 26
    Cambridge, 70, 76, 103, 149–51
    Captain, 85, 87–94, 99–100, 106, 112, 153–4, 194
    Danae, 137, 142–6, 179, 181, 190, 196
    Defiance, xiv, xvi–xxi, 4–5, 7, 10, 15–16, 27, 54–5, 85, 87, 90–1, 94–9, 100–106, 153–5, 160–74, 180, 182, 190–1, 194, 196
    Diadem, 112
    Diomede, xiv, 87, 118–22, 153, 172, 182, 195
    Director, 15
    Dryad, 72
    Edgar, 7–9
    Egmont, 112
    Expedition, 152
    Glory, xiv, 3–7, 41, 85, 87, 90, 94–6, 98–105, 153–4, 181–2, 194
    Goliath, 15
    Grampus, 52
    Hermione, 16, 72, 137–46, 156, 158, 179–81, 196

Impetueux, 122–3
Indefatigable, 63
Inspector, 178–9, 197
Jupiter, 15
Leopard, 12, 14
Le Puissant, 95, 154
Le Tigre, 154
London, 109–111, 136, 194–5
Marie Antoinette, 137, 141–2, 158 196
Mars, 61, 123
Minerve, 25–6
Montagu, 13
Neptune, xiv, 3–4, 14, 85, 87, 90–1, 94, 99–100, 104, 106, 182, 194
Pandora, 148
Phoebe, 79
Pompee, 14, 85, 87, 90–1, 94, 99–100, 104, 106
Porcupine, 6–7, 136
Princess Royal, 69
Queen Charlotte, xiii, 3–7, 85, 87, 94–6, 99
Ramillies, 99
Raven, 84
Repulse, 14, 154
Resolution, 154
Royal George, 7, 69
Royal William, 79
Russell, 123
St George, 7, 87, 110–12, 154
Sandwich, 10, 12, 14–15, 52, 69, 118, 179
Saturn, 9, 73–4, 82, 109, 155, 193
Surprise, 23, 157–8, 196
Tamar, 159
Thames, 25, 191
Tremendous, 70–1
Triton, 66
Ville de Paris, 87, 109–11, 115–17, 195
Naval, French
  Artois, 72
  Indomptable, 46–7
  La Bonne Citoyenne, 133
  Proserpine, 72
  Seduisant, ix, 47
Privateer, French
  La Républicaine, 158, 175
  Lynx, 83

S

Society of the Friends of the Constitution, 52
Spencer, George, 2nd Earl Spencer, First Lord of the Admiralty, 20, 29–30, 65, 109
Spithead, 4, 21, 29, 59–60, 62–3, 65, 68, 154, 192
  anchorage, 4, 62–3, 65, 68, 79, 85, 182
  courts martial, 163, 168
  hangings, 160
  mutiny, 4–13, 50–2, 69, 73–4, 99, 109–110, 113, 142
    United Irish presence, 84, 134

T

Texel, 15, 34, 64–6, 68, 118–19
Tone, Theobald Wolfe, xxi, 190, 192
  Joins expeditions to Ireland, 46–8
  journeys to USA, 45–6
  meeting with Reverend William Jackson, 45
  United Irish envoy in France, 46–7, 66, 71, 181

Tory Island, 48, 68, 183
Toulon, xiii, 61, 67, 108, 119
Transportation, 174
True Britons, 53
Tucker, Benjamin, 110, 114, 116, 118, 194–5
Two Acts, 29, 53, 119

U

United Britons, Society of, 52
United Englishmen, Society of, 53
United Irishmen, Society of, xi–xii, xiv, xvi, 2, 43–7, 49, 51, 134, 139, 144, 149
　anticipating French landings, xii, 67
　emissaries, xxi, 84, 88–9, 94, 98
　funding, 21
　infiltration of British navy, xvi, 20–1, 71
　light horsemen, 100
　links with other societies, 52–3, 81, 180
　mutiny plots, 72, 76, 85, 88–92, 107–119, 142, 160–77
　oath, xvii, 20, 55, 97–8, 161
　plans to take naval warships, 2, 17, 183
　Portsmouth club, 20–1
　propagating the cause, 98–9, 101
　recruiting methods, 88–90
　shipboard club meetings, xix, 90
United Scotsmen, Society of, 53, 185, 192
Ushant, xx, 57, 59–61, 65, 67, 82, 85, 88, 94, 142, 178, 182, 192

W

Wetherell, John, 31
Wight, Isle of, 4, 77

Index by Name:
Rebels, Revolutionaries and Mutineers

Anderson, Peter, 114–16, 195
Atkinson, Thomas, 10, 15, 52

Bott (aka Batt), Thomas, 116–17, 195
Boyd, Thomas, 116, 173–4, 195, 197
Brady, John, 94–6, 100–101, 154, 160, 169, 171–2
Broughall, Dennis, 74–6, 80, 87, 172, 193

Callaghan, Cornelius, 154, 160, 169–71
Cannon, James, 160, 169
Cole, Richard, 110, 195
Connell, Michael, 116, 195

Derbyshire, Thomas, 154, 160–2, 165, 167–9, 173–4
Devoy, Patrick, 160, 169
Dixon, James, 155, 193
Duggan, John, 93–4, 98, 153
Dunn, Terence, 160, 169, 172

Evans, John, 155, 193

Fieney, Ignatius, 142, 196
Foy, Michael, 169

Godfrey, Jacob, 145, 196
Grumley, Thomas, 88, 90, 153
Guthrie, Thomas, 116–17, 173–4, 195

Hines, Edward, 10
Hoare, John, 160, 169
Hollister, Matthew, 10, 15, 52
Hopkins, John, xix, 102, 160, 169, 180
Hynes, Patrick, 169

Jackson, William, 142
Jourdaine, Thomas, 161, 169
Joyce, Valentine, 69

Keenan, Hugh, 144
Kelly, Michael, 154, 158–9, 169
Kennedy, Patrick, 144–5, 196
Kennedy, Richard, xix, 104, 154, 160–2, 169

Laffin, Thomas, 156, 160, 169, 172
Larken, Robert, 72–6, 80, 87, 172, 193
Lawless, James, 164, 169
Lindsey, William, xviii, xix, xx, 55, 94–9, 101–102, 154, 160, 164, 171–2, 180

INDEX BY NAME

McCartey, Owen, 169–71
McCarthy, Charles, 10, 51–2, 192
McGee, Patrick, 89, 93–4, 153
McGuire, Peter, 160, 169
McLaughlan, Edward, 102, 154, 160–1, 164, 169, 171
Mahane, Christopher, 160, 169
Mahaney, Edward, 88–90
Mason, James, xiii, 98, 169, 172

O'Neal, Charles, 94–6, 182

Parker, Richard, 5, 14, 16, 30, 69, 179
Prevot, Jean, 159, 175–7, 196, 197

Reed, David, 55, 154, 160–1, 169, 171
Regan, William, 94–6, 98–9, 102, 106, 181
Ryan, Nicholas, 101, 154, 160, 169

Sweeny, Daniel, 116, 195
Swinney, Edward, 154, 169

Timmings, William, 76–80, 87, 153, 155, 193
Tomms, George, 119–22, 153, 172, 195

Wright, John, 119–22, 153, 172, 195